Global nature, global cu'

Global nature, global culture

Sarah Franklin, Celia Lury and Jackie Stacey

SAGE Publications   London • Thousand Oaks • New Delhi
www.sagepub.co.uk

© Sarah Franklin, Celia Lury and Jackie Stacey 2000

First published 2000

Apart from any fair dealing for the purposes of research or private
study, or criticism or review, as permitted under the Copyright,
Designs and Patents Act, 1988, this publication may be reproduced,
stored or transmitted in any form, or by any means, only with the
prior permission in writing of the publishers, or in the case of
reprographic reproduction, in accordance with the terms of licences
issued by the Copyright Licensing Agency. Inquiries concerning
reproduction outside those terms should be sent to the publishers.

SAGE Publications Ltd
6 Bonhill Street, London EC2A 4PU

SAGE Publications Inc
2455 Teller Road, Thousand Oaks, California 91320

SAGE Publications India Pvt Ltd
32, M-Block Market, Greater Kailash – I
New Delhi 110 048

British Library Cataloguing in Publication data
A catalogue record for this book is available
from the British Library

ISBN 0 7619 6598 X
ISBN 0 7619 6599 8 (pbk)

Library of Congress catalog record available

Text and cover design: barkerhilsdon
Typeset by Mayhew Typesetting, Rhayader, Powys
Printed in Great Britain by The Cromwell Press, Trowbridge, Wiltshire

Contents

This book is dedicated to our mothers:

Susan Franklin, Toni Lury and Daphne Stacey.

List of Figures

List of Figures

Acknowledgements

The idea for this book emerged out of a number of intersecting research and reading groups at Lancaster University and subsequently developed over the course of several years at various other institutions. We would like to thank members of the Department of Sociology, the Institute for Women's Studies and the Institute for Cultural Research at Lancaster University for supporting this project and contributing so significantly to its trajectory. We are indebted to all those who participated in the 'Globalisation and Cultural Change' group 1992–5, especially Deirdre Boden, Mick Dillon, Paul Heelas, Scott Lash, Greg Myers, Colin Pooley, John Urry and Brian Wynne, and to the numerous colleagues in Women's Studies with whom many of these ideas were discussed, particularly Susan Condor, Lynne Pearce, Beverly Skeggs and Alison Young. Sarah is grateful to colleagues at the University of California, Santa Cruz, particularly Jim Clifford and Donna Haraway, for providing a forum to discuss many of the issues in this volume, and for contributing valuable insights to the arguments offered here. Celia would like to thank her new colleagues at Goldsmiths College, especially Les Back and Paul Gilroy, for insightful discussions of the themes of the book.

We are extremely grateful to Lisa Cartwright for her careful reading and incisive comments on the manuscript. Mike Featherstone's commentary significantly helped to reshape the final product. We would also like to thank Debra Ferreday and Judith Wester for their hard work obtaining permission for the visuals reproduced in this book, Fiona Summers for work on the final manuscript, and the Lancaster Sociology Department for financial support. The Lancaster University Photographic Unit was of valuable assistance in preparing the photographs used in this book. Finally, we are grateful to Karen Phillips, Rosie Maynard and Rosemary Campbell at Sage for their patience during the lengthy time it took to bring this text to print, and to Justin Dyer for his enthusiastic precision in copy editing the manuscript.

We are extremely grateful to the following individuals, companies and organisations for generously granting permission to reproduce the visuals in this book:

- *Chapter 1*: Figure 1.1 (Bijan Fragrances Inc.), Figures 1.2, 1.3 and 1.5 (Institute of Noetic Sciences), Figure 1.4 (Third World First), Figures 1.6 and 1.7 (Lennart Nilsson), Figure 1.8 (Department of Human Anatomy and Genetics, Oxford University).

Acknowledgements

- *Chapter 2*: Figure 2.2 (Penguin Books Ltd), Figure 2.3 (Logaston Press), Figures 2.4 and 2.5 (University of Chicago Press), Figure 2.6 (Lockheed Martin), Figure 2.7 (Newbridge Networks), Figure 2.8 (Sun Microsystems).
- *Chapter 3*: Figure 3.1 (Bijan Fragrances Inc.), Figure 3.2 (Design Council), Figure 3.3 (HarperCollins, San Francisco), Figures 3.4–3.6 (Kew Gardens), Figure 3.7 (David Cavagnaro), Figure 3.8 (*The Economist*).
- *Chapter 4*: Figure 4.1 (Promega Biological Products), Figures 4.3–4.4 (Farish Associates, London), Figure 4.5 (Costa Ltd), Figures 4.6–4.10 (The Body Shop), Figure 4.12 (Third World First).
- *Chapter 5*: Figures 5.1–5.19 (Benetton Group S.P.A. and *Colors* magazine).
- *Chapter 6*: Figure 6.1 (*Newsweek* and Universal Studios), Figures 6.2 and 6.3 (Universal Studios), Figure 6.4 (The Dinosaur Society), Figure 6.5 (Carnegie Collection).

Introduction

This book is about the power of nature, not as a static concept or even as a flexible sign, but rather as a shifting classificatory process. It is concerned with an interdisciplinary set of debates about changing definitions of nature, culture and the global. How, we ask, has the relationship between nature and culture been refigured in a global order? What might a feminist analysis of global nature and global culture look like? And what kinds of conceptual frameworks might feminist theory offer to address such questions? This book presents an account of the ways in which the global is performed, imagined and practised across a number of locations, and we analyse these enactments as a set of *effects, entities and embodiments*. We consider the kinds of comparisons a global context makes possible, and the types of differentiation which it renders visible. What is at stake, we ask, in the expanding purchase of the global within the contemporary western imagination? What are the sites, limits and way-finding devices for such a project? What are the worlds, selves, bodies or forms of life described in such a context, and how can they be articulated? We ask, for example, how nature figures in the production of global products, subjects, knowledges and communities. We consider the pasts and futures constituted by and within global-isation, which emerge in shifting cultural economies of scale, context and perspective.

We offer a feminist approach to these questions not simply insofar as nature, culture and the global are clearly all gendered domains, but also because feminist theory offers a set of techniques crucial to the understanding of contemporary forms of social and political change. Instead of offering a definitive statement or a more traditional set of findings, we provide a preliminary exploration of the workings of global nature, global culture from the point of view of feminist cultural theory. We hope to extend some of its core concerns to engage with issues that are only beginning to be discussed as gendered domains, such as the emergence of the global imaginary. This book is thus a collaboration that responds to questions we have encountered in relation to both longstanding and more recent concerns.[1]

Globalisation has become one of the most widely used terms of the last decade.[2] Frequently assumed to condense some of the key changes that characterise contemporary sociality, globalisation in much recent social theory refers to a set of processes that are said to be transforming the social world at an unprecedented speed. Globalising processes have been seen as indicative of a shrinking of the world through new technologies and mobilities, and the speeding up of processes no longer inhibited by national boundaries or by geographical locatedness. Anthony Giddens sums this up as 'an intensification of worldwide social relations which link distant localities in such a way that local happenings are shaped by events occurring many miles away and vice versa' (1990: 64).[3]

For many theorists, globalisation describes the next phase in the development of capitalism (Lash and Urry, 1987, 1994), and/or the extension of modernity into a phase beyond the nation-state (Featherstone et al., 1995; Giddens, 1990). Not reducible to, or interchangable with, the term 'postmodernity', globalisation nevertheless is said to share many of its 'detraditionalising' characteristics (Featherstone and Lash, 1995; Heelas et al., 1996). Studies of global culture have tended to postulate the emergence of a new set of universally shared images and practices (Featherstone, 1990a; Tomlinson, 1999), and thus an *altered condition of universality* (Wallerstein, 1991). As evidenced by the expansive growth of tourism, the intensification of international migration or the homogenisation of commodity consumption, globalisation is used to refer to an increased sense of proximity across national and international boundaries as a consequence of the pervasiveness of common cultures. This sense of global culture is typically associated with products, industries and technologies, including: the growth of international tourism and the airline industries; multinational consumer brands such as Coca-Cola and Holiday Inns; popular media, such as television soaps or disco music; or new electronic networks such as the Internet or satellite telecommunication. The increasing velocity of exchanges across time and space through 'real-time' communication technologies, and the resulting rapidity of the spread of ideas and images (Friedland and Boden, 1994), is said to reconfigure previous 'core' and 'periphery' distinctions: the global cities of London, New York, Tokyo and Delhi restructure rigid East/West divisions in spatial significance as first and third world cities host the same hotel and restaurant chains and their airports play the same background music in their lounges (Hannerz, 1991; Lash and Urry, 1994; Sassen, 1991, 1998).

To oversimplify some highly complex and contested arguments, globalisation in this sense might be read as 'the triumph of the universal' (Featherstone and Lash, 1995: 2). Be it through an analysis of a new structural-economic world system (Wallerstein, 1991), a borderless global economy (Ohmae, 1987) or a global system of 'transnational practices' (Sklair, 1991, 1993), the emphasis has been on the emergence of new universal phenomena. Indeed, it has been argued that replacing the modern world of nation-states is a transnational one of global flows – in the form of media-scapes, ideoscapes, ethnoscapes, finanscapes and technoscapes which have now assumed significance greater than national institutions (Appadurai, 1990, 1996). As a theory of socio-cultural change, globalisation is a thus a shorthand reference for the ways in which 'the global begins to replace the nation-state as the decisive framework for social life' (Featherstone and Lash, 1995: 2).[4]

As well as identifying this emergent, shared culture, globalisation theorists also point to the importance of cultural *diversity* in the production of new universal forms and products. Indeed, specific, localised products (food, music, clothes, television shows) are said to have been taken up, relocated, refashioned and recycled by gobal consumer markets: diversity has become endlessly marketable within global culture. Thus, while globalisation suggests increasing uniformity, it is also seen to depend upon the exportability of local difference, and above all on the interrelation of local diversities within global scapes or flows. As the flows of people, products, ideas and information intensify (Appadurai, 1990; Lash and Urry, 1994), familiarity with 'other cultures' is said to increase, as we all become consumers of new tastes, from the culinary to the philosophical. For some, the global thrives on local diversity, indeed is dependent upon it for its endless production of new markets, brands and identities (the 'universalisation of particularism', Robertson, 1992: 130). For others, the local is in tension with the universal drives of a global capitalist market economy. Processes of recombination through which objects reappear in new contexts carrying some of their original values, but acquiring new meanings, have been variously decribed as processes of 'creolisation' (Hannerz, 1987) and 'hybridisation' (Pieterse, 1995). For Hannerz, 'world culture is created through increasing interconnectedness of varied local cultures whose development is without a clear anchorage in any one territory' (1990: 237). Robertson (1995) even uses the term 'glocalisation' to capture some of these interconnections.[5]

Challenging such accounts are many critics of the globalisation thesis (Grewal and Kaplan, 1994a, 1994b; Jameson and Miyoshi, 1999; King, 1991; Scott, 1997). For Janet Abu Lughod (1991), consideration needs to be given to the unevenness of globalising processes, and for Appadurai, 'globalization is not the story of cultural homogenization' (1996: 11). As Janet Wolff argues in her critique of conceptualisations of culture in debates about globalisation, there are dangers in 'granting these groups or cultures some "essential" existence, denying the linguistic and other strategies through which they are negotiated and produced' (Wolff, 1991: 167). Extending Wolff's critique, John Tagg argues against a view of global culture as an entirety that can be encapsulated by academic theory. Tagg argues that much work on global culture uncritically yields to the desire for totalising theories, be they of modernity, capitalism or human nature: '[T]he very desire for such an account is tied to notions of social totality and historiographical representation that are untenable. If we are to talk of global systems, then we shall have to ask whether concepts of globalization can be separated from theoretical totalizations' (1991: 156). Challenging even the more cultural accounts of globalisation, such as Robertson's concept of 'the world-as-a-single-place', Tagg argues that 'the world that is systematic or one place can never be the world of discourse: this world is never . . . present to itself; it never constitutes an accomplished totality' (1991: 157).[6]

Stuart Hall's analysis of the global and the local, from another angle, similarly cautions against over-generalisations. Whilst Hall's argument situates the local and global within the broad sweep of sociological generalisations about globalisation, his reading of the cultural politics of the constitution of English identity operates as a critique not only of these general trends, but also of theories which fail to specify and locate their claims, and which fail to read culture as a complex and contradictory set of processes. Hall cautions against the 'somewhat closed, somewhat over-integrated, and somewhat over-systematized formulations' of the local and the global within contemporary social theory (1991a: 20). He argues that 'we suffer increasingly from a process of historical amnesia in which we think that just because we are thinking about an idea it has only just started' (1991a: 20). For Hall, globalisation has had many incarnations. If its current mode is one driven by (though, perhaps, not always successfully) North American economic and cultural domination, then its previous mode was one in which the United Kingdom was one of the powerful nation-states dominating colonised countries.[7]

For Hall, then, it is only through an understanding of the changing place of nations within different global configurations that the cultural politics of one particular nation, such as England, might be examined. The place of Englishness within the new global order (the American one, as Hall puts it) needs to be read in relation to the historical decline of its traditional colonial meaning. Moreover, Hall argues, even if the drive behind global culture seems to be a homogenising one (as in global mass media, for example), *the project of homogenisation is never fully complete, successful or straightforward*. While global culture is enormously absorptive, it never simply ingests difference, replacing it with a unified, coherent version: 'a little version of Americanness'. The model of global culture as 'a non-contradictory, uncontested space in which everything is fully within the keeping of the institutions, so they perfectly know where it is going . . . is missing a crucial insight about the logic of capital: that it only advances on contradictory terrain' (Hall, 1991a: 29, 32, 39). Instead, Hall urges us to think of the global-local relation as a 'process of profound unevenness' (1991a: 33). He argues for a reading of the 'new forms of global economic and cultural power which are apparently paradoxical: multi-national but decentred' (1991a: 30).

This book builds on the model of globalisation offered by Hall and others which emphasises its incomplete, uneven and contradictory – even paradoxical – character (Jameson, 1999). In conceptualising global culture as a project, and as a set of effects, we hope to stress that it is endlessly being reshaped through challenges from within, and resistance to its 'invisible hand'. For our purposes, 'globalisation' is not simply an empirical force that has changed the everyday realities of people's lives, but it is *a discursive condition*, currently being reproduced within academia and outside it. Our starting point is that culture is not an object waiting to be found in the external world, which the critic then describes in more or less accurate terms; rather, we analyse the shifting constitution of 'culture', assuming it to be a contested, uneven and relational process.[8]

Like Appadurai (1996: 12), we thus argue that the globalising project is not an object of study we can assume has a single, stable or unified meaning, or even a pre-existent, predictable form. Our analysis does not presume to map a general theory of globalisation, or to specifiy its place in relation to modernity, postmodernity, imperialism, capitalism or postcoloniality. We offer an analysis of the global that is both processual and partial, using the term to indicate an as yet open-ended process without known outcomes. That is, we consider the global to be *an aspiration rather than an achievement*. We argue that the global is as much *an effect as a condition*: it is a project which has yet to be secured and cannot be assumed to pre-exist in a form that is simply reproduced worldwide.

This is, of course, not to argue that the globalisation project is illusory, immaterial or a matter of ideas or the imagination alone – far from it; rather, as the arguments in this book demonstrate, the links between representational and material practice which constitute global nature, global culture are very real and carry high stakes. However, we are concerned to investigate the processes through which 'the global' constitutes its own domains, rather than taking them for granted as self-evident. We thus ask: How is the global manifest at the level of knowledge practices, and the production or recognition of difference? How are commodities, images, fantasies, bodies or identities transfigured by the global? We suggest that the global is repeatedly reinvented through a whole host of what Donna Haraway (1992a) describes as material-semiotic practices. Our approach to the study of globalisation might thus be summed up *as investigating the constitutive power of the global* – as a fantasy, as a set of practices, and as a context. In this book we examine the social formations produced under the sign of the global through analysing specific, localised instances within and through which we argue both *culture* and *nature* are refigured.

In offering a feminist account of how nature, culture and gender are both crucial and underconsidered aspects of the global, we investigate the multiple ways in which the global produces de- and renaturalised identities, subjects, properties and worlds. We explore these processes in terms of a *traffic in nature*, that is, in terms of the constitutive effects of naturalised idioms as they are transferred across domains, revised, extended and made newly productive as part of the global project. For example, we investigate the repeated reinventions of nature within contemporary global practices of the biological, the bodily, the visual, the technological and the subjective. Consequently, we also ask how the global is made manifest in changing dimensions of time, space, scale and perspective, and we examine the images, techniques and imagined futures through which such transformations become perceptible, possible and even ordinary. We suggest that such investigations comprise part of a long overdue feminist critique of globalisation *as a set of effects or registers*.[9] We are thus attentive to the ways in which the natural is deployed in the production of both everyday and specialised knowledges and practices – in the production of transgenic breeds and global brands, in self-conscious practices of health and well-being, in emergent fashion styles and film genres, as well as in the formation of global commodity markets and transnational flows of people, ideas and capital. Throughout this book, we advance and explore the claim that in *the traffic in nature* constitutive of the global imaginary certain switching points – criss-crossings between nature and culture; nature and history; and nature and technology – emerge as especially important. Understanding the global thus becomes for us an exemplary means of developing an analysis of *the ordering of kind and type* that is constitutive of what counts as real, self-evident or categorical, be it in the form of commodities, bodies, property or life itself.

Historically, feminist theory has addressed a number of topics, such as gender, sexuality, race, class, reproduction and production, politics, health and bodies. Feminist work has been central to the development of contemporary debates about identity, subjectivity and the politics of difference, and to the critique of concepts such as the social, the natural and the cultural. Indeed, it is increasingly clear that there are no topics or phenomena to which a feminist analysis is not relevant – at which point it is useful to consider feminist theory as a hermeneutical tradition, or as a set of techniques, rather than as a fixed set of positions or models. The perspectives we generate in this volume enact feminist theory in this way: as an analytical tradition concerned with the production of difference, not only of male and female, but of *kind and type* – as in the grammatical function of the term 'gender' to describe types of words in many languages.

Our use of gender in this way extends the arguments of Haraway who argues that: '"alterity" and "difference" are precisely what "gender" is "grammatically" about, a fact that constitutes feminism as a politics defined by its field of contestation and repeated refusals of master theory' (1991: 147). The usage of 'gender' we propose here, as grammatical, syntactic, or lexical, also extends the model of it proposed by Monique Wittig as a system of 'marks' (1992), which is similarly used by Collette Guillaumin to describe both race and nature as 'a system of marks' analogous to a grammar (1995). This same analogy is developed by Hortense Spillers (1987) in relation to the markings of race and the 'grammars' of gender, kinship and genealogy through which it has historically been imposed upon the populations (formerly) owned as slaves in the United States.

Feminism offers a long tradition of recognising the power to define, to make distinctions, and to create categories as key to a host of other power effects. Central to this critical analytical politics is the recognition that 'worlds in the making' are also imagined worlds, just as worlds denied, forgotten or made invisible may be unmade (Castañeda, 1996, 2001). This book is concerned both with worlds in the making through specific practices linked to the project of the global – such as the human genome project – and with the emergent new universalisms through which such ventures reshape the limits of the thinkable and the real in the world at the turn of the millennium. To explore these concerns, we foreground the question of what forms of life are being imagined, created and valorised in relation to the future of a panhuman world. Against this, we ask what are the risks, the catastrophic modes of thinking and the tools and techniques which set the terms of non-life? In addition we look at the pleasures, spectacles and celebratory images which comprise the popular consumption of global culture.

Central to our approach to global nature, global culture is a concern with technologies – not simply in the sense of the technologies commonly associated with the project of the global, such as digital, virtual and visual technologies, and the growing range of biotechnologies, but also in the Foucauldian sense of technologies of the self (Foucault, 1988a and b).[10] In this second sense, gender itself may be considered a technology, as in the 'technologies of gender' outlined by Teresa de Lauretis

(1987) and Judith Butler (1990, 1993). We build also on the model of gender as a technology outlined by Donna Haraway (1997), in which, for example, she compares the ordering of kind and type through gender to the regulation of commodities through branding.[11]

The emergence of an understanding of gender as a technology, which is productive not only of particular kinds of difference, but also of their *naturalisation through forms of embodiment*, has brought with it a set of recognitions that are crucial to the analysis we offer in *Global Nature, Global Culture*. In theorising the constitutive effects of the global in making worlds, bodies, selves and futures, we rely closely on the way gender has come to be theorised over the past two decades within feminist work. To overgeneralise, we might argue that a definitive shift in the conceptualisation of gender in the last decade has been the turn towards theorising what gender *does* rather than what it *is*. This shift reflects a concern not only with gender as a process, rather than a state or a condition, but also with gender as a *productive mechanism* or *enabling device* (Franklin, 1996). In suggesting that the project of globalisation involves the production of renaturalised subjects, we offer an extension of feminist concerns not only about nature and culture, but about what it means to secure naturalised kinds by *doing* rather than *being*. In other words, our analysis of the global closely parallels recent debates in feminist cultural theory about gender, and in particular the renaturalisation of kind and type.

In arguing that neither gender nor sex is a naturally occurring, pre-social regime of difference, Judith Butler makes a compelling case that a reconceptualisation of gender as performative, as something that enacts itself, exposes the artifice of its foundational claims. Butler describes her project in *Gender Trouble* 'as a strategy to denaturalize and resignify bodily categories' (1990: x). She writes:

> I describe and propose a set of parodic practices based in a performative theory of gender acts that disrupt the categories of the body, sex, gender, sexuality and occasion their subversive resignification and proliferation beyond the binary frame.
>
> (1990: x)

Gender is denaturalised in Butler's account through a conceptualisation that seeks to challenge the place of cause and effect, and of origins, in the teleological explanation of 'natural facts' such as sexual difference. Butler's intervention urged feminists to rethink gender as an enactment, a process, and a performance. There is no such thing as 'being female', according to Butler's analysis, because there is no pre-social domain of 'natural facts' which establish sex as binary, as biological, or even as 'real'.

Arguing that gender is instead an effect or consequence of a system of compulsory sex binarism, Butler uses the example of drag to argue that gender might be conceptualised as imitation, rather than as inherent: '*In imitating gender, drag implicitly reveals the imitative structure of gender itself – as well as its contingency*' (1990: 137, original emphasis). For Butler, such subversive moments reveal 'sex and gender denaturalized by means of a performance which avows their distinctness and dramatizes the cultural mechanism of their fabricated unity' (1990: 138). Butler's argument is not simply that sex and gender might be uncoupled from biology in such a moment, but, further, *that these gender performances expose the very textures of their imbrication.* She continues, 'gender is an identity tenuously constituted in time, instituted as an exterior space through *a stylized repetition of acts* (1990: 140, original emphasis).

Although some rather reductive interpretations of her work imply otherwise, Butler is not suggesting that because gender is not written in natural law it is simply a choice. To argue that gender is an enactment is not to conclude it is merely an act; to argue that gender is always already a copy is not to suggest it is inauthentic or superficial; and to argue that gender is an unstable or contingent identity is not to say that it has no power to define and regulate. Indeed it is Butler's argument that gender must be regulated *all the more because of its instability* rather than in spite of it: after all, if gender binarism were so obvious, why would there be such intensive activity devoted to making it appear in very particular ways and prohibiting its appearance in others?

Reflecting upon the 'gender as performative' model, in the introduction to *Bodies that Matter*, Butler writes:

> For if I were to argue that genders are performative, that could mean that I thought that one woke in the morning, perused the closet or some more open space for the gender of choice, donned that gender for the day, and then restored the garment to its place at night. Such a willful and instrumental subject, one who decides *on* its gender, is clearly not its gender from the start and fails to realize that its existence is already decided *by* gender. Certainly, such a theory would restore a figure of a choosing subject – humanist – at the center of a project whose emphasis on construction seems quite opposed to such a notion.
>
> (1993: x)

What is important here for us is Butler's argument that gender is both contingent and regulatory – *indeed that the regulation of gender is precisely driven by its non-obviousness.*[12] We similarly suggest that what we are calling global nature, global culture in this book can be subversive and parodic, while at the same time it can also be regulatory and exclusive. Our arguments about the traffic in nature occurring within the context of the global parallels Butler's analysis of gender, in suggesting a greater flexibility of the natural to secure certain kinds of difference or comparison. In the same way that the theory of the performativity of gender should not detract from the power of its inscriptions, so we have cautioned against the conclusion that the denaturalisations of the globalising project have made nature redundant.

Our concern in this book builds on and responds to recent debates addressed to the traffic between nature and culture, the borrowings between one domain and the other, and the ways in which a distinction or contrast between these two terms continues to be productive. In mapping this traffic we examine their co-production in some depth, foregrounding the complex and often paradoxical ways in which *nature and culture have become increasingly isomorphic while remaining distinct*. Our use of the term 'global nature, global culture' is intended to describe both this process *and the effects it can generate*. Such a view – of the increasing isomorphism of nature and culture, their ongoing redifferentiation, and the generative power of this process – has close links with a number of other positions, all of which are linked by the shared belief that the long-standing traffic, or borrowings, between nature and culture is undergoing a significant transformation.

One way to summarise these debates is in terms of the assertion that the differences between nature and culture have collapsed. Hence, for example, Haraway (1997) uses the metaphor of 'implosion' to describe how she sees nature and culture becoming increasingly densely interpolated with one another. In contrast, Paul Rabinow (1992, 1996a and b), also writing largely in relation to the new genetics and biotechnology, argues that nature and culture have been 'inverted', so that culture is now the model for nature, which has become equivalent to technique. Marilyn Strathern (1992a and b) argues that nature has been increasingly 'assisted' by technology so that it can no longer provide a prior ontological status to culture. Both Jameson (1991) and Lyotard (1984), like Baudrillard (1994a) and other postmodern theorists, argue that culture has become 'everything', that there exists nothing we might describe as 'nature' any more. As stated above, we extend these arguments further in this book, demonstrating that while nature and culture are increasingly isomorphic, in that they are acquiring each other's powers, their distinctiveness continues also to remain crucial. It is in these processes of overlap and opposition, of borrowing from each other and yet remaining distinct, where we argue a particular set of generative effects can be seen to lie. By asking how these processes of comparison and contrast are put into motion, within particular contexts, and in pursuit of specific aims, we argue the meanings indigenous to global nature, global culture become visible. In this book, we are primarily concerned to trace the engenderings of global nature, global culture which result from these processes of comparison, contrast, ricochet and contextualisation.

It is thus the examination of *the production of difference* which links our analysis of the global to recent feminist theories of gender. Another important example of this is Haraway's recent argument about a shift 'from kind to brand' (1997) in which the classifications of type and kind are reinvented. Haraway suggests that while classifications of kind and type have been denaturalised through proprietary marking, as is the case with the patenting of transgenic organisms, the commercial brand or trademark has, in the same process, been naturalised through an attachment to the reproduction of new life forms. This argument thus connects the spatial and temporal dimensions of kinds, or kin, related by genealogy, to the branding of the genome itself as mark of commercial propriety, as in new genetically engineered seeds whose 'natural' reproduction is regulated by patent law and protected by genomic markers.[13]

In this book we extend Haraway's argument by exploring further the implications of the shift from kind to brand, by asking how new life forms become commercial property, and indeed how new forms of commercial property are engendered as life forms. In exploring the implications of such shifts through a range of examples, we ask: How might we need to reconceptualise the nature–culture axis as a classificatory process if nature as a referent system cannot secure the ground it once did, as a taken-for-granted limit point or horizon, while at the same time forms of capital, properties and commodities are themselves increasingly naturalised? If nature is no longer fixed, and ceases to guarantee the same 'natural' borders of sex, race, gender, reproduction, the human or the body, then how might such transformations be evaluated, analysed, represented or interpreted? How is nature being re-created in the space of its own displacement? And if culture can now be reproduced biologically – for example, in the life forms of patented property – how will its transmission be regulated? Can its reproduction be made secure? Or do such promiscuous minglings collapse the very terms of reference by which they might be defined, regulated or owned?

Initially, such transformations might seem to indicate a flexibility that would be welcome to those critics keen to unanchor nature's authority: feminist critics, for example, have a longstanding concern with challenging the naturalisations of gender, race, class and sexuality that have been employed to justify forms of inequality. Thus, from a feminist point of view, the dislodging of nature's laws within globalising cultures might appeal to a desire to argue for the possibility of social transformation. If nature re-appears as a sign that is visibly being put to work, then perhaps its contingencies are more explicit, and the constructedness of its forms might be assumed to undermine the universality of its claims. Indeed, this book repeatedly demonstrates how nature is being commodified, technologised, re-animated and rebranded in ways that expose its artifice. No longer able to authenticate or pre-exist culture in the predictable ways it once could, nature could be seen to have moved out of the picture in the multiple and intertextual significations of globalising cultures.

We argue throughout this book that such denaturalisations have been accompanied by processes of renaturalisation which continue to foreground nature as pivotal to the new universalisms of global culture. As our discussions will demonstrate, if nature becomes a technique in the reproduction of the new life forms of the global, it does so in such a way that, far from undermining its authority, re-establishes it. For nature and culture are neither polar opposites, nor are they simply changing places. The longstanding borrowings between nature and culture which Marilyn Strathern (1991) describes in terms of partial connections no longer require acknowledgement; they operate as complex substitutions. Consequently, their seemingly isomorphic capacity to achieve autogenerative legitimation requires an analysis of precisely how they attain such effects in the new global orders that surround us.[14]

In our analysis we conclude these effects are such that both nature and culture appear to become self-generating, *to be able to reproduce themselves*. We argue this paradoxical capacity is integral to their working, and that it is this specific capacity which indicates how the apparent isomorphism of nature and culture is a part of the project of the global. For the global provides the model *for a context which is isomorphic with itself*: as the novelist Borges (1964) describes, the global is co-terminous with itself – it acknowledges no boundaries but its own. But our analysis also seeks to trouble this process of auto-reproduction: by redescribing the emergence of global nature, global culture as both partial and processual, we draw attention not only to its successes, but to the contestation of origins, the squabbles of ownership, the unequal distributions of risk and responsibility.

● ● ●

This book is divided into two principal parts. In three co-authored chapters in Part One, entitled 'Second Nature', we seek both to introduce readers to the key debates with which our project is engaged, and to begin to elaborate our analysis through a range of exemplary case studies we use as indicative indices to the wider processes we seek to explicate. We introduce a range of specific products, texts, images, practices and technologies through which to build our arguments about contemporary social change. The case studies we have chosen, however, are not meant to be read as the *only* or the *most* important examples of the phenomena we use them to interpret, and in this sense our examples are not chosen with a view to be *representative*. They are used as *indicative* instances, and their selection is not meant to imply their definitive status (as reflecting the essence of the contemporary moment). The resulting discussions thus produce certain hermeneutical vectors, which are offered as routes to the changing significance of global nature, global culture. Specifically, we analyse some of the changing effects of dimension, scale, comparison and context in the production of the new global orders. Through a discussion of these examples, we ask: What happens to nature and culture when they are recontextualised within the global? In short, we offer a preliminary analysis of the kinds of traffic whereby global nature, global culture are effected.

In Part One, then, we outline our approach to questions of global nature, global culture in a number of ways. In particular, we intersperse theoretical and conceptual discussions with a series of 'readings' of icons which in different ways foreground some of the central dynamics with which we are concerned. Drawing from cultural studies, anthropology, gender theory, science studies and sociology, we introduce a range of debates and concepts we then develop in greater depth in the more extended case studies presented in the three single-authored chapters comprising Part Two, entitled 'Nature Seconded'. Our use of a series of global 'icons' is intended to create a set of orienteering devices for moving through the landscapes of turn-of-the-century global nature, global culture. In our analysis we seek to show the ways in which these icons function variously as figurative condensations of the traffic between nature and culture in the processes of global world-making. Altogether we discuss three sets of icons: the blue planet, the foetus and the cell; the fossil and the pixel; and the seed and the breed. These sets of icons are chosen for the ways in which they facilitate our exploration of global nature, global culture.[15]

The blue planet, the foetus and the cell are our starting points in Chapter 1 since, we argue, each of these iconic visual images is indicative *of the changing facts of life in a global context*. We discuss this set of icons in Chapter 1, entitled 'Spheres of Life', which explores how they have come to represent the macrocosm and the microcosm of humanity – the fragility of the blue planet, the foetus and the cell appearing to stand in for a sense of humanity's exposure to risk. The technological reproduction of each icon effects the erasure of context, uniting a common humanity through the aura of distance and proximity respectively. The icon of the blue planet offers a view from beyond; the icons of the foetus and the cell offer a view from within. Put crudely, these icons are indices of the changing constitution of life itself from outside and inside. These privileged (and impossible) perspectives offer the viewer ways of moving beyond conventional means of visualising life, and they position viewers as witnesses both to new spectacles of life itself and to the technological capacities which made such images possible. As such, they signal the disappearance of traditional horizons, as well as the celebration of technological prowess and accomplishment. They suggest new ways of imagining the parameters of human life: its beginnings, its endings, its limits and capabilities, and above all its vulnerabilities.

The second set of icons, the fossil and the pixel, is used as a means of examining the changing configurations of temporal boundaries in global nature, global culture. We pair these icons in Chapter 2 as 'Imprints of Time' which have come to represent the complexity of relations of past, present and future. In both the fossil and the pixel, the relations between nature, history and time are foregrounded as a question of reproduction. We examine both icons as transitional objects indexical of the temporal uncertainties of their respective eras: the fossil is for modern linear time what the pixel is for the non-linear temporalities of postmodernity. Historically, the fossil was a figure which represented the fragmented pre-modern temporality of nature when it had no history: the past to which the fossil now belongs (natural history) did not exist until the fossil helped to secure it.

Presenting us with an unfamiliar temporality, the pixel falls outside the time of natural history. Refiguring photographs, for example, the pixel is the unit through which it becomes possible to reach into the past and change what was assumed to be permanent. This not only interrupts the linearity of time, but also disturbs the traditional ownership of images. In the natural history museum the fossil offers an apparently stable version of frozen past time. As the unit of digital technologies from cameras to compact discs, the pixel is the ultimate emblem of recombinant temporality: it seems to undo time and to negate its fixtures. The relation between the fossil and the pixel thus opens up to interrogation questions of authenticity, authority and authorship and reveals the displacement of genealogical time characteristic of the global age.

The third pair of icons is the seed and the breed. Juxtaposed in Chapter 3 as 'Units of Genealogy', these are examined in relation to the prominent and highly visible ways in which biodiversity figures in the constitution of global nature, global culture. We consider the seed and the breed as they invoke a contrast of traditional and recombinant models of genealogy. In the current climate of controversy about the genetic modification of crops, the purity of the seed has taken on an increased significance. As public debate rages about safety, regulation and responsibility, previously trustworthy and reliable aspects of nature are now thrown into question and are seen to be at risk. In this context, the preservation of seeds branded as pure and natural through their association with ancient and traditional cultures (so-called 'heirloom-variety seeds') has the appeal of guaranteeing an authenticity that exceeds contemporary western cultures. Here the preservation of global cultural diversity is promised through natural products.

Similarly, but also in contrast, techniques such as cloning and transgenic reproduction alter the breeding of domestic livestock, which no longer secures a familiar pedigree or follows a natural generational order. The postmodern genealogies engendered through genetic engineering undermine familiar traditions and offer recombinant models of plant, animal, human and microbial lineages in the name of global health and agricultural interests. Both the traditional and the detraditionalised versions of nature coexist within global nature, global culture: whilst the heirloom-variety seed promises to secure nature, the transgenic breed troubles familiar definitions of purity and uniqueness, of inheritence and kinship, and of paternity and progress.

Through our analysis of these sets of icons, we aim to foreground some of the complexities of global nature, global culture. It is as much the dynamics produced by these pairings (their relationalities), as it is the individual icons themselves, that provide us with ways of reading these complexities. Our analysis of the seven icons is interspersed with our discussions of a number of theoretical and conceptual debates. In each chapter we present brief, critical discussions of recent debates in social theory concerning ideas of nature and the natural, from a range of perspectives including feminist anthropology, gender theory, science studies, the sociology of the environment, the Frankfurt School and critical theory.

Opening Part Two, 'Nature Seconded', Jackie Stacey's chapter is concerned with what might be called the 'intimate global': those dimensions of global culture relating to subjectivity, fantasy and embodiment. Asking 'how the global gets within', Chapter 4 discusses how particular products and practices connect consumers to different versions of globality and traces the simultaneous commodification and yet renaturalisation of an imagined universal nature operating in the project of global culture. Located within these broader debates, the chapter focuses on changing models of health and disease in contemporary western societies, and asks: What are the forms of new universalism that operate within these health practices? Who are their new global subjects? And how are such subjectivities embodied? Here 'second nature' is explored through the ways in which 'self-health' deploys aspects of global cultures to confirm its authority. The chapter thus examines the changing relationship between nature and culture in contemporary constructions of the body, its interiority, and the imaginative connections between outside and inside, and between self and other.

In Chapter 5 on the global brand Benetton, by Celia Lury, the shifting status and implications of the refiguring of the natural and political kinds of race, gender and national identity are analysed as questions of style and matters of individual choice. It is argued that such natural and other kinds are reconstituted *as cultural essences* through a range of branding practices by the fashion company Benetton. Indeed, many of Benetton's photographic practices invite an understanding of gender remarkably close to that proffered in the reductive readings of Judith Butler discussed above, namely that 'gender [is] like clothes, . . . that clothes [make] the woman [or man]' (1993: 231). Their effect is to make it seem possible that categories of difference which had been seen as naturally given or as fixed are open to choice, and may be taken on and off as easily as one changes jumpers. Furthermore, through the representation of catastrophic thinking in its advertising, Benetton suspends and enters the global time of exposure, marking this new space as its own, and providing the possibility of transcendence. The famous images of a man dying from AIDS, an oil-covered duck and international and/or racialised conflict both pose decontextualised risks for the consumer and offer the possibility of consumer global citizenship via the opportunity to participate in the 'United Colors of Benetton'. In this process, gender as kind is displaced, only to be re-introduced in the kinships of the brand.

Chapter 6 addresses changing definitions of life, or life itself, in the context of turn-of-the-century genetics and biotechnology. Following a review of recent literature on the technologisation of human, plant and animal life forms, Sarah Franklin turns to the production and reception of the film *Jurassic Park* in order to explore several dimensions of what is described as an emergent genetic imaginary. In turn, this genetic imaginary is argued to be based upon an altered understanding of the facts of life, such as those depicted in *Jurassic Park*, the film that makes extinction 'a thing of the past'. At the centre of various forms of cultural production, *Jurassic Park* offers an imaginary re-animation of extinct life forms, as the basis of a global cinematic spectacle, linked to distinctive forms of marketing, branding and distribution. In addition to being a Hollywood box office phenomenon, the film was also celebrated by natural history museums internationally, and has become the subject of several popular books and a film sequel since its release in 1993. Using the analysis of *Jurassic Park* as a lens on the production of global nature, global culture thus offers a means of exploring a range of issues, including the shift from kind to brand, new definitions of paternity and gendered property, the respatialisation of genealogy, and the recurrence of themes of catastrophism, extinction and resurrection in contemporary forms of popular, material and visual culture.

Together, the three chapters in 'Nature Seconded' enable us to consider in more depth and with greater specificity many of the concerns raised in Part One and in this Introduction. The three extended case studies in Part Two parallel our earlier use of icons in the first three chapters by enabling us to ground many of our more exploratory claims in specific, indicative examples. At the same time, our analysis remains preliminary in many respects, especially insofar as we do not provide here a more detailed account of the complex ways in which specific individuals or communities incorporate or resist forms of global nature, global culture as ways of life in a more quotidian sense.

By moving in and out of specific case studies of products, images and texts, and by foregrounding largely institutional practices, such as breeding, branding or banking, our aim is to contribute to debates about the making of worlds, properties, selves and life forms within the project of the global. By drawing upon an inter-disciplinary set of theoretical sources, and a wide range of scholarly arguments addressed to nature, culture and the global, our aim is both synthetic and provocative: we use these terms to 'trouble' one another, as well as to complement other theories of what globalisation is, means and does. Navigating the difficult path between engagement and misplaced concreteness in the analysis of the global poses many challenges we have not resolved. Our depictions of the worlds, selves and life forms in the following sections thus perform, among other things, both an excessiveness and a circumspection which are themselves fitting tributes to, and enactments of, feminist knowledge production at the start of the new millennium.

Notes

1   This book extends many of the arguments initially developed in collaboration for *Off-Centre: feminism and cultural studies* (Franklin et al., 1991a). See especially Franklin et al. (1991b).
2   Over 100 books on the topic of globalisation were published in 1995 alone (Busch, 1997, cited in Urry, 2000). Globalisation was the subject of the Reith lectures in 1999, delivered by Professor Anthony Giddens from numerous locations around the world. Also in August 1999 the *National Geographic* produced a special themed issue on 'Global Culture'. These are but a few of the many indications of how the term 'globalisation' has become increasingly important within both academic scholarship and more generally.
3   For a discussion of 'time-space compression' as a characteristic of postmodernity, see Harvey (1989), and of 'time-space distanciation' as a characteristic of globalisation, see Giddens (1990).
4   Even for those aware of the limits of reading the global as a systemic worldwide unity, ethno-graphic models of the lived cultural experience of globalisation often operate within a vocabulary of the universal; for example, Roland Robertson writes of 'the human global condition' and of a 'global consciousness' (1992: 183). Global culture here refers to the compression of the scale of the world into a more uniform and graspable unit (the 'world-as-a-single-place') and the intensification of a consciousness of the world as a whole (Robertson, 1992: 185).
5   In different ways, Ulf Hannerz's theories of cultural processes at the periphery also seek to counter the theories of global homogenisation with more nuanced accounts of complex connection between first and third world countries (Hannerz, 1990, 1991).
6   Indeed, Tagg argues, a number of critics have quite rightly situated the desire for the world to be a single place within a theory of the subject; for example, Lacanian psychoanalysts might read such a desire as 'the projection onto an isolated image of the planet . . . an Imaginary wholeness that represses the multiple and heterogeneous positioning effects of language' (Tagg, 1991: 157).
7   Hall's account of Englishness demonstrates the dangers of the reinscription of a regressive and defensive, racist version of Englishness in a global order in which England has lost its (previously triumphant) place as a world leader. Writing of the the 1980s in Britain, Hall argues: '[A]t the very moment when the so-called material basis of the old English identity is disappearing over the horizon of the West and the East, Thatcherism brings Englishness into a more firm definition, a narrower but firmer definition than ever it had before' (1991a: 26).
8   In these respects, the approaches taken here follow some of the traditions of cultural studies and anthropology in addressing sociological questions.
9   There have been several important critical feminist accounts of globalisation, most notably those of Grewal and Kaplan (1994a, 1994b), outlining a transnational feminist studies which explores 'the

relationship of gender to scattered hegemonies such as global economic structures' (1994b: 17), and see also Kaplan, 1996 and Kaplan and Grewal, 1994. In a related case study, Sasha Roseneil (1997) describes the global, local and personal dynamics of the women's peace movement in the 1980s. Saskia Sassen criticises what she describes as 'narratives of eviction' in current theories of global economics, against which she proposes a model aimed 'to specify sites for the strategic instantiation of gendering and for new forms of women's presence' in the world economy (1998: 82–3). Such critical feminist studies have so far had little impact on dominant conceptualisations of the globalisation process.

10   Questions of how technologies enable the emergence of something called 'the global' seem almost inevitable, so closely associated are certain forms of technological enablement with the concept of globalisation and the presumed forms of cultural change it signifies. However, we describe technologies in a broader sense, asking how techniques of self-management, technologies of representation and new reproductive technologies combine to enable forms of enactment specific to global nature, global culture.

11   In deploying gender in this way, our method too is a technology of sorts – a means of enablement through which certain ways of apprehending, exemplification and analysis are put into motion. We thus acknowledge, and seek to make visible, the ways in which our analysis is inevitably caught up in the very processes it seeks to describe.

12   For Butler, the recasting of gender performativity as 'individual volition' overlooks the ways in which gendered embodiment is a 'compulsory practice . . . but not for that reason fully determining'. Instead she argues that 'embodying is a repeated process. And one might construe repetition as precisely that which *undermines* the conceit of voluntarist mastery designated by the subject in language' (Butler, 1990: 138, original emphasis).

13   Haraway's depiction of the shift from kind to brand takes as its primary example the marking or branding of transgenic commodities by breeding a proprietary corporate signature into their genome, so that companies, such as Monsanto, can determine, for example, which specific soybean plants were grown from their patented seeds (and thus claim remuneration from any farmers who have used such seeds illegitimately). Chapter 6 in Part Two of this book addresses these themes in greater depth.

14   Similarly, Butler's suggestion that the notion of gender is more usefully understood as doing not being neither ignores the continuing significance of the natural nor makes critique of its essentialist consequences impossible. The focus on gender as technology facilitates the analysis of the potential flexibility of nature and its extended powers of reproduction that are a consequence of the movements between the natural and the cultural, the kind and the brand. This is not the same as a loosening of its grip – rather, as we shall show, it may be precisely the opposite.

15   Our use of global icons parallels, but is distinct from, the Lancaster Global Citizenship project, which pursues many questions about global imagery and the media we do not explore here (see, for example, Szerzynski and Toogood, 2000; Toogood and Myers, 1999). Similarly, although our use of global icons is directly inspired by the use of 'figures' in Donna Haraway's (1997) writings (in which some of the same images are used, such as the seed and the foetus), her use follows more closely the work of Eric Auerbach on mimesis, by which she draws attention to conventions of Christian figurative realism structuring the nominally secular worlds of modern technoscience. Our icons are used as case studies to illustrate our arguments and as 'roadsigns' to exemplify our interpretive technique.

Part One / **Second Nature**

Sarah Franklin / Celia Lury / Jackie Stacey

Chapter 1 / Spheres of life

It has become commonplace to associate the present era with environmental damage, global warming, mass extinction of plants and animals – indeed 'the end of nature' (McKibben, 1989). The advent of new reproductive and genetic technologies, such as cloning, similarly evokes images of 'post-natural' and 'posthuman bodies' (Hayles, 1999). In contrast to such claims, it is a central argument of this book that nature has been given new life at the turn of the millennium – both refigured and revitalised in projects such as the human genome project and celebrated in films such as *Jurassic Park*. Countering the view that nature has been displaced by culture, or simply the commodity, is the view explored here that nature is being put to work in new ways that signal not so much its disappearance as its transmogrification. Nature, in a sense, has been remade. It is this reworking of nature – and its ability to acquire new traits – which we explore in Part One of this book.

Our interest in ideas of the natural extends this area of longstanding import-ance for feminist theory and politics by positing a *processual* model for understanding how nature is used to ground cultural meanings and practice. The specific theorisation of ideas of the natural we propose comprises a threefold process of *naturalisation*, *denaturalisation* and *renaturalisation*. This processual model emphasises the move-ments enabling ideas of the natural to signify with the notable fluidity, contra-dictoriness and power that is their distinctive feature. As Raymond Williams (1976) noted in his pioneering work on ideas of the natural in the context of Englishness, 'nature' is among the most complex and polysemic signs in the English language. This indeed often seems to be the source of its power: nature is a kind of workhorse referent-system in the reproduction of distinctions, demarcations and classifications. Yet, this magical capacity to function as a multi-purpose foundational logic is difficult to specify. Our analysis here is derived from our understanding of the natural as a distinctively powerful and transformative idiom, continually reinvented in the pro-cesses of naturalisation, denaturalisation and renaturalisation as a means of grounding the orders of meaning and practice we understand as culture.

Our understandings of culture are similarly focussed on processes of redefini-tion and change, and, in examining the movements through which idioms of the natural are mobilised to produce specific effects, we are inevitably also positing a model of culture *as a form of animation*. Here, too, it is the ways in which culture is not fixed, but refers to a dynamic set of processes, which enable us to examine how meanings are put to work. The ways in which culture must be recognised as changing lead us to theorise culture as a set of techniques and processes, through which forms of distinction, classification, differentiation and comparison are enabled or precluded.

In examining these conjoined processes, we also foreground the importance of an understanding of nature as *context*, a term we also define in terms of process. At the heart of our analysis is the question of displacement, since we claim that as definitions of the natural are displaced, *so too the very model for context they afford is altered*. Using various examples, we seek to show how definitions of nature which functioned as models or analogies for context are being transformed.[1] Such models include not only conceptions of the body (which has, for example, informed concepts of the city, society and the globe) but also the organisation of dimension, perspective, movement and matter. We argue that nature has established a model for context in terms of temporality and scale – securing the way-finding device of the horizon, or the genealogical orientation of descent, which inform the natural order of history, and the relationality of life itself. Such orienting devices organise relationships between past, present and future, the relation of originals to copies, and of reproduction to progeny. We argue that the ways in which nature has been able to establish context is currently being both displaced by, and overlaid with, new means of stabilising similarities, connections or differences – in short, relations. This leads us to consider, for example, new kinds of universalism through which the global can be said to refigure what a context means and does. To what extent does the global displace familiar notions of the universal as a set of dimensions ordering space, time, scale, context or connection?[2]

If the uses of nature as models for context are indeed shifting, and if this is in part what the term 'globalisation' signifies, then it seems likely that the kinds of life which are brought into being through this changing relationship will themselves be transformed. As Marilyn Strathern (1995a and b) suggests, and as we seek to elaborate here, the appearance of a global order *that is able to constitute its own context* is dependent upon both a concealing of its own social, political, cultural and economic dimensions and the production of new universalisms which perform specific types of connection. We argue that the emergent universalisms of global nature and global culture comprise 'worlds in the making', and do so through specific processes (Castañeda, 1996, 2001). Like others who have raised critical questions about how the global refigures context, we suggest that the new universalisms of global nature, global culture are achieved through forms of displacement, exclusion and classification (Jameson, 1999). As with ideas of the natural, with which they have certain key features in common, articulations of globality are means through which both established and novel inequalities become inherent ways of life. In the same way that ideas of the natural have long been used to defend and to legitimate forms of social exclusion and restriction as innate – as facts of life – so it becomes important to consider the specific mechanisms which animate global nature, global culture. In this book, we thus ask: *What are the facts of life through which a global imaginary is becoming an environment, a universe, an identity, a habit or a 'second nature'?*

As Raymond Williams famously noted: '[T]he idea of nature contains, though often unnoticed, an extraordinary amount of human history' (1980: 67). There is no 'proper meaning' for nature; instead it is 'a case of a definition of quality which becomes, through real usage, based on certain assumptions, a description of the world' (1980: 68). In a lecture written in the 1970s, Williams argued that:

> [The] sense of nature as the inherent and essential quality of any particular thing is, of course, much more than accidental. Indeed there is evidence that it is historically the earliest use. In Latin one would have said *natura rerum*, keeping nature to the essential quality and adding the definition of things. But then also in Latin *natura* came to be used on its own, to express the same general meaning: the essential construction of the world. Many of the earliest speculations about nature seem to have been in this sense physical, but with the underlying assumption that in the course of physical inquiries one was discovering the essential, inherent and indeed immutable laws of the world.
>
> (1980: 68)

Central to Williams' account of ideas of the natural is their overdetermination: as they are able to describe the essential constitution of the world, so they also describe the essential principles through which it is ordered. Although, as we shall discuss below, more recent debates about ideas of the natural, especially in relation to environmental change and technological intensification, differ from Williams', we draw attention here to his emphasis on nature as a form of essentialism; we too are concerned with the relations between objects and their contexts, and the world-building consequences which flow from these relations and which produce *the effect of being self-evident*. Agreeing with Williams that naturalisations are a particular form of essentialising discourse, it is one of the central aims of this book to examine the kinds of material-semiotic effects they can be mobilised to produce in a global context, *and indeed how a context of globality is thus established*.

● ● ● Seconding Nature

The concept of 'second nature' is useful to us as an idiom through which we attempt to hold together a range of critical perspectives on nature, the natural and their histories. We explore the idea of 'second nature' not only in its more traditional Marxist sense of a nature that has been worked upon, but also in the broader sense of its classificatory power. We suggest that many of the debates about 'second nature' in the past have strong parallels with questions about nature and the natural in the context of globalisation; indeed it is precisely certain kinds of questions about 'nature' and 'naturalness' which inform understandings of the global, such as the idea of global warming.

Common to many critiques of contemporary global environmental destruction is the view that there is no longer any such thing as 'nature' at all (see Robertson et al., 1996). Bill McKibben, writing of the 'end' of nature, for example, argues that man-made global climate change has made 'every spot on the earth . . . artificial' (1989: 54). Other theorists, such as Alexander Wilson (1992), argue that nature is no longer preserved as anything other than a sign of what it used to be – a signifier only of its own loss. The very term 'nature *preservation*' makes explicit that nature now depends on human management: nature is not so much dead as Disneyised. For Wilson, it is not nature but technology through which the essential constitution of the world, and the principles which reveal its essential properties, are perceived, witnessed and made known. He writes that today: 'technology is not merely a collection of tools and machines or a representation of power. It is also a sensorium, a field of perception. If the land is wired, so are we' (1992: 258). This view of nature as displaced by technology, existing only as a sign of its own obsolescence, evokes a habitual reflex of nostalgia often associated with both modernity and postmodernity, and consequently characteristic of much of the literature on nature concerning environmental change. Similarly motivated by an earlier politics of crisis, the meaning of second nature developed within the Frankfurt School, by theorists such as Theodor Adorno, Walter Benjamin and Georg Lukács, referred to nature transformed by human agency and renaturalised as everyday life. Second nature for Benjamin, for example, was the shopping arcade; today an exemplar would be the Nature Company or the Body Shop, in which denaturalised nature can be renaturalised as a commodity.[3]

In re-animating the concept of second nature (informed by, but not restricted to, the crisis-laden determinism outlined above), we consider nature in relation to the meaning of 'to second' as a transitive verb:

> **second tr. v. 1.** *To attend (a boxer or a duelist) as an aide or assistant.* **2.** *to promote or encourage; reinforce.* **3.** *To endorse (a motion or nomination) as a required preliminary to a vote.* **4.** (si-kond'). Chiefly British. *To transfer (a military officer, for example) temporarily.*
>
> (*American Heritage Dictionary*, 1992: 1629)

The first sense of 'to second', meaning 'to attend' or 'assist', has been explored by both Marilyn Strathern (1992a and b) and Paul Rabinow (1992, 1996a) in their accounts of nature remade through technology, or 'assisted nature'. As they note, insofar as many of the primary etymological and contemporary meanings of nature and the natural denote a separate domain, subject to its own laws and orderliness, the notion of 'assisting' nature is somewhat paradoxical. This paradox also has consequences for social actions and identities, and in particular, for relationality. As Strathern notes:

> The new reproductive technologies . . . seek to assist natural processes . . . but this . . . assistance creates new uncertainties . . . The more facilitation is given to the biological reproduction of human persons, the harder it is to think of a domain of natural facts independent of social intervention. . . . [This] will not be without consequence for the way people think about one another.
>
> (1992b: 30)

In other words, new forms of technological assistance to 'nature' not only raise ethical, legal, technical and social issues, they also raise questions at the level of meaning, and thus effect the constitution of relationality.

In addition to this definition of 'to second', we also borrow from the second and third definitions, 'to promote' and 'to endorse', drawing attention to the uses of the natural as a means of *reinforcement*. Many of the naturalisations, denaturalisations and renaturalisations we describe in this book involve the way nature is 'seconded' by culture, where nature is used as a legitimating 'vote' or grounding essentialism. Similarly, the paradoxical depiction of environmental protection as 'wilderness management' represents human agency as *extending*, or *building upon*, 'nature itself', thus conflating human activity with its objects. Finally, we borrow from the 'chiefly British' meaning of 'to second' to describe the secondment of nature through its use as a means of *transfer or replacement*. Second nature is also defined as nature seconded into a variety of forms of service; indeed, culture may be described *as* nature, as in the claim that genetically modified foods are produced through 'natural processes'. Similarly, the use of designs 'found in nature' to create packaging for products are instances of seconded nature – such as the perfume DNA, packaged in a helical bottle and sold as a beauty product (see Figure 1.1). To understand either the commercial feasibility of DNA perfume, or its desirability as a means of self-expression, a series of interpretations and analogies must be mobilised. Since no one knows what DNA smells like, the denomination of this product is not literal.[4] DNA is a scientific representation of a chemical structure, specifically the architecture of deoxyribonucleic acid. In turn, the helical structure of DNA has acquired the power to signify a kind of essence or source, a universal foundation for all living things. Although DNA may be understood as a 'natural essence', its representation as a double helix is denaturalised, insofar as it is extracted from its 'natural' context, much as a museum display of a human cell abstracts its architecture for the benefit of edification. In this case, though, the transfer of a molecular model of DNA into the design of commercial packaging effects a renaturalisation: this *eau de parfum* is analogous to the essence of life itself. These transfers are literal at the same time as they are playful, suggestive and timely. As Strathern notes:

> [I]f culture consists in established ways of bringing ideas from different domains together, then new combinations – deliberate or not – will not just extend the meanings of the domains so juxtaposed; one may expect a ricochet effect, that shifts of emphasis, dissolutions and anticipations will bounce off one area of life onto another.
>
> (1992b: 3)

A further example of 'nature seconded' is provided by another contemporary cosmetic product, Virtual Skin, from the company Prescriptives. In a promotional feature about this product entitled 'What Now, What Next?', the changing technology of cosmetic foundations – and, we suggest, of foundations more generally – is outlined:

Figure 1.1

Although Bijan's DNA perfume 'does not contain deoxyribonucleic acid', its packaging makes reference to the molecular structure of DNA, both by using a helical bottle and by incorporating a helix into the perfume's logo.

Once upon a time, foundation was supposed to be seen. It's true. Women wore base to cover up their skin. But make-up priorities have changed – we want foundation to hide blemishes, disguise shadows and be imperceptible. It has to look, act and feel like skin.

What is notable here is a shift from the use of culture to assist nature to *the replacement of the one by the other*, or their substitutability *as* one another. 'Women want liquid skin in a bottle,' says Anne Carullo, Vice President of Product Development for Worldwide Prescriptives. As transparencies, nature and culture mimic each other's qualities such that they can hardly be differentiated, while the difference between them is precisely what makes this seconding or substitution desirable. Instead of covering the other up, culture acts and feels like nature. Transparent foundations are available from Prescriptives as a second skin: 'Virtual Skin's patent-pending formula is our most natural-looking, natural-feeling foundation ever.'

What is especially interesting about this transfer are the trafficking processes between the natural and the cultural which make it possible. The problem for other foundations, it seems, the reason they continue to be visible, is that they are designed in 'a one-dimensional way, as if they were going to be applied to a flat surface, like paint'. The face, however, is not flat: 'With this in mind, Prescriptives created a three-dimensional foundation, the inspiration for which came not from skin, but from a car!' While at a car show in Tokyo, Carullo came across a painting process that gives bodywork a 3D finish. From this discovery it was apparently but a short step to 'a new era in foundation': 'The techno-wizards at Prescriptives took the technique, modified it and used it to create Virtual Skin. . . . Carullo describes the finish as super-natural.' There are twenty-three shades available in this Prescriptives spectrum in the UK, while Colorprinting in the US enables you to find 'your Exact Foundation from over 100 choices – and your Exact Colors for lips, cheeks, eyes'. 'Have you been Colorprinted?'

The transfer identified here in which 'a new generation of foundation erases the line between foundation and skin' is only made possible by a complex series of interchanges or ricochets. The acceptability of skin in a bottle – transparent, artificial skin that has visible effects, but is itself imperceptible – arises from the use of a technique developed in relation to the bodywork of cars and its adaptation to the bodywork of the human face. However, this seconding of a technical application follows from the 'realization' that the human face is three- rather than one-dimensional: 'It has peaks and curves and is made up of lots of translucent layers, colours and tones.' This relay results in a virtual application that replaces nature by acquiring the property of transferability not simply from one to two dimensions but to three dimensions and then back again. This fluidity is captured in the logo, slogan or brand which can be transferred across promotion, packaging and products, allowing for what Margaret Morse describes as 'liquidity': 'the exchange of values between different ontological levels and otherwise incommensurable facets of life' (1990: 194).

As stated earlier, we approach the representation of nature and culture in the age of globalisation as a means of analysing changing orders of scale, dimension, limit and horizon through which contexts of comparison are produced, with corresponding effects on how the world is perceived, enacted and defined. As worlds are remade and re-imagined, so too are analytic techniques for tracing their emergence made possible, and necessary. In thinking through the specific processes whereby DNA can be marketed as a perfume, or cosmetic products described in terms of the sleek exteriors of cars, we seek to develop methods and terminologies to help us specify the movements, or stages, through which such comparisons make sense. What are the patterns linking DNA perfume to Virtual Skin? How are both of these products and their representations linked to the increasing visibility of technologies designed to assist the human body? What does it mean for DNA to become a brandname?

● ● ●

In the analysis of the icons in Part One of this book, we seek to show how the definitions of nature which functioned as models or analogies for context in western self-understandings are being transformed. In this chapter, we consider three icons which are definitive of the changing facts of life in the global context. The blue planet, the foetus and the cell are used here to create a set of critical orienting devices for millennial global nature, global culture.[5] They help us to demonstrate how familiar universalist essentialisms, such as 'the human species', or 'the family of man', are altered through the processes of recontextualisation evident within globalisation. How might we compare the differences between the universalising shared-human-nature and shared-human-culture essentialisms of mid-twentieth-century western discourse with those viewed through the turn-of-the-millennium panoptics of the foetus, the blue planet and the cell? Using these overdetermined contemporary images as our lenses, we raise here a number of questions to which we return in each of the chapters in Part Two.

Framing this discussion of 'spheres of life' is a concern with the ways in which the global refigures a sense of both scale and connection through the depiction of life forms. The icons of the blue planet, the foetus and the cell can be seen to represent an emergent universalism we describe as *panhumanity*, illuminated by a specific way of seeing life (as a glowing blue orb, as a vulnerable being, or as a permeable bodily unit) and defined by new forms of universal human connection (not only as a family or a species, but as a global population at shared risk of global environmental destruction and united by collective global images). Panhumanity, in this sense, describes the shared subject position produced by risks such as global warming, through which the 'right to life' of individuals can stand metonymically for and beside the survival of the Earth, as a planet, itself. Panhumanity is thus a term to describe a different measure of the universal human subject, contrasting, for example, with that depicted within the 'family of man' (see Celia Lury, this volume and 1998). Panhumanity, a term to describe the effects of a different ability to represent, to scale and to visualise life as global, planetary and endangered, is thus the kind of perspectival shift we seek to explore by attending to the recontextualisations at work in the production of global nature, global culture and their corresponding subjects and objects.

● ○   The Blue Planet

The image of the blue planet became one of the most widely distributed icons of the late twentieth century, appearing on PC screens, on sports clothes, on coffee mugs and on book and magazine covers. Be it the dynamic, revolving planet that opens the BBC news every evening in Britain, the symbol of the vulnerable Earth in the environmental pressure group Greenpeace's literature, or the shrinking globe that invites international travel in British Airways advertisements, the blue planet continues to be one of the most pervasive visual icons of globality, persistently adopted and adapted in western advertising, media iconography and environmental politics.

Taken by astronauts in the late 1960s, the original footage of the blue planet was shot from the point of view of 'looking down' or 'looking back' at the Earth (see Figure 1.2). This perspective on the Earth has come to convey a sense of both connectedness to, and disconnectedness from, earthly concerns. The aerial God's-eye view of the blue planet confirms not only the Earth's uniqueness (it is described as the only planet that glows), but also the relative insignificance of humankind itself (what value could one individual, family or nation have in a scale of these proportions?). Suspended in space, in infinite stillness, the blue planet has been much discussed as an image that encapsulates contemporary understandings of 'life on earth' (Cosgrove, 1994; Ingold, 1993; Myers, 1999a; Sachs, 1994). Evoking both endangered fragility and the vitality of a luminescent life force, glowing with energy, the image of the Earth as the blue planet signifies both isolation and commonality.

Responses to the image of the blue planet have been governed by a combination of vulnerability and wonder: on the one hand, the technological developments that brought this sight to a global audience reinforce the sense of a continuing mastery over nature (scientific vision is no longer terrestrial); on the

Figure 1.2

Suspended in space, in infinite stillness, the first photographs of the Earth taken from outer space have been much discussed as images that encapsulate contemporary understandings of 'life on earth', making of 'the blue planet' an iconic image of both contemporary technological progress and fears about endangered human futures.

other hand, 'man' is humbled through this visual reminder of his insignificance (see Figure 1.3). Integral to the popular excitement surrounding the landing of the first man on the moon, the photographs and televised images that have since become global icons of space travel convey something of that 1960s ethos: a technologised pioneer spirit in its cosmic incarnation. Then, still mid-century, science promised to open up new possibilities, and technology materialised the means to realise them; together they would produce great achievements to benefit humankind. Seeing and knowing were bound together in these frozen moments of photographic evidence which captured history in the making. Western civilisation's progress narrative could be confirmed through this visual icon of discovery and exploration, in which space was still understood as another (perhaps final) frontier, a common horizon, a limit whose anticipated transgression both motivated a movement forwards and defined the limits of human endeavour.[6]

Since its first appearance as an image, the blue planet has been deployed as a symbol of global unity, international collaboration and shared planetary interdependence. Instead of the horizon being the natural limit of humanity's expectations, a limit set by the curve of the earth and its movements around the sun, 'mankind' encountered a planet made visible as a whole, discrete entity. Space became a new location from which to view ourselves, and this *perspectival shift* has produced both a new context for universalisms and an added visual dimension by which the universe scales the order of things. In other words, the project of exploration in space now appears to offer the chance to transcend earthly geographies, marked by 'man's' petty squabbles over land and property, and to shift perspective – indeed to move beyond the notion of perspective associated with the acceptance of a natural horizon altogether – opening the possibility of inhabiting a territory beyond: a space previously reserved for powers beyond humankind. This is the space of *panhumanity*, of a newly imaged and imagined form of global unity. The panoptical lens of space photography both extends and restricts the possibilities of what it is to be human; it establishes a space of *visualisation without horizon*, a space which Gilles Deleuze (cited in Rabinow, 1992: 234) describes as unlimited finitude (*fini illimité*).

A foundational text of blue-planet imagery is the large, glossy, atlas-like book *The Home Planet* (Kelley, 1988), which unites photographs from Soviet cosmonauts and American astronauts in the name of global collaboration. Dedicated to 'all the children of the world', this publication aims to encapsulate the spirit of the age in which a new planetary consciousness does not simply promise, but anticipates, a better future. Endorsing this spirit of shared exploration, Jacques-Yves Cousteau opens his introductory remarks thus:

> Like most fathers, by clear star-studded skies I used to take each of my two little boys in my arms for a glimpse at infinity. The splendor of the unreachable silenced their chatterboxes for a few seconds. They raised their arms and closed their little fingers in a futile attempt to grasp one of the twinkling sparks that dot our dreams. The little fellows obeyed the command reported by Ovid: 'God elevated man's

Figure 1.3

*Photographs and televised images of space travel
convey at once a sense of technological mastery
over nature and 'man's' vulnerability and relative
insignificance.*

forehead and ordered him to contemplate the stars.' . . . My father was ninety-one when the Apollo program was deployed. He never believed that a human being would ever reach the moon.

(1988: Foreword)

Progress is narrated here as an intergenerational exchange, an expression of paternal expectation, and a confidence that with each new generation 'man' will benefit from his increasing access to the universe and hence deeper understanding of himself. Looking up into the infinite universe, father and sons stand silenced, awestruck and enabled in contemplation of an unending, untouchable and formerly unchartable, night sky. Through an implicit analogy to his own undersea explorations, and as a kind of unofficial ambassador for panhumanity, Cousteau concludes:

[O]ur planet is one . . . borderlines are artificial . . . humankind is one single community on board spaceship Earth. . . . The meaning of the space conquest is symbolized by the famous set of pictures taken from the moon, celebrating the birth of global consciousness that will help build a peaceful future for humankind.

(1988: Foreword)

But there is also a sense in which these pictures are understood to offer more than this: they bring the future forward into the present. In a world in which the horizon is recognised as artificial, as no longer natural, it is as if, as global subjects (as fathers and sons in the same time and space, not separated by technological advances from previous generations), we can all now reach out and touch 'the twinkling sparks that dot our dreams'. As editor of *The Home Planet*, Kevin Kelley, writes:

Already the vision of a distant, beautiful, vulnerable home planet has, for many of these astronauts and cosmonauts, forever altered their consciousness of themselves, of Earth, and of our place in the cosmos. And now, through their own words and through the spectacular images they captured on film, these space explorers offer us all the possibility of a similar transformation. . . . *The Home Planet* is the result of uncommon international cooperation at every turn . . . [it] brings together the essential humanity we take with us into space, and which is so fully enhanced by the experience.

(Kelley, 1988: coverleaf)

This 'essential humanity', when viewed from outer space, is recontextualised as what we call *panhumanity*: a collectivity transformed, 'forever altered' in its consciousness, by being after the fact of an earlier universalism, the boundaries and horizons of which have been transformed. Panhumanity is united not only by a shared human nature, or family tree, but by a shared culture, composed of images such as the blue planet which convey a sense of vulnerability and risk. The image of the blue planet is thus both a transformative image in its own right, and an icon of an era defined by the 'altered

Figure 1.4

Like the image of the mushroom cloud, deforestation has become a symbol of human global vulnerability, providing a counter-image to the glowing blue planet. In this poster from a conference sponsored by Third World First, the image of an impoverished black child standing against an orb-like chainsawed cross-section of tree-trunk is used both literally and symbolically to represent the shared threat to panhumanity.

consciousness' of the panoptical, heavenly gaze which captures the planet as a glowing blue orb. As Fred Hoyle predicted, 'Once a photograph of the Earth, taken from the outside, is available . . . a new idea as powerful as any in history will be let loose' (1948, quoted by Kelley, 1988, on inside coverleaf).

Panhumanity is thus defined by a mixture of pride in technological achievement and simultaneous appreciation of its associated risks. The awe evoked by the first extra-terrestrial photographs of a planet glowing in the darkness of space was heavily tinged with fears concerning future human survival, and the technological risks necessary to produce such images in the first place. The image of the Earth as self-regulating, glowing and radiant is overlaid by a simultaneous sense of its vulnerability and need for protection. The counter-icon to the blue planet that has shaped postwar consciousness is the image of the huge mushroom-cloud explosion of the Hiroshima bomb – the atomic threat that could destroy humanity on a global scale.[7] The dangers of modern scientific and technological projects, already present in the popular imagination when the blue planet came into cultural circulation, increasingly define the notion of a 'shared planet'. At the turn of the millennium the risks of environmental degradation, famine and poverty are increasingly associated with the very technologies that epitomised human progress in an earlier era, such as combustion engines and refrigerators, which have now produced ozone depletion and global warming. This is a defining contradiction of panhumanity under the sign of the blue planet, in which deforestation has become another contemporary counter-image to the glowing blue orb (see Figure 1.4).

As well as illuminating the Earth's vulnerability to the dangers of scientific endeavour, the image of the blue planet condenses contemporary anxieties about the negative effects of growth, industrialisation and consumption on a global scale. With the displacement of the Earth's horizon as the natural context for understandings of progress, there is no longer a clear sense of an outside or deferred future on to which the rejected, the unwanted, the disowned effects of progress can be displaced. For example, when adopted by the environmental group Friends of the Earth, the blue planet came to represent the dangers of reckless growth and consumption. From this environmentalist perspective, the blue planet – held still, suspended in space, on the verge of catastrophe – radiates an urgency for global unification around the problems of pollution, global warming and environmental risk (Macnaghten and Urry, 1998).[8]

The advent of panhumanity symbolised by the blue planet thus seems to offer the possibility of both a future that can be anticipated and a future that might never happen: tomorrow, *and* the possibility that tomorrow might never come. Both scenarios are the consequence of the loss of familiar and reassuring horizons and bring with them uncertainties and insecurities. As Barbara Duden suggests:

> One of the most fundamental but least noted events in the second half of the twentieth century is the loss of horizon. We live somewhere between satellite TV, which knows no skyline, and the telephone, which allows us to reach beyond our line of vision to connect with any number we choose. . . . It was just yesterday when the whole earth suddenly 'appeared' as the Blue Planet and we began to accept the fact that all would be exposed to recording equipment from far above this Tower of Babel. (1993: 10)

We extend Duden's claims about the loss of a horizon as a perspectival shift definitive of global culture, global nature to suggest that such shifts have consequences too for our perception of collective human existence, and for the time and space co-ordinates through which human life is understood at the turn of the millennium (see Figure 1.5).

Figure 1.5

The loss of familiar horizons, and the new perspectives offered by an extra-terrestrial panoptics, exemplify a shift definitive of global nature, global culture – as is suggested by this image of the Earth, taken from the surface of the moon, offering a kind of recontextualised horizon against which to view the 'home planet'.

The Foetus

Such changes in orientation – or shifts in the uses of nature to ground familiar registers of perspective, scale or panoptics – are not restricted to how we understand the cosmos and our place within it. They also shape emergent notions of the human body. So, for example, Barbara Duden suggests that the image of the foetus might be understood 'as one among the modern results of living without horizon' (1993: 14). As Duden and Donna Haraway have both argued, there are striking parallels between the iconic power of the blue planet and that of the foetus:

> The idol of the fetus has only one competitor at present, and that is the Blue Planet. Just as the sonogram of the fetus stands for one life, so the TV satellite picture stands for all life.
>
> (Duden, 1993: 110)

> The fetus and the planet earth are sibling seed worlds in technoscience. If NASA photographs of the blue, cloud-swathed whole Earth are icons for the emergence of global, national, and local struggles over a recent natural-technical object of knowledge called the environment, then the ubiquitous images of glowing free-floating human fetuses condense and intensify struggles over an equally new and disruptive technoscientific object of knowledge, namely 'life itself'.
>
> (Haraway, 1997: 174)

The most celebrated foetal images are those produced by Swedish photographer Lennart Nilsson. First appearing in *Life* magazine in 1965, and since then the object of sustained popular fascination, Nilsson's photographs offer a vivid documentary portrait of unborn life (see Figure 1.6) A series of Nilsson's photographs are reproduced in *Being Born* (Kitzinger, 1986) to illustrate an account of the development of the foetus from conception to birth, accompanied by a text in which the well-known British anthropologist Sheila Kitzinger addresses the reader directly. The image accompanying the 'once upon a time' beginning of the story of the origins of life shows a foetus attached to a placenta by an umbilical cord, floating in a globe-like sphere of white light. The planetary connotations of the spherical foetal container are amplified by the super-imposition of the foetus on to a black and white background resembling a starry galaxy.[9] The foetus is suspended in the glowing amniotic orb that radiates the promise of a new life, and the amniotic sac itself is suspended in space, connecting this new life to the life forces of the universe. Both the foetus and its planetary encasement are represented here against an infinite cosmos suggesting limitless time and space (see Figure 1.7)

The comparison between the foetus floating in a 'void' and the vulnerable astronaut drifting in space has been much commented upon by feminist critics. As Barbara Katz Rothman famously remarked: 'The fetus in utero has become a metaphor for "man" in space, floating free, attached only by the umbilical cord to the spaceship. But where is the mother in the metaphor? She has become empty space' (1986: 114).[10] Images of the foetus shown in 'curled-up profile, with its enlarged head and fin-like

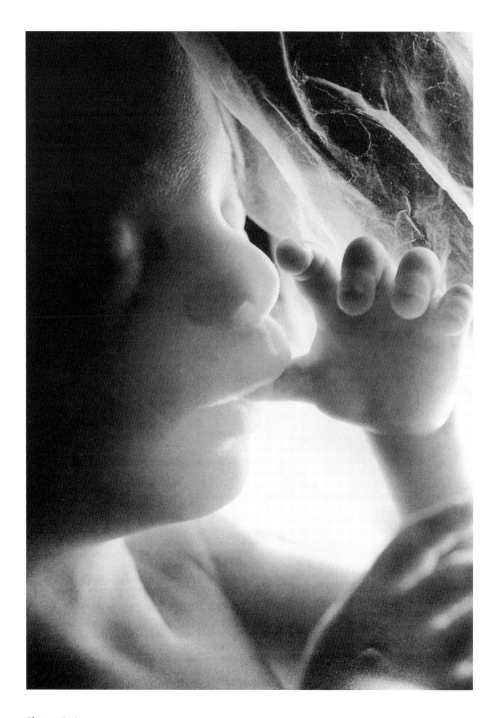

Figure 1.6

*Swedish photographer Lennart Nilsson's images of
'life before birth', first published in* Life *magazine in
1965, are among the twentieth century's most well-
known photographs, and have made of the foetus a
definitive icon of both panhumanity and life itself.*

Figure 1.7

The foetus is shown in this Nilsson photograph suspended in the glowing amniotic orb that radiates the promise of new life, set against a starry background, as if connecting it to the forces of the universe. Together, the image of the foetus and the blue planet comprise icons of the inner and outer space that belong to global nature, global culture.

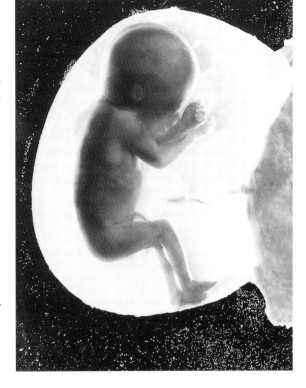

arms, suspended in its balloon of amniotic fluid' can be traced back to the same period in which the image of the blue planet was produced (Petchesky, 1987: 61). For Duden, the connections between foetus *in amnio* and 'man' in space are hard to ignore. Writing of the 1965 *Life* magazine photographs, she comments:

> I look at the figure in its trans-parent balloon, the limbs drawn up to the torso. A background appears, like a starry sky. A glossy umbilical cord connects the creature to a pink bubbly shape and I am reminded of photos of astronauts floating in space.
>
> (1993: 11).

As Duden's reading demonstrates, foetal imagery comprises a formative discourse linking outer (planetary) space and inner (amniotic) space. In the 1990 *Life* magazine account of how life begins, the newly fertilised egg is described as an 'eerie planet floating through space' and the blastocyst is referred to as having 'landed' at eight days, '[L]ike a lunar module, the embryo facilitates its landing on the uterus with leg-like structures composed of sugar molecules on the surface' (Duden, 1993: 14).

The fantasy of autonomy from the mother is extended further in popular representations that have fetishised technologies as modes of reproduction in themselves (Petchesky, 1987: 63). In *2001 Space Odyssey* (Kubrick, 1968), for example, autoreplication renders the maternal body redundant as the 'starchild' lives on as the sole survivor of cosmic extermination; like an embryo in outer space, this cyborg becomes the symbol of life and fertility (Sofia, 1984).

The pervasiveness of the metaphorical interchanges between foetal and planetary imagery, and their substitutability for one another, offer an example of recontextualisation in which different orders of life itself become analogies for one another. A further parallel might be drawn between these two icons insofar as they both exclude particular manifestations of life whilst simultaneously symbolising, even fetishising, 'life' in the abstract. Just as the grounding function of nature as context, the horizon, disappears in relation to the icon of the blue planet, so too does the woman who was the context for the icon of the foetus: the mother. In both their places is the space of the 'environment'.

The combination of autonomy and permeability in understandings of the foetus and the planet leads to a particular configuration of risk and responsibility, which is in turn correlated to questions of national and imperial sovereignty (see Ginsburg, 1989; Hartouni, 1992; Petchesky, 1987; Phelan, 1993). Open to the potentially negative influences of their relative environments, the foetus and the blue planet both invoke discourses of individual and collective responsibility for the future of life itself: as Duden has argued, 'just as the Blue Planet – "seen" from space – is the environment for all life, so woman is the environment for new life' (1993: 2). Within this move is evident what Duden calls the 'transmogrification of the unborn into a part of an endangered eco-system . . . the protection of life' (1993: 2). The duty of the mother becomes managerial: she is the custodian of a new life, of life itself, and this imperative must be manifest in her behaviour during pregnancy (see McNeil and Litt, 1992). In this series of shifts, facilitated by the convergence of changing technologies and political discourses over the past ten or fifteen years, pregnancy has been transformed into a 'process to be managed, the expected child into a fetus, the mother into an ecosystem, the unborn into a life, and life into a supreme value' (Duden, 1993: 2). The icon of the foetus thus condenses wider imperatives of global systems management that will sustain the planet for future generations; as a sacralised and fetishised image of endangered life, the foetus stands in for the whole of life itself and symbolises the future. The sustainability of life on planet Earth and the viability of the life of the foetus outside the mother's body become the focus for the discursive management of bodily and global risks, threats and catastrophes. As Duden argues:

> As the pink disk of the zygote appeals for the maintenance of one immune system, so the blue disk of the biosphere appeals for the survival of the global system. Both disks act like sacraments for the 'real presence' of life, for whose continuation a global 'we' is made responsible. Thus a misplaced abstractness, which makes the fetus into an object, creates the *sacrum* in which the futile pursuit of survival overpowers contemporary consciousness.
>
> (1993: 110)

Here, the 'global perspective' identified by Ingold (1993) is accompanied by what might be called the invention of a 'foetal perspective' which both complements and inverts it.[11] What is at stake here, both politically and culturally, is the way in which these icons successfully reconfigure our contemporary notions of horizon or natural limit, thus redefining understandings of inner and outer, of self and other, of human and non-human, of life and death. In both images, the use of nature as a model for context may be understood in terms of displaced horizons and the consequent respatialisation of both outer and inner universes.

● ● ●   **The Cell**

Like the foetus and the blue planet, the cell is one of the most iconic 'spheres of 'life' at a bodily level. The cell is commonly conceptualised as the most basic unit of life, be it plant, animal or human. Accounts of our 'biological origins' lead us back to the cell as the original 'sphere of life' inside the maternal body.

The cell is arguably the fundamental unit of our bodily communication network in the contemporary imagination. As historian Michael Holquist suggests: 'We are awash in streams of information that course through single cells to different organs and systems in our bodies, a constant flood of communication' (1989: 1). If we conceptualise the cell as the basic unit of life, then

> the cell is to body communication . . . as the phoneme is to linguistic com-
> munication, the minimal unit of meaningful difference. . . . The cell, like the sign, is
> a means for keeping stasis and change in dialogue. . . . Communication within the
> body occurs much as it does outside the body.
>
> (Holquist, 1989: 5–6)

Seen as a visual referent for our ongoing negotiations around such borders, the cell is the iconic signifier of life itself at its most bodily level. To generalise, we might say that 'cell theory' has been one of the most influential scientific formulations of the concept of life which pervaded twentieth-century western thought. As Holquist points out, 'since the work of Schleiden and Schwann in the 1830s biology has taken "cell theory" as one of its basic paradigms' (1989: 5). And as numerous studies have demonstrated, the conceptualisation of the cell as the basic unit of life has not been restricted to biological discourse but has permeated our understandings of contemporary social life.[12]

Like the blue planet and the foetus, the cell radiates ambiguities about its relative autonomy and permeability. It is a sphere that confounds Ingold's model of surface and core, and of separation and integration. Writing of the changing historical significance of different conceptualisations of orbs and spheres, Ingold proposes that we now live in an age characterised by a belief in 'global environmentalism' which, 'far from marking humanity's reintegration into the world, signals the culmination of a process of separation. . . . The global environment is not a lifeworld, it is a world apart from life' (1993: 31–2). For Ingold, our increasing sense of the planet as a globe that supports life on its surface contrasts unfavourably with a previous sense of it as a sphere that contained life in a more integrated way: '[T]he lifeworld, imaged from an experiential centre, is spherical in form, whereas a world divorced from life, that is yet complete in itself, is imaged in the form of a globe' (1993: 35). It is partly the prevalence of certain kinds of visual imagery of the globe that produces such an effect: from the geography lesson to the astronauts' photographs and television footage, visual images of the globe as something to be looked at from afar have conferred a sense of separation and objectification. Accompanying this shift has been the general assumption that the planet is an environment to be managed, to be colonised and to be either exploited or preserved; whatever its form, the global environment is nature separated from 'humanity'. Our changing relationship to nature within this framework, according to Ingold, might be seen as a 'movement from revelation to control, and from partial knowledge to calculated risk'. This is accompanied by the 'undermining of cosmological certainties and the growing belief in, and indeed dependence upon, the technological fix' (Ingold, 1993: 41).

In light of Ingold's argument, contemporary conceptualisations of the cell both extend previous models of spherical integration and yet also belong to this more recent image of the global environment. The cell is not separate from life, but rather is seen to hold the 'secrets of life' within it (Keller, 1990); indeed, life is not located on its surface, but rather is seen to emanate from its centre (Ingold, 1993: 37). Unlike the globe, the cell contains human life literally and symbolically; the permeability of the egg cell's surface by the 'penetrating' sperm is required for processes of procreation and reproduction to begin. Like the globe, however, the cell is endowed with self-regulating properties that are central to its survival, and, furthermore, it is represented as an independent entity whose protective surface defends it against invasion from the outside. There are, nevertheless, important ways in which our image of the cell is informed by a sense that this sphere, whilst being defended, is also subject to influence (interference): for example, viruses enter cells and yet are often impossible to reach since they are protected by the cells' borders; and genetic engineering seeks to transform the cell by interfering with its DNA and yet to preserve some of its original form.[13]

But it is not only metaphors of permeability that characterise our conceptualisations of cell mutability, it is also the activity of cell division. In scientific accounts of the beginning of life, embryonic development progresses as cells continue to divide. For example, in the origin story that addresses the child reader in *Being Born*, Kitzinger writes: '[T]he one cell split into two cells. The two cells split into four. The four cells split into eight. And the ball of cells grew and grew till it looked like a shimmering, silvery blackberry' (1986: 14–15). The egg cell is thus conceptualised as transformable both through the permeability of its surface and through the doubling process that characterises its generative activity. Embryo development is perhaps the most common image of cell division and has become an image closely connected to notions of 'life', but cells are more generally conceived of through their self-replicating activities and their interactions with other cells around them (see Figure 1.8). These autogenerative processes raise important questions about the cultural connotations of the cell as a sphere. For in the case of the cell, whilst the surface is disturbed as one cell becomes two, it is not broken by an external being or substance when the cell divides. Uniquely, then, the composition of the cell remains unchanged as it duplicates itself and generates life.

Current perceptions of the permeability and transformability of the cell are embedded within particular historical developments affecting ideas about the cellular body. In the history of immunology, for example, there are important changes in the

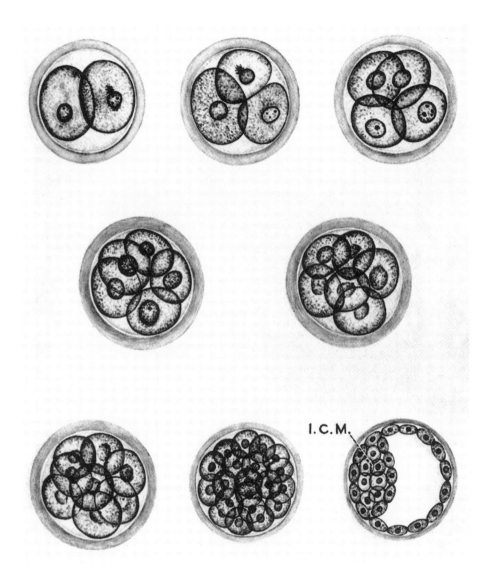

I.C.M.

Figure 1.8

In the classic account of the beginnings of life,
embryo development progresses as cells continue to
divide, as shown in this photomicrograph of the
process of cleavage.

conceptualisation of inner and outer spaces and of the cell's role in maintaining bodily equilibrium. As Alfred Tauber details, a leading theorist in turn-of-the-twentieth-century immunology, Elie Metchnikoff (1905), applied Darwin's evolutionary model of 'competitive struggle and the survival of organisms better adapted to their environment' to his own embryological research in which he viewed 'the developing organism as composed of competing cell lineages, thus applying the idea of Darwinian struggle to the internal environment of the organism itself' (Tauber, 1994: 19). In so doing, Metchnikoff shifted the notion of struggle between species into a conflict '*within* the individual organism', claiming the 'struggle of the phagocytes with intruders' is only part of the immunological picture, the 'surveillance of malignant or senile cells' being another. According to this view, the immune system as a whole (phagocyte) 'determined what was not to be destroyed or eaten, whether foreign or native' (Tauber, 1994: 19). The legacy of such a model changed our understanding of the properties of cells generally and shaped the conceptualisation of their activities as being in dialogue with their environments: '[A]ll cells are able, by modifying their function under the direction of susceptibility, to adapt themselves to changes in the surrounding conditions. All living elements are able, therefore, to acquire a certain degree of immunity' (Metchnikoff, quoted in Tauber, 1994: 19). Tauber reads Metchnikoff's approach as suggesting that organisms are '*in principle* defined . . . as ever-changing. In such a context, health cannot be defined absolutely' (1994: 24).

Although these theories were heavily contested and have been reworked considerably, certain basic assumptions have continued to shape our associations with the cell today. The construction of the cell as a unit of an immunological environment is central to our contemporary understanding of health, illness and bodily boundaries. As Holquist argues, the cell is conceptualised within these frameworks as part of an interactive universe. It can be conceived as

> a matrix of elements, such as cytoplasm, chromosomes and ribosomes, organized around a nucleus that contains the source of information in DNA. It is a little universe not unlike the tiny world of the atom, which, with its electrons and neutrons circulating around the nucleus, also images centering as a necessary fiction.
>
> (Holquist, 1989: 5)

This new bodily environmentalism signals a departure from previous mechanistic images of the human body and has led to a metaphor of the body not as a machine but an ecosystem: '"[H]omeostasis" . . . [referred to] how internal alterations in the body work to maintain the constancy of the whole system in the face of changes in the external environment' (Holquist, 1989: 8). In biological discourse the cell is conceptualised as being in dialogue with its environment:

> Cells are highly specialized; in order to do their work consistently they must be freed from the constant changes of the fluids that sweep about them in a constant

flux. Thus the cell membrane acts much as the epidermis of the total body does: as a border between an internal environment dedicated to stability and an external environment charged with ever-changing differences.

(Holquist, 1989: 6)

This environmental metaphor has been widely taken up in theories of the body and its well-being. For example, in his analysis of 'cancer and the self' Roger Levin develops the notion of 'cancer as an environment of bodily felt experiencing' (1987: 166). He suggests that cancer research has increasingly focused on 'the regulatory environment of abnormal cell growth' (1987: 167). Indeed, Levin argues that the twentieth century witnessed a paradigmatic shift towards a concern with the body as an environment (1987: 168). Within this model the cell is a semi-autonomous unit that is responsive to its surroundings. It is hard to distinguish between the environment and its inhabitants in this model of the body. The cell has its own environment: it is a separate sphere that must defend itself against invasion; but it is also part of the more general environment of the body's interior which is composed of, amongst other things, millions of more or less healthy cells that are endlessly dividing.

Furthermore, this model of the cell as the carrier of bodily meanings has bestowed upon it a kind of selfhood. As Tauber has argued, within immunological discourse this 'conception of organism posited a dynamic, teleologically based notion of selfhood', and the phagocyte as 'possessor of its own destiny and mediator of the organism's selfhood' resonates with contemporary understandings of the cell (1994: 26). As Emily Martin suggests, these constructions reconfigure the imaginative limits of self and other:

> [W]hereas in earlier time, the skin might have been regarded as the border of the individual self, now these microscopic cells are seen as tiny individual selves. . . It is possible that in the 1990s what was the patient (or person) has itself become *an environment* for a new core self, which exists at a cellular level.
>
> (1992: 415, emphasis in original)

But it is not simply that the cell is invested with an almost human motivation or agency, but also that this bodily unit is often seen in relation to the personhood of its host. Indeed, as Jackie Stacey argues in Chapter 4, within some alternative medical discourses of health and illness the cell is seen as a microcosm of the self. It may represent the embodiment of emotional distress; it may be a sign of one's lack of defences; it may be proof of one's healthy boundaries. It is significant that these new environmental metaphors of the cellular body bring with them certain imperatives: the responsibility to maintain balance, the need to keep oneself informed, the duty to calculate risk. Whilst the connections between cell and self build outwards towards a global environmentalism and might therefore seem to bring them a sense of community and collectivity, there is another outcome of these relational dialogues across changes of scale in the ways that individuals come to be held responsible for the maintenance of their own internal environments. The reworking of western scientific notions of the cell within discourses of self-healing effects more than a change of scale or location; it produces the following discursive moves. The cell is a unit that has been designated environmental qualities – *we are thus connected to planetary forces through our innermost forms of embodiment*. The cell's separateness and strength may be crucial to our individual survival, but its integrity is under constant threat from both inside and outside the body – *we are therefore responsible for monitoring all influences of our own immune harmony*. Condensing all kinds of information about our histories, the cell is the unit that must be relied upon to achieve autonomy and yet its permeability reminds us that we are always at risk – *we embody the biographies of our own well-being*. These are the recalibrated bioscapes of global nature, global culture.

● ● ● **Notes**

1   Our concern with contextualisation differs from theorists of globalisation such as Giddens (1990, 1991). In our view, the emergence of globalisation is linked not simply to an increase in processes of dis- or re-embedding, that is, in motility, *but to radically transformed notions of contextualisation or embedding themselves*. Our argument in this respect more closely resembles that of Strathern (1992a and b), who has similarly claimed that nature provides an important model for context in western societies.

2   As Marilyn Strathern has noted: '[C]ontextualisation was never a neutral activity, [and] is not without its consequences' (1995b: 153).

3   For an analysis of the Nature Company, see Smith (1996), and of the Body Shop, see Kaplan (1995) and also Chapter 4 below.

4   The label on the bottle says it contains no deoxyribonucleic acid. Significantly, the bottle itself is comprised of a triple helix, unlike DNA, which is structured along two helices.

5   These are life forms in which understandings of context and shared future are not naturally limited by the distant horizon; instead they are defined by the permeability of borders, and shifting differences between inside and outside, between life and death. This understanding of borders or limits is most clearly exemplified in contemporary systems thinking, in which systems define their own boundaries. In such understandings, systems differentiate themselves and thereby constitute whatever lies outside the boundary as an environment (a process Niklas Luhmann [1989] describes as context control).

6   It was supposedly his understanding of the implication of seeing a ship disappear below the horizon which convinced Christopher Columbus that it was worth setting sail for what were to be named the Americas.

7   In his compelling account of the image of the blue planet both as specific geographical or cartographical image and as a symbol of US imperialism, Dennis Cosgrove (1994) analyses the close links between the optimism conveyed by these images from space science and the growing pessimism towards other aerial technologies produced during the Cold War, in the aftermath of Hiroshima and Nagasaki, and the beginnings of the Vietnam War.

8   However, the displacement and marginalisation of human life in this use of the global icon of the blue planet had uneven and destabilising political effects. As anthropologist Tim Ingold (1993) argues, the image of the suspended blue orb can be seen to suggest a distancing of humans from an apparently sealed and separate geographical entity. Indeed, Friends of the Earth stopped using this image in their promotional material for this very reason.

9   This image of the foetus is Nilsson's personal favourite, which he calls 'the spaceman' (personal communication, Mrs Nilsson).

10 These photographs have been of particular concern to feminists for over two decades, in part because of their widespread use by anti-abortion campaigns to promote foetal rights. For a

comprehensive review of feminist debates about the foetus and foetal imagery, see Morgan and Michaels (1999).

11   Indeed both perspectives are closely related to the emergence of a genetic perspective on nature and life, which is arguably one of the most significant perspectival and technological shifts for which the twentieth century will later come to be known (see Chapter 6).

12   See, for example, Martin (1992, 1994), Spanier (1991), Tauber (1994), Weindling (1981). For an example of the personification of the cell, see Gary Taubes' 'Conversations in a Cell' which discusses Stuart Schreiber's research on 'how a cell talks with the outside world' (Taubes, 1996: 49).

13   Of course, the relative autonomy or permeability of the cell varies according to type and function. The egg cell is the ultimate permeable sphere in our cultural imagination. The most prevalent scenario in popular and biological narratives of procreation is that of the large ripe egg passively awaiting penetration by the most eager of competing sperm. As Emily Martin highlighted in her classic critique of conceptualisations of the egg and the sperm, such models legitimate conservative notions of femininity as essentially passive and masculinity as essentially active: the typical supposedly 'objective' account in biological textbooks describes the egg as static and as 'large and passive', and the sperm as moving with energy, velocity and purpose (Martin, 1992: 412; see also Spanier, 1991: 338).

Chapter 2 / Imprints of Time

In discussing the foetus, the blue planet and the cell as icons, we began by considering their importance as symbols of life, or life itself, as has been suggested by numerous commentators, most notably Barbara Duden (1993) and Wolfgang Sachs (1994). Such iconic shifts must also be appreciated in the light of an earlier reconfiguration of life, labour and language argued by Michel Foucault to instantiate the modern era. In his famous passage in *The History of Sexuality: Volume 1* describing the shift from consanguinity to population, Foucault argues that governmentality was realigned with a reversal in the capacity to define life and death:

> For a long time, one of the characteristic privileges of sovereign power was the right to decide life and death. . . . Since the classical age the West has undergone a very profound transformation of these mechanisms of power. . . . This death that was based on the law of the sovereign is now manifested as simply the reverse of the right of the social body to ensure, maintain, and develop its life. . . . The atomic situation is now at the end point of this process: the power to expose a whole population to death is the underside of this power to guarantee an individual's continued existence.
>
> (1980: 135–7)

In addition to describing the shift from the individual to the population as the object of sovereignty over life, Foucault also describes here a new 'right of the social body to ensure, maintain, or develop its life' (1980: 136). New definitions of life are thus important not only as iconic signifiers, but as forms of governmentality, as Duden illustrates in her discussion of foetal rights in Germany. Having become 'life' or 'a life', nature is reinscribed as the social body in need of management, protection and surveillance.

One interpretation of how nature has begun to signify a different sense of context, therefore, may be *that nature is increasingly understood in terms of life as a project, an ordering principle, or a constitutive purpose to existence.* Raymond Williams describes a similar shift to Foucault, when he suggests that:

> From the late eighteenth century, and very markedly in the nineteenth century, the . . . personification of nature changed. From the underlying image of the

constitutional lawyer, men moved to a different figure: the selective breeder; Nature the selective breeder. Indeed the habit of personification, which except for rather formal uses had been visibly weakening, was very strongly revived by this new concept of an actively shaping, indeed intervening, force.

(1980: 73)

According to Williams, 'what changed this emphasis was of course the evidence and the idea of evolution: natural forms had not only a constitution but a history' (1980: 73).[1] If the Victorian idea of nature concerned not only constitution, but the order by which such a constitution was principled, then, as Robert M. Young (1985) has claimed, it is evident why Darwinism not only changed understandings of 'man's' place in nature, but also reordered the perception of nature's place in 'man'. Formerly providing a context for the emergence of human civilisation out of primitive savagery, the idea of belonging to a state of nature is *internalised*, becoming human nature – an inner wilderness requiring management, cultivation and discipline. The need to become civilised thus imposes a new, modern govermentality upon the human subject, for whom animal ancestry became, as Williams perceives, *both evidence and idea* for changing conceptions of selfhood and society.

Williams argues that a separate domain of nature emerges in conjunction with early eighteenth-century European conceptions of it as a material realm governed by principles and laws (hence the notion of a 'natural order' so essential both to natural history in the early modern period and to modern biology). Lawlike, mechanical nature is both personified and unified within European science in a manner which parallels monotheism – in particular the Judaeo-Christian model of a deity that is singular, personified and originary. With the advent of Darwinism, nature replaces, though complements, God as the origin of the diversity of life, including humanity itself (Williams, 1976, 1980).

The emergence of a separate domain of nature in the Enlightenment period has been extensively critiqued by feminist historians in terms of how this process can be read as both gendered and sexualised, with significant implications for understandings not only of women and reproduction, but of knowledge production, objectivity and truth.[2] Scholars such as Carolyn Merchant (1980) have documented the ways in which nature came to be feminised by the 'masculine philosophy' associated with founders of the Royal Society, in particular Robert Boyle and Francis Bacon. Accompanying the rise of Cartesian mechanistic philosophy, Merchant (1980) describes 'the death of nature', and an attendant sexualisation of the relationship between nature's 'secrets' and the penetrating gaze of scientific epistemology (Merchant, 1980; see also Easlea, 1980, 1981). As Ludmilla Jordanova writes in a revised version of her classic 1980 essay on 'Natural Facts',

Human history, the growth of culture through the domination of nature, was represented as the increasing assertion of masculine ways over irrational, backward-looking women. The very concept of progress was freighted with gender.

(1989: 37)

Women's association with nature and the natural, both in terms of being more defined by their 'unruly' natural capacities than men and insofar as the feminine and the natural became metaphorically linked, has been the subject of ongoing debate within several fields of feminist scholarship. Linked to the extensive feminist historical literature on the associations of nature, culture and gender which shaped the birth of modern science (and indeed the project of modernity itself) is the critique of biological determinism within feminist science studies – a concern which emerged as one of the most important arenas of feminist debate in the 1980s and 1990s.[3] Here again, as in feminist historical studies, the critique of biology is aimed both at its subordinating effects on women (who remain closely tied to definitions of their biological natures, much as by their feminine natures in the more distant past), and at how biology shapes its objects as the dominant science of our time (as is especially evident in the resurgence of genetic determinism at the turn of the millennium).[4] Consequently, the feminist critique of ideas of the natural within biology, and in particular of the model of biological sex difference which lies at the heart of narratives of human evolution and behaviour, has become pivotal in uncovering the means by which naturalisations serve to legitimate inequality.[5]

From this perspective, the historical emergence of a domain of the natural, replete with sexualised imagery of male domination and superiority, continues to have effects into the present day. Evelyn Fox Keller (1992) suggests, for example, that nature remains defined by notions of secrecy and feminine elusiveness within the contemporary sciences, where the secrets of life remain powerfully defined by the secrets of death, as is particularly evident in the linkages connecting the production of the atomic bomb and the emergence of modern molecular genetics. Writing of one of the most famous narratives of scientific discovery in the twentieth century, the unravelling of the double helix, she argues that:

> The story of the double-helix is first and foremost the story of the displacement and replacement of the secret of life by a molecule. Gone in this representation of life are all the complex undeciphered dynamics that maintain the cell as a living entity; 'Life Itself' has finally dissolved into the simplest mechanisms of a self-replicating molecule.
>
> (1992: 51, references deleted)

'The Death of Nature', its mechanisation, the familiar gender dynamics of this process, and the elaborate sexual and reproductive idioms which inform both the practices and the representations of science are thus argued by many feminist scholars to comprise one of the definitive features of modernity. Like Williams and Foucault, Keller claims that the idea of nature as a distinct domain, comprised of lawlike principles amenable to scientific discovery, is 'a metaphor indelibly marked by its political and theological origins' (1992: 29).

Complementing these historical approaches, feminist anthropology has been of particular importance in exploring questions about ideas or domains of nature and the natural (Rubin, 1975). This is in part because of the way questions of sexual inequality repeatedly lead into discussions of biology, and the question of whether women's subordination is universal, or the result of the universal 'natural facts' of sex difference. The work of Marilyn Strathern has been central to the critique of a universalising model of nature since her early and prescient essay, 'No Nature, No Culture: the Hagen case', was published in 1980.[6] In it Strathern pointed out that not all societies can be presumed to share the idea of a domain of nature as separate from culture. 'There is no demarcated "nature" or "culture" in Hagen thought,' she suggested, continuing that:

> Consequently, there is no such thing as nature or culture. Each is a highly relativised concept whose ultimate signification must be derived from its place within a specific metaphysics. No single meaning can in fact be given to nature or culture in western thought; there is no consistent dichotomy, only a matrix of contrasts.

> (1980: 177)

Rereading De Beauvoir's classic arguments about women's subordination in *The Second Sex*, Strathern proceeds to challenge the ways in which male–female has been brought into relation with nature–culture as a 'symbolic operator' in very particular ways within both feminist theory and anthropology. She concludes that male–female represents a kind of difference readily mapped on to nature–culture *in a way that would not be possible in other societies.*[7]

This model of nature, and the implications of how it is tied to other concepts, such as male and female, or individual and society, is the subject of Strathern's *After Nature: English kinship in the late twentieth century* (1992a) – a comprehensive discussion of ideas of the natural in English, Euro-American and global culture.[8] For Strathern, as for Young (1985) and Williams (1976, 1980), the emergence of a domain of the social defined as *after nature* stems, in part, from the Darwinian model of genealogy. In this view, according to Strathern, humanity comes to be seen as both descended from, and consanguinous with, nature, at the same time that human society comes to be seen as modelled on a departure from a state of nature through the invention of social laws (Figures 2.1 and 2.2). What is *partial* about these connections is the way in which, for example, society both belongs and does not belong to nature; what is merographic about these linkages is the different ways nature and culture *overlap*. The preservation of the after-nature model of society, as both part of and distinct from the order of nature, is, in Strathern's view, evident in the hybrid institution of kinship, understood to be composed of ties of blood and ties by law. It is through kinship as a 'hybrid' that Strathern demonstrates a two-way traffic: ideas of the social are installed in nature through concepts such as genealogy (before Darwin's usage not a naturalised concept), and ideas of the natural are installed in the social, for example, through the idea of a biological relative (Strathern, 1992a and b). As in her earlier work on gender, Strathern's writings on kinship foreground ideas of the natural as one of the key sites in which to examine the possibilities of difference which structure cultural life.

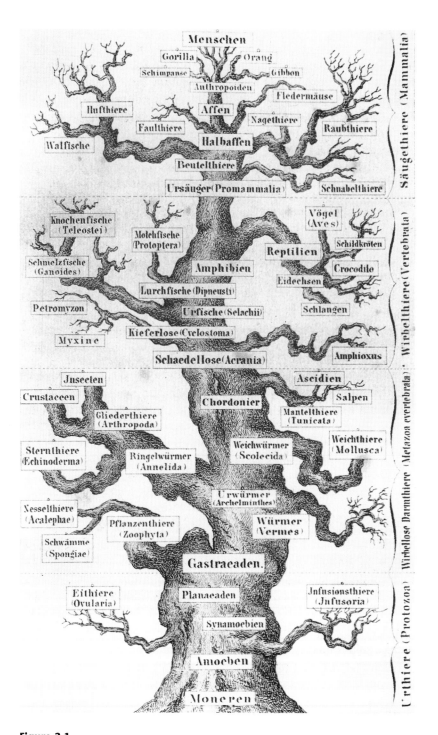

Figure 2.1

*Haeckel's genealogical tree demonstrates the
interconnectedness of all life forms, emphasising
their (vertical) descent from a common ancestor, as
theorised by Darwin.*

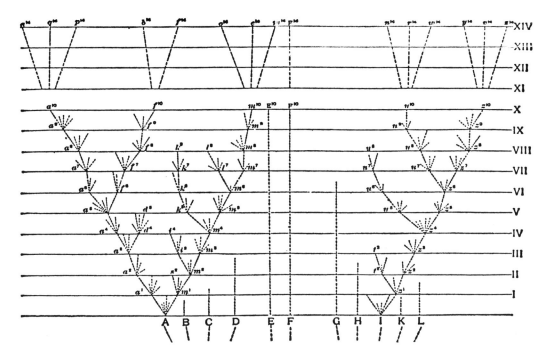

Figure 2.2

In the only illustration in The Origin of the Species, *Darwin offers a horizontally calibrated genealogical tree emphasising the divergences within and among species which combine to produce the variation through descent necessary to evolution.*

The importance of the natural to models of origins, kinship, creation, generation and lineage has remained a central theme within feminist anthropology for over three decades. In *Naturalizing Power*, for example, the editors note that: 'The social was embedded in the natural, but a particular version of it . . . the Hobbesian variety [of a] struggle for survival in a situation of scarce resources, with self-interest as a motivating force' (Yanagisako and Delaney, 1995b: 5). They cite Marx, who noted 'how Darwin recognizes among beasts and plants his English society with its divisions of labor, competition, opening of new markets, "inventions" and the Malthusian "struggle for existence".' Hence, they argue, 'In Darwinian theory the natural order retained both the hierarchical order of Creation and its god-given quality; the difference is that the power no longer came from God, it came from Nature' (1995b: 5). As a consequence, it became possible to look to nature for explanations of human behaviour, for example in models of human reproduction and sexuality which came to be seen to be governed by the rules of nature, as among animals and plants.[9]

Echoing the earlier claims of Sherry Ortner (1974), Yanagisako and Delaney argue that: 'In contemporary Euro-American belief, "reproduction" has been reduced to its natural character and is associated with women; women have been defined by and come to represent the reproductive role' (1995b: 9). In turn, they argue that 'feminist cultural analysis challenges the assignment of sex and reproduction to the category of "biology"' (1995b: 9). This move evinces the identical conclusion to that described by social theorists Macnaghten and Urry, namely that such a challenge 'calls into question the analytic domains conventionally used by social scientists' (1995b: 9). For feminists, however, the aim was not merely to challenge the overdetermination of the natural facts–social facts distinction. Feminist attentions to the natural were also motivated by a recognition of the extent to which definitions of 'woman's nature' confirmed, legitimised and reproduced gender, class and racial inequalities.[10]

A defining concern within much scholarship on ideas of the natural within the western tradition has been the extent to which nature signifies both a domain in need of discipline, and a force which inevitably exceeds the effort to 'tame' its powers. In her contribution to *Naturalizing Power*, feminist anthropologist Anna Tsing argues that the distinctive characteristic of the natural is paradoxical in the form of its *dual agency as both manageable and independent*. 'Naturalizing power', Tsing writes, 'requires empowering nature [and] empowering nature means attributing to nature forms of agency we can understand' (1995: 114). The trade that criss-crosses back and forth between ideas of nature and ideas of society finds its currency in forms of power and agency that are, she suggests, always-already recognisable. Yet, she adds, '"nature" is, by definition, that which escapes human attributions. . . . The work of nature in US American culture is to create a space for a tension between those forms of agency we best know and those we imagine to be outside our ken' (1995: 114). Tsing's figure for materialising this traffic in ideas of the natural is the honey bee, a domesticated nature-worker whose activities both exemplify and exceed domestication. An ideal industrial worker, living within a highly organised and domesticated division of labour and capable of surplus production, the bee also behaves unpredictably by cross-breeding, migrating, escaping and going wild (Figure 2.3). From this bee's-eye view, nature is thus a potent border zone of two-way traffic. It is a material world animated by an agency that is both knowable and harnessable, but also unpredictable and autonomous – with a life of its own.

In many respects, Tsing's analysis harmonises with that of Donna Haraway, for whom nature has always existed inseparably from its function as a zone of appropriation for culture: 'Nature is only the raw material of culture, appropriated, preserved, enslaved, exalted, or otherwise made flexible for disposal by culture in the logic of capitalist colonialism' (1989b: 13). For Tsing and Haraway, it is precisely the extent to which nature persists as more than the sum of its appropriations which gives it the majesty and awesomeness necessary to ensure its ongoing survival. Both accounts locate the capacity of nature to operate as a magical sign by appealing to its movement, its trafficking capacity, and its border-function as a kind of conversion device. The materiality of nature is dually signified: as an inscription device or coding system, capable of shaping objects and subjects, such as bodies and landscapes; and as an agentic domain independent of culture that is unpredictable, beyond reach of domestication and unknowable. There are, in this sense, two natures: the one that 'belongs' to culture, and the one that is its alterity.

Figure 2.3

The honey bee's attractions as a domesticated nature-worker have made it the subject of a long-lasting amateur and professional bee-keeping culture, as depicted in British bee enthusiast Frank Slater's classic study, The Humble Bee.

● ● Nature and History

It is the first of these understandings of nature – that is, the nature that belongs to culture – which German critical theory called 'second nature'. As developed within the Frankfurt School, second nature describes the ideologically effective renaturalisation of the social order. In some contemporary critical accounts of second nature, such as Fredric Jameson's, nature is entirely reduced to culture, effecting an implosion of the terms. For Jameson, second nature is postmodern culture: 'Postmodernism is what you have when the modernization process is complete and nature is gone for good. It is a more fully human world than the older one, but one in which "culture" has become a veritable "second nature"' (1991: 121). This is similar to Rabinow's description of nature in the context of the new genetics as 'known and remade through technique [so it] will finally become artificial, just as culture becomes natural' (1992: 241–2). Yet the Frankfurt School's own analysis was less stark, recognising that the meaning of nature is not fixed: as well as undergoing its own internal development, it is also produced through multiple couplings: nature and society, nature and technology, and nature and history. Indeed, these earlier discussions of second nature were developed principally in relation to critical conceptions of temporality, including, most notably, the idea of history (see Koch, 1993).[11] In the interpretation of the dialectic between nature and history, however, there were important differences between members of the Frankfurt School, notably between Theodor Adorno and Max Horkheimer (1979), Georg Lukács (1968), Walter Benjamin (1970, 1983) and Siegfried Kracauer (1995).

Georg Lukács terms technology 'second nature' in order to criticise the presumption that the world in its given form was 'natural' in the ontological sense. Although intentionally a Marxist category, second nature was understood by Lukács in a strongly Hegelian frame; it referred to alienated and reified subjectivity, a world created by humans who did not recognise it as their own. There were no longer two natures in capitalist society, only second nature. For Walter Benjamin, in contrast, nature is always both created by humankind and something 'other' than the subject, and this remains true no matter how much (or how little) human labour has been invested in it. Moreover, for Benjamin, real change – as opposed to the changes of history – may be achieved through the operation of mimesis, by being receptive to the expressive power of matter or the natural. Nevertheless, Benjamin argues that while nature *can* be actualized in this way, it has tended to appear only as the perversion of history that is called progress, or as the domestication of the wilderness, as development or as evolution. He charts the emergence of this nature that belongs only to culture in both the objects and contexts of the modern world – in the commodity, and the arcades, panoramas and world expositions of contemporary consumer culture, and its formal or objective techniques of scale – giganticism and miniaturisation.

Siegfried Kracauer too believes that what he calls 'bare nature', a nature which naïvely asserts itself, affirming its own omnipotence, is most often a mythological cult, a paradoxical response to a 'system oblivious to differences in form' (1995: 78). But his pessimism is not absolute. As he notes, 'if human beings were merely exploiters of nature, then nature would have triumphed over nature' (1995: 80). He believes that there is 'a space for the intervention of reason' and the possibility of recognising 'the resplendence of the things of nature' (1995: 81, 82). Nevertheless, so intense are the powers of domination and abstraction that he is able only to advocate the mimicking of the dead as a strategy of survival: this is redemption via reification or self-eradication, what he terms 'active passivity'.

For Benjamin, though, natural history is never simply the transposition of neo-Darwinianism on to history as progress – never only the panorama of evolution or the taming of the wilderness; there is also always the possibility of identifying 'failed material' as a trace of prior life or alternative ways of living. Furthermore, he believes it is possible to reverse the direction of progress, turn away from the vindication of the forward course of history by viewing it with the backward gaze of the Angelus Novus. While the inherent potential of second nature typically remains unrecognised, unconscious traces of the not-yet of nature are to be found in 'archaic images', the 'petrified ur-forms of the present'. Central to both these interpretations is the emblem or hieroglyph – 'a montage of visual image and linguistic sign, out of which is read, like a picture puzzle, what things "mean"' (Buck-Morss, 1989: 161). For Adorno, however, Benjamin's conception fails to pay adequate attention to the ways in which the symbol or emblem turns into fetish, and is itself implicated in a developmental, almost immanent, relationship to a utopian future.

It is the apparent immanence of the future in the continuous present of the global imaginary – as is manifest in the rise of catastrophic thinking or the colonisation of the future which is characteristic of the production techniques of global capitalism – which has led many contemporary critics to assume the absolute hold of seconded or alienated nature at the turn of the millennium. As we noted earlier, one of the most significant ways in which nature is being refigured in contemporary culture is through the displacement of the horizon, as suggested by the icons of the blue planet, the foetus and the cell. At the same time, drawing on the recognition of ambivalence we have identified in the writings of feminist anthropology and critical theory, we do not presume the homogeneity of the effects of the multiple and cross-cutting processes of naturalisation, denaturalisation and renaturalisation. Nor do we take for granted the uncontested nature of the history which has produced the conjuncture of the global as the site of a future unavoidably brought into the present. Rather, we take the alignment between the natural and the global as a symptom of changing cultural landscapes and histories that help shape global subjects, global citizens and a global imaginary with as yet uncertain consequences.

In what follows we explore further the defining features of global nature, global culture through an analysis of the paired icons, the fossil and the pixel. In our earlier discussion of the global icons of the blue planet and the foetus, the processes of denaturalisation and renaturalisation were tied to a concern with issues of difference and similarity, with the disappearance of the horizon as a natural spatial limit, and the emergence of a notion of panhumanity. Here it is not spatial but temporal boundaries, the horizons of natural history, that are at issue.

The history of the interpretation of fossil objects recapitulates a much broader set of shifts, from the sixteenth century onwards, linking nature, history and life into the familiar patterns that are understood as matters of scientific fact (Rudwick, 1976). In the imprint of the fossil, then, was gradually deposited an entire cultural landscape of connections, linking the emergence of life to the passage of linear, progressive and one-directional time we might describe as the time of natural history, or simply as 'natural time' – the time of genealogy. The fossil, in its very shape and form, became an index of these changes, as appearances became affinities, and affinities became kinds. It is in the same period, in sixteenth-century England, that the time of genealogy is also beginning to ground, or naturalise, cultural conventions such as authorship, modelled on the genealogical relation of father to offspring, and of property, through copyright (Battersby, 1989; Rose, 1993). It is in this way that the 'facts of life' of nature, natural history and genealogy are seconded into cultural service – doing time, as it were, for modes of cultural reproduction.

Because of the importance of 'natural' or 'genealogical time' not only to the history of life forms, but to cultural institutions, such as authorship and property, this temporality must be seen as a foundational narrative of modernity, and, we suggest, a foundation which is 'exposed' in the context of globalisation. Global nature, global culture is not rooted in history, but rather comes into being in a 'time of exposure', a time described by Paul Virilio (1994) as one of danger, uncertainty and risk, as the speeded-up time of a scaled-down globe in which history is condensed into fleeting instants, a time that is no-time-at-all, and over which no control is possible, as in the boom and bust cycles of equity markets which ultimately signify persistent instability. Similarly, Baudrillard (1994a) argues that the time of nature or genealogy has been eclipsed by the time of the 'posts-', creating the effect of a dissolve between after and before, which brings with it a collapse of the distinction between originals and copies and the redistribution of authorship. For example, this new ('catastrophic') time of the posts- upsets the genealogical order and unilinear temporality of photographic realism, in which images were secured by an indelible relation of emulsion to the passage of natural time – the emulsion impression, like the fossil, a hollowed-out trace of 'real' life – and to authors, who composed, shot and thus created photographs.

Against the fossil, we contrast the pixel, as an icon of the emergent temporalities of global nature, global culture. We ask how the pixel, described as a digital cell or 'fossilised light', mediates between before and after, original and copy, authorship and image. In contrast to the temporal order secured by the hollowed-out imprint of the fossil, the pixel authorises an unfamiliar and disturbing temporality which seems insecure, unstable and fleeting. In both instances, then, we explore how the traffic between nature and culture brings into being certain understandings of time. As in the aptly named digital practice of cloning, a technical term for replacing 'lost' parts of an image, the 'facts of life' in cultural reproduction are upset by new technologies, which enable new, non-genealogical, 'unnatural' relations. We ask what forms of life, what life forms, occupy the space of the pixel, a space we propose as definitive of global nature, global culture? How are regimes of property altered in such a context? As the kinship which belongs to genealogy is replaced by other kinds of affinity and connection, what new family relations emerge in cultural reproduction and among commodities? Along with these and other questions, we explore the fossil and the pixel as icons of the new temporalities of global nature, global culture.

The Fossil

The longstanding capacity for the natural emblem of the fossil to service cultural conceptions of progress and development is explored by historian Martin Rudwick (1976) in his account of changing conceptions of fossils as natural facts, or facts of life, from the sixteenth to the nineteenth centuries – during what is generally known, that is, as the period during which modernity took shape. In the first of his chosen episodes in the history of palaeontology, Rudwick addresses the work of sixteenth-century naturalist Conrad Gesner, especially *On Fossil Objects*, completed in 1565. Rudwick notes that in the mid-sixteenth century, the word 'fossil' meant simply 'dug up', and the criteria adopted for distinguishing what are now termed fossils were non-existent. Gradually, as more specific criteria were developed, objects with what was seen as a causally significant resemblance to organisms came to be termed 'organised fossils' or 'extraneous fossils', to distinguish them from the rest of the broad range of 'objects dug up'. However, it was not until the early nineteenth century that 'the word "fossil" . . . finally became restricted' to its modern form (1976: 2–3). In mapping this process of restriction, Rudwick claims that the fossil has been an important artefact through which modern ideas of nature and history took shape.

Rudwick identifies three important innovations in Gesner's early book: 'the use of illustrations to supplement verbal description, the establishment of collections of

Figure 2.4

In this illustration from The Meaning of Fossils, *Martin Rudwick's caption draws attention to the way in which sixteenth-century naturalist Conrad Gesner distinguished between fossil objects on the basis of their physical affinities, or shapes, using detailed woodcut illustrations to support his classificatory efforts.*

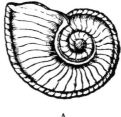 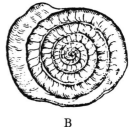

A   B

specimens, and the formation of a scholarly community cooperating by correspondence' (1976: 15). Gesner's book was the first in which illustrations were used systematically to supplement a written text on 'fossils' (Figure 2.4), and Gesner himself said he was 'including as many illustrations as possible "so that students may more easily recognise objects that cannot be very clearly described in words"' (1976: 15). What is striking here, though, is the way in which visual representation was the means by which objects came to be put into, or rather under, names. As Michel Foucault describes this shift,

> Natural history finds its locus in the gap that is now opened up between things and words – a silent gap, pure of all verbal sedimentation. And yet articulated according to the elements of representation, those same elements can now without let or hindrance be named.
>
> (1970: 129–30)

Indeed, as Rudwick goes on to point out, technologies of representation played a key role in the history of palaeontology, 'similar to that of improvements in instrumentation in the physical sciences' (1976: 9), providing visual criteria by which different classes of fossil objects could be distinguished and classified not only by a proper noun but also by *kind*, that is, by a common noun or genus.

Once introduced, such classificatory devices further shaped the impulse to *visualise* nature, to develop specialised techniques of observation and taxonomic display. Indeed, Foucault contends that the eighteenth century saw a new nature, 'stripped bare of all commentary', in which words, texts and records are replaced by the herbariums, gardens and collections in which things are examined *in and of themselves*, 'bearers of nothing but their proper names'. He argues: '[W]hat had changed was the space in which it is possible to see them and from which it was possible to describe them' (1970: 131). Foucault describes this space of description as a *non-temporal rectangle* in which, stripped of all commentary, the objects of interest are purified and 'present themselves one beside another, grouped according to their common features, and thus already virtually analysed' (1970: 131). Instead of a spectacle or performance, as it had been in the Renaissance, nature in the Classical eighteenth-century period is arrayed as a table: 'What came surreptitiously into being between the age of the theatre and that of the catalogue was not the desire for knowledge, but a new way of connecting things both to the eye and to discourse. A new way of making history' (1970: 131).

This space of the non-temporal rectangle made possible a process of de- and recontextualisation in which nature was purified of its former attributes, such as what the sixteenth-century natural philosopher Girolamo Cardona termed the 'natural magic' of fossil objects. In situating the classification of fossil objects in relation to a 'magical' conception of their agency or power, Renaissance scholars were engaging an altogether different temporality of nature, history or life from either their eighteenth-century or their modern counterparts. According to their Neoplatonic philosophy, the whole universe was 'a network of hidden affinities and "correspondences", which might be made manifest by resemblances not only between microcosm and macrocosm but also between the heavens and the Earth, between animals and plants, and between living and non-living entities' (Rudwick, 1976: 19). In their world, culture was to learn from nature, perhaps acquiring some of its awesome power by drawing distinctions, establishing resemblances, and making connections. But the traffic went two ways, and in the exchange, the genealogical history of modernity was to emerge. Moreover, this history was tied to an understanding of *kind* which had its basis in the reproduction of *form*.

In his work *On the Nature of Fossils*, published twenty years before Gesner's book, Agricola attempted a visual scheme of fossil classification based on their purely physical properties. On this basis he distinguished 'gems' (a category which included both pearls and gallstones), 'earths', 'rocks', 'metals', 'hardened fluids', and finally 'stones' (including not only lodestone, gypsum and mica but also 'several objects that were commonly believed to fall from the heavens' [Rudwick, 1976: 23]). Rudwick notes that what grouped all such objects with other 'fossils' was primarily their common physical property of 'stoniness'. It is in this notion of petrification that we can begin to identify ideas of reproduction and generation later shaping the modern concept of life as an evolved system driven by the passage of time, in the form of natural history. Rudwick comments,

> [W]ithin the Neoplatonic framework all the evidence of a petrifying process could be interpreted as signs of the 'growth of stones'. In Neoplatonic thought the distinction between living and nonliving was simply unreal: all entities shared in some sense in the quality termed 'life', however much they differed in the mode of its expression.
>
> (1976: 25)

Gesner, like many of his contemporaries, accepted this notion of *petrification* as the process responsible for fossils' common property of 'stoniness'. What marked him out, however, was that he chose to illuminate this natural process by adopting *form* as his principle of classification, thus drawing on one of the most longstanding western conventions – the separation of form from matter. As Susan Oyama notes,

Whether one traces our present conceptions of life to Aristotelian notions of form and matter . . . or . . . to Newtonian and Cartesian definitions of matter as inert and therefore as requiring outside animation, it is clear that our preoccupation with organisms as material objects whose design and functioning must be imparted to them has a long and complex past.

(1985: 12)

Gesner's classification of fossils in terms of *form* is the first stage in the emergence of what Foucault describes as the visible relief of fossils. For Gesner, physical resemblances were a consequence of the bonds of affinity resulting from a pervasive moulding force or 'plastic force' (Rudwick, 1976: 45). However, others offered an alternative interpretation of organic resemblances: they were held to be a result of a process similar to that which was believed to occur in simpler organisms, that of 'spontaneous generation' (*generation aequivoca*), or the implantation of specific seeds within the earth. Rudwick explains, 'For example, if a specific "seed" of a fish were washed into the ground it might be able to grow from "stony" material and generate a fish-like fossil in the rock' (1976: 35). In these considerations of the nature of fossils, then, the problem of resemblance over time and across space is initially resolved by the adoption of either a theory of formal correspondence or one of generation by seed. Resemblances – or affinities of kind – are identified through the development of techniques of differentiation and then recontextualised in understandings of reproduction and an emergent notion of natural history. In the periods of intense debate which followed, this natural history came to be understood in terms of developmental processes, marked by periods of disruption and rapid transformation; at issue was the problem of reproduction, the commingling of questions of continuity and discontinuity, and thus of time itself, with those of difference and identity.

In his discussion of later episodes of the history of palaeontology, Rudwick shows further how the emblem of the fossil came to be linked to novel narratives of the earth's development. For example, he demonstrates how the studies that comprise Buffon's *Epochs of Nature* (1778) enlarged conventional chronology and detached human history from the history of life, or, rather, relegated it to a small part, albeit the culmination, of a much longer sequence of events, thus contributing to a separation of natural history from other histories, of nature from culture. By 1830, Rudwick suggests, the findings of several naturalists, but most notably the results acquired by Georges Cuvier (Figure 2.5) by means of comparative anatomy and reconstruction, meant that this natural history was seen to be common to all corners of the planet. As Rudwick describes it,

[T]he geological time-scale was firmly established as almost unimaginably lengthy by the standards of human history, yet documented by an immensely thick succession of slowly deposited strata. The successive formations of strata, and even in some cases individual strata, were clearly characterised by distinctive assemblages of fossil species, which enabled them to be identified and correlated over very

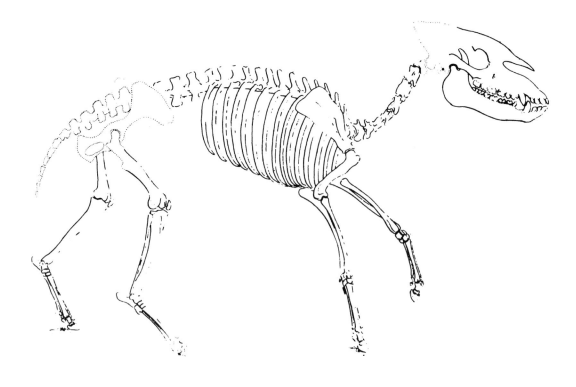

Figure 2.5

This detailed image of Palaeotherium, or 'ancient beast', was based on fossilised remains recovered from a gypsum quarry at Montmartre in the early 1800s. Remains such as these, from an extinct vertebrate, enabled Cuvier to suggest a new geological time-scale for natural history.

wide areas. This correlation proved that in its broader outlines the history of life had been the same in all parts of the world.

(1976: 156–7)

In later episodes of the interpretation of fossils, the natural history they revealed came increasingly to be tied to progressive, linear conceptions of time and an understanding of the world which had seen not just one Great Flood but a series of major changes in physical geography. This latter point was a philosophy propounded by Cuvier in particular following his investigation of fossils from a gypsum quarry at Montmartre, and was later termed 'catastrophism' (although Cuvier himself preferred the term 'revolutions', with its more Newtonian flavour) (Rudwick, 1976: 124–33). However, although a directional or 'progressive' element was beginning to emerge from the study of the history of life and the earth itself, the relationship between extinction and evolution was still then, in the early nineteenth century, one of antithesis.

The aim of this discussion of the fossil, however, is not to show how fossils came to be correctly understood nor to show how uncertainty was reduced about how best to classify fossil objects; it is rather to demonstrate how their interpretation reveals the interrelated conception of nature, culture and history, and the use of one as the model or context for the other in the emergence of the notions of development, progress, genealogy and evolution: in short, to see how fossil objects are dug up as 'signs of life'. These signs are seen to reveal life's organisation, as the linear, brachiating, genealogical system Foucault describes as 'life itself' – a conceptual shift that, he argues, instantiates the modern era.

Yet, as Jean Baudrillard notes, these 'signs of life' continue to change:

> If modernity, in its day, gave rise to anthropological exploration, post-modernity, for its part, has spawned a positive craze for the neolithic and the paleolithic. The extraction of relics has become an industrial undertaking. . . . Ironically, we might say we are watching the liberation of fossils, just like everything else. . . . They too want to express themselves.
>
> (1994b: 73)

For Baudrillard, this craze for fossils is driven by the remorse humanity feels as it loses the thread of its own (cultural) history, producing a 'vague sense of criminal responsibility towards our ancestors and our fantasies' (1994b: 72). He thus suggests that the familiar natural history in which humanity situated itself now falters, in need of artificial resuscitation. This time, however, Baudrillard contends,

> All the relics, all the traces which were shrouded in the greatest secrecy and which, by that token, formed part of our symbolic capital, will be exhumed and resuscitated: they will not be spared our transparency; we shall turn them from something buried and living into something visible and dead.
>
> (1994b: 72)

Baudrillard argues that contemporary relics are divided into 'originals' and 'copies' (a reconfiguring of the recurring problem of resemblance or affinity). Moreover, it is the copy or substitute which is now 'the only version appropriate to our universe, where every original constitutes a potential danger and all singularity runs the risk of hindering the free circulation of value' (1994b: 75). The originals are preserved, but this preservation is not in recognition of the testimony they bear to some great flood in the past (as was theorised in the later moments of the natural history Rudwick describes), but in preparation for a flood – a global danger – that is yet to come:

> All the originals are put under lock and key (the Lascaux caves, the Tautavel skull, the underwater cave at Cassis). More and more things are exhumed to be immediately reinterred, snatched from death only to be cryogenized.
>
> (1994b: 73–4)

For Baudrillard, the second class of today's fossil objects comprises copies of dug-outs, bones and wall paintings drawn from earlier times, a time before the posts- which describe the contemporary era. In this respect, the posts- are the temporal equivalent of the artificial, permeable boundary or horizon described earlier in relation to the icons of the blue planet, the foetus and the cell. They are the boundaries which do not simply allow a distancing from the past, a sense of perspective, but enable a new, more strategic and instrumental, relation to history. They do not simply enable distinctions to be drawn between 'before' and 'after', but also make it possible for the one to be introduced into the other in specific, carefully controlled ways by which they open up access to the unlimited yet finite time of the global imaginary. This time, of global nature, global culture, of exposure and survivalism, is also dependent on the fiction of another non-temporal rectangle: the computer screen.

● ●　**The Pixel**

One example of the contemporary 'liberation of fossils' described by Baudrillard is photography, a medium which William J. Mitchell describes as 'fossilised light' (1992: 24). And, as with other fossil objects, the digital photographic image, whilst sometimes described in terms of artificial life, is certainly 'doubtfully organic' and unquestionably beset by 'uncertain affinities'; here, too, the originals are either irrelevant or non-existent while the copies are put into circulation. Not surprisingly, given the rapid expansion of this new field of fossil objects with the proliferation of computer-aided techniques, there is growing confusion about how best to classify the things now being 'dug up' and their relationship to developmental, genealogical or 'natural' time, and consequently to understandings of 'before' and 'after', or cause and effect. Nevertheless, just as the non-temporal rectangle adopted by eighteenth-century natural philosophers enabled comparisons to be made and distinctions drawn, so too does the non-temporal rectangle of the computer screen.

　　　The pixel is the name given to the individual 'cells' into which a photographic image is subdivided and encoded digitally by a computer. This encoding specifies the intensity or colour of each cell or pixel by means of an integer number. Thus, the manipulation of the pixel, digital information and its sequences which is the basis of computer-aided imagery offers what Mitchell describes as a 'temptation to duplicity' in the post-photographic era. This temptation arises from the capacity of digital imagery to interfere with the photograph's 'aura of superior evidential efficacy' based on conventional understandings of 'the special bond between fugitive reality and permanent image that is formed at the instant of exposure' (Mitchell, 1992: 24). This digital re-authoring of the photograph is achieved by replacing it with an informational code. The replacement of a special bond – the instantaneous unfolding of figurative reality in natural time captured as a 'moment of exposure' – by the temporary fix afforded by the pixel is inevitably decried by some as the loss of nature as a referent, a context or a ground for the image. The potential fluidity of a digital *imitation of photography* signifies for some a dangerous unmooring, while, for others the temptation is to believe in the possibility of re-creating this ground, this nature, retrospectively – that is, to make second nature by intervening in the instant of exposure.[12] As Renaud points out, digitalization, like the use of comparative anatomy elaborated by Cuvier in the earlier period, opens 'a subtle and, in the mathematical sense, catastrophic gap in the functioning and the paradigm of the inherent formal development of this kind of image' (1995: 182).

The computer screen, like Foucault's non-temporal rectangle in which nature had no history, opens up new possibilities for understandings of kind, reproduction and temporality. The moment of exposure is held open for intervention and extends in all directions. It becomes the unbounded but finite time of global nature, global culture. In turn, this new 'history' recontextualises definitions of life itself, by altering its systemic connections to generation, genealogy and reproduction.

While there is still great uncertainty and even the possibility of catastrophe in the notions of time emerging in global nature, global culture, form is once again being adopted as the basis of classification, specifically the form of in-formation, through its elaboration in the principles of shaping and animation as applied in modern visual technologies. Indeed, information is what Susan Oyama (1985) describes as 'the modern source of form' and is deployed across a diversity of contemporary living and non-living entities. It is inscribed in both nature and culture, in biotechnology and the visual technologies of contemporary society, in 'molecules, cells, tissues, "the environment"' and digital photographs, computer programs and brands.[13] Moreover, while information is often latent, it is also held to be causally potent, allowing these entities 'to recognize, select and instruct each other, to construct each other and themselves, to regulate, control, induce, direct and determine events of all kinds' (Oyama, 1985: 2). Thus, it provides the imaginary possibility of auto-construction that is definitive of global nature, global culture.

Moreover, just as previous classifications of fossil objects proceeded by dividing form and matter, making one active and the other passive, so too new forms of life and non-life, including the animated imagery of computer-aided photography, are made to appear to come into being independently of matter. Indeed, the very dimensions of matter are being called into doubt: so, for example, the processes of magnification and diminution are redundant in many of the new visual technologies for they reveal no further information. More generally, Paul Virilio suggests that not only scale but the very concept of physical dimension – so fundamental to Cartesian conceptions of space – has been displaced:

> And suddenly the ancient distinctions among the dimensions disappear. The dimensional dissection of classical geometry – where the point cut the line, and the line cut the plane, which then cut through the solids – has lost a critical part of its practical utility. . . . The last 'dissection' is not so much a fact of physical dimensions as it is a fact of the selection of speeds of perception and of representation, slowed down or sped up, that cut up the depth of time . . . .
>
> (1991: 32–3)

However, this 'last dissection' is not only a process of denaturalisation; it is also a process of renaturalisation: it illuminates matter, nature or 'the real' in new ways. So, for example, alongside the well-established technique of image cropping, there is now the possibility of what Fred Ritchin calls 'reverse cropping', the extension, or cloning, of the edge of an image. Ritchin describes this technique as a 'modification in time':

> [T]he photographic image is no longer time-specific, the result of the momentary and privileged meeting of subject and photographer. Now, time is not fleeting. The editor's revisionist ability can extend to interfering even with the already completed relationship of the photographer to his or her subject. One can reach backward in time, repudiating the photographer's judgement, to 'rephotograph'.
> (1990: 30–1)

The second nature depicted in digital photography is the product of an instrumental reaching backwards in such a way as to refigure the future. In this process, nature and history are related in ways which exemplify the instabilities opened up by the artificial resuscitation of natural history or the renaturalisation of history through the detour of information in the non-temporal rectangle of the computer screen.

For Ritchin, the intervention into the moment of photographic authorship made possible by digitalisation is disturbing insofar as the creativity, artistic judgement and ethics of the photographer are erased. He wishes that the relationship between observer and observed could always remain confined in the 'already completed' temporal relationship of chemical photography. But for Paul Virilio, the introduction of computerised technology simply makes visible what had previously been assumed: the fleeting moment of exposure in 'instantaneous' perception is now the basis of a new temporal order. Virilio is not suggesting that the introduction of computerised technology inaugurates a time of exposure into photography, but rather that it makes time newly visible, and, importantly, newly productive. He writes that in retrospect we can see that even the 'most instinctive, least-controlled glance is first a sort of circling of the property, a complete scanning of the visual field that ends in the eye's choice of an object' (1994: 61). The time of seeing, of editing, is now itself visible and is the locus of intervention, commercial exploitation and the claims of intellectual property. So, for example, in a recent advertisement for Lockheed Martin, the ability to view changes in the weather across the globe by means of radar – symbolised by a fine line superimposing a screen on to a landscape – is described as a 'moment of accurate weather prediction' (Figure 2.6). That the weather which is to be viewed is 'flash floods' and 'unexpected storms' is yet one more example of the ways in which the gobal is brought into being as a response to some imagined threat (Baudrillard, 1994b, and see Chapter 5 below). As in the case of the earlier icons then, questions of origins, control and responsibility are significantly implicated in the processes of de- and renaturalisation afforded by the pixel.

Such interventions can be seen to be more than a matter of technological power. So, for example, in a recent advertisement (Figure 2.7), network provider

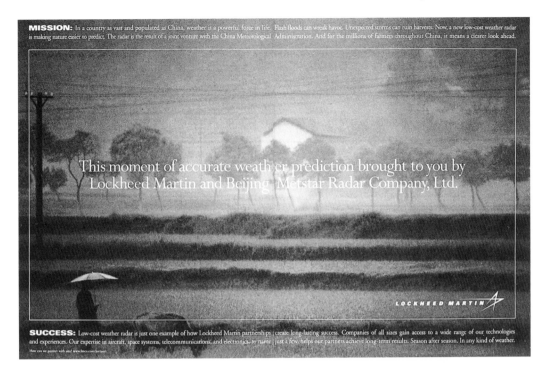

MISSION: In a country as vast and populated as China, weather is a powerful force in life. Flash floods can wreak havoc. Unexpected storms can ruin harvests. Now, a new low-cost weather radar is making nature easier to predict. The radar is the result of a joint venture with the China Meteorological Administration. And for the millions of farmers throughout China, it means a clearer look ahead.

This moment of accurate weather prediction brought to you by Lockheed Martin and Beijing Metstar Radar Company, Ltd.

LOCKHEED MARTIN

SUCCESS: Low-cost weather radar is just one example of how Lockheed Martin partnerships create long-lasting success. Companies of all sizes gain access to a wide range of our technologies and experiences. Our expertise in aircraft, space systems, telecommunications, and electronics, to name just a few, helps our partners achieve long-term results. Season after season. In any kind of weather.

How can we partner with you? www.lmco.com/partners

Figure 2.6

In this advertisement from Lockheed Martin, global weather prediction technology is depicted through references to catastrophic change, linking a specific means of visualising global time and space to the promise of controlling the future, and thus increasing wealth accumulation.

Newbridge promote themselves by claiming that it is they who can be depended upon to keep open the electronic channels which operate in the time of exposure, sustaining the global economy: 'In 2.7 gigabytes, the financial markets will close. Your network, however, is still open for business.' The ability of Newbridge to enable the consumer to take action in the time of exposure is now, somewhat clumsily, indicated by the fractions of a second it takes for a hammer to fall. But such interventions could not be sustained if they did not produce a space fit for inhabitation. And life forms or forms of life which inhabit this space are classified by brand rather than by kind.

The pixel, as the unit of animation of the non-temporal rectangle of the computer screen, is the device by which the time of exposure is opened up for occupation by global brands. The aspiration to occupy the time of exposure is demonstrated most obviously in the use of promotional tag lines for global brands which present the overcoming of both space and time as little more than a matter of choice: 'Toshiba: In touch with tomorrow'; 'Microsoft. Where do you want to go today?'; and, perhaps most famously, 'Solutions for a small planet. IBM'. A recent advertisement for Sun Microsystems (Figure 2.8) encapsulates the global thinking

IN 2.7 GIGABYTES, THE FINANCIAL MARKETS WILL CLOSE. YOUR NETWORK HOWEVER, IS STILL OPEN FOR BUSINESS.

.0
.1
.2
.3
.4
.5
.7
.8
.9
.10

56,789 buy options ordered

$12 million in T-Bills sell

18,603 shares traded

ARE YOU READY? To outsiders looking in, it is a ballet of chaos and frenzy with global consequences. On the floor of any major stock exchange, the volume of information transactions fluctuates wildly as gigabytes of data circulate worldwide within fractions of a second. | As the demand for information peaks, one issue stands alone – can the network handle the volume? | Financial sector businesses require an information infrastructure that is ready for anything. It is probably the most important investment they'll ever make. It's also why they choose Newbridge to deliver their network.

NEWBRIDGE  www.newbridge.com/go   1-800-343-3600

Figure 2.7

Newbridge's advertisement for their network services offers to provide financial information in the 'time of exposure' that now characterises the global economy through an image of the fractions of a second it takes a hammer to fall.

Who's dot-comming the world?

Today, it's ".com" this, ".com" that.

You're more than a little familiar with .com. But how about the company behind it? At Sun, we've been taking companies into the Network Age for the better part of 16 years. Everything we make, everything we do (and everything we've always done) is about network computing.

And that's what dot-comming is all about.

Our computer systems, technologies and services enable companies to get to the Net, and .com their business processes. From ISPs like UUNET and EarthLink to entertainment companies like Sony. From e-commerce businesses like Music Boulevard to portals like Excite. And with our Java™ technologies, we're extending the Net – all the way to consumer devices. By dot-comming everything from smart cards to cell phones to home appliances, we're ushering in a whole new world

of interaction. With our technologies behind them, hundreds of companies, some decades-old, some hours-old, are dot-comming themselves overnight. Reinventing themselves overnight. We're the dot in .com. What can we .com for you?

We're the dot in .com.

Sun
microsystems

Figure 2.8

In this advertisement for Sun Microsystems computer products, the conventions of website addresses are animated to become an active brand strategy ('Who's dot-comming the world?'), with the dot connecting the global image of the blue planet, or whole earth, to 'com', while Sun Microsystems' corporate trademark substitutes for the dot itself.

which suggests that a new world-order is being created and occupied by the brand; it asks 'Who's dot-comming the world?' to reply 'We're the dot in .com.', connecting the dot to 'the world' with an image of the blue planet. The text elaborates:

> by dot-comming everything from smart cards to cell phones to home appliances, we're ushering in a whole new world of interaction. With our technologies behind them, hundreds of companies, some decades-old, some hours-old, are dot-comming themselves overnight. Reinventing themselves overnight. We're the dot in .com. What can we .com for you?

Such brand rhetoric not only invokes the temporalities of global culture (see Lury, 1999), it is also the means of making connections, drawing distinctions and finding resemblances or affinities between the objects of second nature and the commodities of global nature, global culture.

● ●   **Notes**

1   As Strathern similarly comments:

> Perhaps it was . . . around 1860 or so, when the cultivation of nature was replaced by its own grounding naturalism, that is, by apprehension of nature as a natural system. Given a concern with reproduction ('inheritance') of organisms, one might suggest that evolutionary thinking also facilitated the equation of procreation and biology. The 'natural facts' of life were natural in the sense of belonging to the biology of the species.
>
> (1992a: 119)

2   In addition to Carolyn Merchant's groundbreaking study *The Death of Nature* (1980), see also Brian Easlea (1980, 1981) and Ludmilla Jordanova (1980, 1986, 1989) for feminist accounts of 'nature' in the history of science.

3   The substantial body of feminist work on both the biological sciences and biology as a cultural system has important and distinctive links to the feminist analysis of naturalising processes. See, for example, Birke (1986); Birke and Hubbard (1995); Fausto-Sterling (1985); Haraway (1989b, 1991, 1997); Hubbard (1990, 1995); Hubbard et al. (1982); Keller (1990, 1992, 1995, 1996); Oudshoorn (1994); and Spanier (1995).

4   For the latter in particular, see Hubbard and Wald (1993).

5   For a review of several versions of the feminist critique of the natural and the biological, see Franklin (2001a).

6   This essay was published in the same anthology as the Jordanova essay on 'Natural Facts' mentioned earlier. Both pieces appeared as chapters in the now classic anthology edited by MacCormack and Strathern, *Nature, Culture and Gender* (1980). The critique of ideas of the natural was of particular importance to this anthology as it was written in response to two of the most influential early feminist anthropological essays on gender, by Edwin Ardener (1972) and Sherry Ortner (1974), both of whom drew heavily on structuralist presumptions of a universal nature–culture dichotomy, which they saw as grounding understandings of gender difference. It is in turn Strathern's prescient critique of this conceptual arrangement of nature, culture and gender which underpins much of Butler's later argument, in *Gender Trouble*, about the discursive power of the natural or biological in producing gender as an effect (see Butler, 1990: 37).

7   In her conclusion, Strathern summarises that for Hageners:

> There is no culture, in the sense of the cumulative works of man, and no nature to be tamed and made productive. And ideas such as these *cannot be a referent of gender imagery*. Hageners do use gender idioms to talk about social as opposed to personal interests, and the cultivated as

distinct from the wild. But these two domains *are not brought into systematic relationship*; the intervening metaphor of culture's domination over nature is not there. . . . Neither male nor female can possibly stand for 'humanity' as against 'nature' because the distinction between them is used to evaluate areas in which human action is creative and individuating.

(1980: 219, emphasis added)

8   Strathern's depiction of nature, culture and gender as a 'matrix', and her concern with processes of domaining, distinction and kinds of difference, are described in her later work in terms of partial analogies she defines as 'merographic' (1992a: 72–87). In terms of nature–culture, Strathern draws attention to the ways in which they can become contexts for one another, and overlap, as a means of producing a range of perspectives, by which they may appear to be oppositional, complementary, or indeed part of one another.

9   For Delaney (1986), the unexamined power of naturalising processes has important implications in relation to powerful Judaeo-Christian themes, such as Creation, which she argues index concepts such as that of paternity. For Yanagisako (1985), the axiomatic importance accorded to 'the biological facts of sexual reproduction' within social theory is one of the major ways in which naturalisation obscures other social processes. In both respects, naturalisations are seen to obscure the cultural specificity of highly influential and often 'self-evident' concepts structuring dominant or mainstream models of, for example, human reproduction by making these appear to be self-evident.

10   An important difference of focus distinguishes much feminist scholarship on ideas of the natural from more recent literature produced within sociology, philosophy and anthropology, which is primarily concerned with a domain of nature implicated in ideas about the environment (Cronon, 1995; Dickens, 1996; Wilson, 1992) and ecology (Descola and Palsson, 1996). While a concern with land, the environment and 'natural' resources was critical to early feminist discussions of nature and the natural, such as those by Carolyn Merchant (1980) mentioned earlier and more recently the work of Vandana Shiva (1989), feminist scholarship on 'the nature question' has in general been primarily addressed to ideas of the natural related to women's bodies, and in particular their reproductive and sexual capacities (Plumwood, 1993). Within feminism, 'natural facts' have been most often queried where they have been used to legitimate repressive notions of 'women's nature'. In sum, a great deal of feminist work on ideas of the natural has been about biology, very much in contrast to more recent work on ideas of nature and the natural, such as Macnaghten and Urry (1998), which is largely focussed on the environment.

11   As Foucault notes,

> For natural history to appear, it was not necessary for nature to become denser and more obscure, to multiply its mechanisms to the point of acquiring the opaque weight of a history that can only be retraced and described, without any possibility of measuring it, calaculating it, or explaining it; it was necessary – and this is entirely the opposite – for History to become Natural.
>
> (1980: 128)

By this he means that up to the mid-seventeenth century all that existed was histories of distinct plants and animals. Natural history could emerge only when 'the history of a living being was that being itself, within the whole semantic network that connected it to the world' (Foucault, 1970: 129).

12   It is perhaps not surprising that one of the most well-known cases in which this technology has been put to work is in the creation of digitally imaged dinosaurs of *Jurassic Park* (see Chapter 6), for dinosaurs are complex symbols of aspects of earlier commonsense understandings of the temporality of natural history: of what came before, what is no longer, and should be on the other side of the 'post-', in the past.

13   Our understanding of the brand as a sign of second nature is motivated in part by Walter Benjamin's claim that '[t]he span between emblem and advertising image lets one measure the changes that have taken place since the seventeenth century in the world of things' (in Buck-Morss, 1989: 429).

Chapter 3 / Units of Genealogy

The importance of the pixel to the open-ended temporality of global brands adds an important dimension to Haraway's proposal of a 'shift from kind to brand' (1997), which shapes the new grammars and genders of technoscience.[1] In this chapter we explore further how brand strategies are explicitly constituted through familial, genealogical and sexual connections, which, we argue, exemplify distinctive features of global nature, global culture more widely. The ways in which the reproduction of commodities, markets, capital and brands now have their own explicit 'facts of life' is made particularly evident in the context of bio-commodities, such as genetically modified foods, where the brand is not only written into the product's DNA, but consumed in the double sense of being both purchased and eaten. We explore these questions briefly here in the context of global branding, before returning to these themes in the last pair of icons, the seed and the breed.

Asking how it is that brands establish relations of naturalised kind, we explore the ways in which the brand is reproduced not only in commodity kinship (relations of affinity between products) but also in kinships of the commodity (relations of affinity between consumers and brands). We thus draw attention to the ways genealogies are used to organise, and naturalise, relations among products and their purchasers through brands. What is of interest to us here are again the switching points whereby one kind of naturalised connection (family bonds) can be transferred to produce an analogy for a different set of relations (among products, and between products and their consumers). For us, it is both the increase in the traffic between naturalised idioms and commodity culture, and the intensive policing of the passing-points for this traffic, which demonstrate again why global nature, global culture is a necessary and unavoidable context for a feminist occupation. Continuing the tradition of feminist cultural analysis in which gender is understood to mark, perform or enact what Haraway describes as the material-semiotic effect of naturalised kind,[2] this account of how the global brand creates its own context for naturalisation demonstrates its indexicality of the workings of global nature, global culture.

The time of the brand is that of the *instantaneity* of recognition and thus discrimination: brands work through the immediacy of their recognisability. This recognition is achieved through proprietary marks, including hieroglyphs or logos, such as the curly script and curvaceous bottles that encourage us to drink Coca-Cola[3] or the Golden Arches that invite us in to have a BigMac Meal; these scripts both distinguish the brand and produce brand families, or contexts. Logos operate as what Paul Virilio (1991, 1994) calls *phatic images*, images that target attention, synthesizing perception. As a phatic image, the brand works to displace or decontextualise bodily or biographical memory, which had been a naturalised aspect of the (apparently instantaneous) processes of perception, and recontextualise it within its own (technologically mediated) body of expectations, understandings and associations built up through market research, advertising, promotion, sponsorship and the themed use of retail space. What is significant about the brand as a phatic image is thus the extent to which it can recoup the effects of the subject or consumer's perception as the outcome of its own powers through an assertion of its ability to motivate the product's meaning and use. This is achieved through the ways the brand operates to link the subject and object in novel ways, making available for appropriation aspects of the experience of product use *as if they were properties of the brand*.

According to Paul Virilio, the 'parasitic persistence' of 'geometric brand-images, initials, Hitler's swastika, Charlie Chaplin's silhouette . . . or the red lips of Marilyn Monroe' is not merely an effect of technical reproducibility, but a means of message-intensification (1994: 14). To underscore the capacity of the brand to condense its message into its mark, product logos are deliberately targeted, and are intended to force the viewer to look; indeed Virilio argues they are the result of an 'ever-lighter illumination, of the intensity of its definition, singling out only specific areas, the context mostly disappearing into a blur' (1994: 12). While this capacity is partly the result of an extensive process of market research and promotion, the proprietary powers of the brand are also established through the ways in which its phatic inscriptions create and maintain links among product items, product lines and product assortments.

Integral to the power of successful global brands, such as Ford, Nike, McDonald's and Benetton, is the creation of so-called 'family resemblances' among products, through which commodities come to be seen as sharing essential character traits: the shared substance of their brand identities. In these and other cases, brand work may be seen to produce a form of *commodity kinship*. Brands both include and exclude, producing a diacritical kinship of family resemblances through distinctive proprietary marks. Brand-development strategies typically associate a range of products with a brand as a source or origin, establishing a relation of ownership to the 'parent' company and a form of commodity affiliation among several generations of products. At the same time, such strategies may also de-emphasise family connections where they may harm the parent brand, as in the case of Reebok's acquisition of Rockport shoes, which were not renamed 'Reebok' but were added separately to the company's portfolio as additional brand capital. The creation of new brands by the parent company itself is a related strategy of brand diversification, as in the case of Toyota's introduction of the Lexus species of motorcar. Brand-extension strategies, like marriages to foreign royalty, involve a calculated risk in the selection of what products to add or delete to strengthen the brand, for example how many variations on Pepsi are compatible with greater brand strength before product reliability and recognisability begin to be compromised. Brands thus rely on both connection and disconnection, in-laws and outcasts, for their successful reproduction over time and across generations of product.

The life of a brand may also be closely connected to a particular individual. Unlike the relations established by copyright, in which the author's works are analogous to offspring, brands tied to individuals, such as those named after various fashion designers, establish an identity between the brand and its personification. For example, although Richard Branson is the creator of the Virgin brand, his connection to it is not that of an author so much as that of a living embodiment, or guarantor, of the brand. While there is no obvious connection between a record label, travel services, clothing and financial products, these are united as a brand family under the distinctive Virgin logo. Virgin has become a brand associated with a particular entrepreneurial style, and this is in turn inseparable from the attributes of Richard Branson. The Virgin brand establishes a relationship to Richard Branson, which customers literally buy into when they purchase the range of Virgin services and products. In this instance, the 'life' of the brand depends crucially upon the life of its creator, as if of one body.[4]

Authorship and paternity are combined in the advertisement for the perfume DNA marketed by the designer Bijan which makes a very explicit comparison between this product and his children (Figure 3.1). Bijan is shown with his children in the ad, the top caption of which reads: 'DNA . . . it's the reason you have your father's eyes, your mother's smile, and . . . Bijan's perfume.' Below this the sub-caption continues: 'Bijan with his DNA . . . son Nicolas and daughter Alexandra.' DNA perfume by Bijan thus equates the product with his offspring, while the brandname, 'Bijan', is, like the designer himself, a progenitor. Consequently, although brand:product :: genitor:progeny, this relation explicitly contradicts the possibility of brand:product :: genitor:brand.

So close is this connection that the life of the brand can be imagined as at risk of accidental death. In a 1998 interview in *Wired* magazine, 'living brand' interior designer Martha Stewart is compared to a 'force of nature' and directly questioned about her brand survival should she 'be hit by a bus'. Her introduction as a prolific entrepreneur emphasises a flow of output, as if from her own body: '[W]ith a 2.3 million-circulation magazine and syndicated column bearing her name, a river of books, and a stream of television shows, Martha Stewart is a force of nature, the most influential person alive giving shape to our living spaces' (Kelly, 1998: 114). Yet this very productivity, as if itself an expression of personal vitality, raises the inevitable spectre of the danger to the brand of the possibility of Martha Stewart's sudden death:

> **Kelly** Management guru Tom Peters preaches the 'brand of you' – if there is anyone this applies to, it's you. What happens if you get hit by a bus? Does the brand of you continue?

DNA...it's the
reason you have
your father's eyes,
your mother's smile,
and...

bijan's perfume.

DNA
PERFUME

by bijan

bijan
with his DNA
son nicolas
and daughter
alexandra!

DNA fragrances at Nordstrom or call 1•800•695•8000

Figure 3.1

*In this advertisement for his product DNA perfume,
the designer Bijan is shown with his two children,
linking the theme of paternity to his brand name.*

Stewart: I'm trying to make sure that my brand extension is broad enough that if anything happens, or I decide to check out, it can continue. We have taken the next five years of photographs of me already, so if anything happened to me we have those closets full of photos.

Kelly You could have yourself scanned to create a virtual character.

Stewart Cloning hasn't worked yet, but I'll be the first. The first human Dolly will be me.

(Kelly, 1998: 114)

The intertwining of the 'life of the brand' with the lifetime of the person seen to embody it is at first evident in the name, 'Martha Stewart', and is suggestive of the importance of names to reckonings of descent and ancestry (patrimony), as well as personal value and worth ('a good name'). Martha Stewart is literally a 'name brand' in these familiar, and here doubled, senses. However, what is significant about this interview too is the ease with which concern about the life of the brand moves into the frame of reproductive and information technologies, in the suggestion of 'a virtual you' and cloning.[5] These 'facts of life', enunciated in response to the question of brand survival, illustrate precisely the movements within and between naturalised, denaturalised and renaturalised contexts of brand existence.

In the same way that brands are reproduced and naturalised through close analogy to both living persons and naturalised families of products, so too are brands repeatedly promoted through conventional forms of heterosexuality and family life, such as traditional family scenarios, normative gender roles and a domestic division of labour. A well-known example in the UK is the OXO family, whose trials and tribulations are resolved as they sit down at a family meal to eat a dish flavoured by OXO stock-cubes (Celia Lury, 1993). Brands may indeed be seen *to replace* family ties, offering participation in a commodity kinship system in which the brand provides the shared bodily, or reproductive, substance. A suggestive example of the way brands stand in for family ties is provided by novelist Sara Schulman, in a critique of some parts of the gay press that represent their audiences to advertisers not only as groups with high disposable incomes, but also as 'the most brand-loyal consumers in the country'. Schulman cites a prospectus used by one US popular gay magazine which claims that gay people are particularly open to recruitment into kinships of the commodity because of their exclusion from heterosexually-based family structures, or their own families of origin: 'Many gay people are separated from their families . . . therefore the mechanisms that normally lead people to choose a product are absent' (1994: 2).[6] Here, as in its connections to both its living embodiments, and the products with which it shares family ties, the brand is closely defined by the inclusions and exclusions marking its contexts of circulation.

While brands establish familial, sexual and genealogical ties to products, consumers and producers, these naturalised relations do not perform straightforward or traditional versions of family, sex or genealogy; we might even say the brand performs some of these as unnatural acts, or in drag, as when 'proper' descent lines are erased, outsiders become part of the family, or brand loyalty connects queer consumers to new markets. These aspects of the life of the global brand thus provide a means for us to extend the more explicit use of branding by 'parent companies' as a kinship strategy by asking what kind of 'family resemblances' among commodities, lineages of product evolution or 'brand families' are being engendered in the pursuit of building brand capital, or name recognition? While brand-marketing strategies borrow liberally from established definitions of kinship to provide analogies for the ways in which products are 'related', *these analogies can also travel back* (Strathern, 1992b). In other words, the relations connecting products to their 'parent company', such as their brand or trademark, might be seen to refigure what counts as a naturalised kind, or kin.

This two-way traffic, which is both excessive and paradoxical in ways that closely resemble Butler's account of gender performances, is particularly evident in the manufacture of globally branded biological products which bear the mark of their parent company in their genetic blueprint. For example, Michael Pollan (1999) describes how Monsanto, the chemical and would-be life sciences giant, inserted a 'marker' gene into its New Leaf Superior potatoes, reprogamming them to produce their own insecticide. The marker, which Pollan describes as 'a kind of universal product code' (1999: 11), allows Monsanto to identify its plants after they leave the laboratory, enabling the 'parent' company to enforce its patent licence to those who purchase its products to grow potatoes to eat or sell, but *not to reproduce*. As Pollan continues:

> Soon [Monsanto] is expected to acquire the patent to a powerful new bio-technology called the Terminator[7] which will, in effect, *allow the company to enforce its patents biologically*. Developed by the USDA [United States Department of Agriculture] in partnership with Delta and Pine Land, a seed company in the process of being purchased by Monsanto, the Terminator is a complex of genes that, theoretically, can be spliced into any crop plant, where it will cause every seed produced by that plant to be sterile. Once the Terminator becomes the industry standard, control over the genetics of crop plants will complete its move from the farmer's field to the seed company – to which the farmer will have no choice but to return year after year.
>
> (1999: 12, our emphasis)

Like the kinships of the commodity described above, the branding of life itself refigures what can count as natural kin, or kind. We can suggest, using brands as just one example, that in the same way naturalisation and denaturalisation produce distinctive forms of global culture, so too can *the renaturalisation of kind* secure different relations, such as ownership and control of non-genealogical reproduction. Developing on Haraway's suggestive proposal of a 'shift from kind to brand' (1997) to describe the proprietary marking of bio-commodities allows us to pursue her invitation to read the global brand as a type of global kind, or kind-making technology, indeed *as a kind of global gender*. This is not only one way to explore what is meant by the condition (material, discursive, or as viable offspring) of globalisation; it is more specifically a way of linking an account of global nature, global culture to 'global genders', such as brands.[8] This is another way of saying that kinship and gender are connecting different orders of things than they used to, and that they also mean differently: instead of signifying *naturally different kinds*, gender- and kinship-as-brand now signify *kinds of naturalised difference* and connection. Through brand extension, brand reproduction and brand hygiene is thus also created a new grammar for the calibration of life as a productive force.

● ● ● Context, Control and Choice

In her work on models of organic form and the role of information as a 'causal' factor in development, Susan Oyama (1985) identifies a fundamental question of context control. In a discussion of cybernetic systems that is highly relevant to an under-standing of the pixel and the gene as units in a code of communication, Oyama identifies a tendency to conflate communication with causation, pointing to the ways in which information is frequently characterised as 'the power to direct what is done', and to the argument that communication 'occurs when events in one place or at any one time are closely related to events in another place or time' (1985: 67). In turn, Oyama links this conflation to contemporary understandings of animate systems, and the belief amongst some life scientists that life processes comprise 'the storage, readout and transfer of information, the processing of information in logical opera-tions implemented in molecular interactions', and are 'intelligent' at the molecular level (1985: 64).

In other words, the conflation between communication and causation, present in everyday understandings of plan and instruction, is also exemplified in definitions of in-formation in cybernetics, genetics and computing in which the 'code' is understood to operate independently of context – an understanding critical to the model of the gene as a message, the utility of the pixel to digital imagery, and the commercial implementation of the brand as a proprietary mark. Oyama argues the conflation between communication and causation is problematic insofar as it yokes together ideas of pre-existing form and teleological control, thus establishing a calculus of causes and inevitability, and of risks and responsibilities, which encourage us 'to predict limits in situations whose critical parameters may be unknown' (1985: 63). As Pollan points out in his discussion of genetically modified potatoes, the consequences of their introduction into agriculture are highly uncertain. He makes the wry point that while biotechnology depends on the ability to move genes freely among species and even phyla, its environmental safety depends on the very opposite principle: on the integrity of species in 'nature' and their rejection of foreign genetic material (Pollan, 1999: 11).

Oyama and Pollan thus both point to problems associated with *the erasure of context* which underpin the emergence of global nature, global culture. Oyama believes that what has become more unstable is the cultural ordering of causation, direction and control, and, like Baudrillard, she links this instability to a denial of origins. Baudrillard further suggests this disavowal is gendered: made to function as a fetish, the fossil conceals a refusal of difference (of gender, of type, of the partial analogies of nature and culture and their links to paternity and genealogy). Standing in as the hallucination of an origin, the fossil indexes a continuing masculine anxiety about reproduction, the relation between cause and effect, before and after, copy and original.

Oyama too argues that the contemporary definition of information as instantiated in the gene reduces life to 'an ever more complicated set of metaphorical plans and images to assist the creator homunculus in its labors' (1985: 111). This creator – who has appeared earlier in our discussion of the blue planet and foetus as the representative of panhumanity – appears to achieve the impossible, pulling himself up by his own bootstraps. Moreover, in concealing a refusal of difference, the contemporary understanding of fossils and pixels promotes a belief in the possibility of a mechanism of 'replication, a way in which like could be produced from like' (Keller, 1996: 118). Yet, as Keller points out in her study of the biological sciences, the '"secret of life" to which we have so ingeniously gained access [is] no pristine point of origin, but already a construct at least partially of our own making' (1996: 121).

One important example of a rhetoric which denies this partial determination is to be found in the vocabulary of choice. It is the requirement of the exercise of will which is the decisive means by which the global citizen is established. Theorists such as Benedict Anderson (1983) and Homi Bhabha (1994) argue that the unchosen underpins the naturalness of the distinctive formations of national identity that characterise Euro-American history. We suggest, in contrast, that emergent global networks offer the chosen – or, rather, choice itself – as the origin of the imagined community of global citizenship; indeed, they render choice itself a necessity. In other words, in place of the 'determining power of the indeterminate' that Bhabha identifies in stories of national origins, the invitation to be a global subject depends upon the the naturalisation of compulsory choice and (artificial) selection. We would thus contrast the consuming subject of the enterprise culture, of global nature, global culture, whose identity is confirmed through choice, against the 'unchosen' identities of race, nation, kinship and other naturalised connections.

In this process of world-making, as Strathern remarks, 'Choice becomes conventional, and conventions are for the choosing' (1992a: 152). Within the global imaginary, difference is subject to the dictates of lifestyle, of consumer culture and commodification. The biological, historical and social differences which had informed the categories of type or kind, the categories of gender, race, class, sexuality and age, are rendered amenable to choice. Once placed within the grasp of choice, previously biological, political and social attributes of the individual and collective body, including not only aspects of personal identity, but also reproductive futures, individual health and well-being, and national identity, are increasingly understood within a discourse of strategic, voluntary transformation (Celia Lury, 1998). Such transformations, however, are, as argued above, already foreseen in the creation and operation of global brands.

A local example of identity-by-design is the joint effort by British Prime Minister Tony Blair's 'New Labour' government and Demos, a British 'think-tank' which published a report in 1998 entitled *Britain^{TM}: renewing our identity*. In the face of anxiety that 'there is no single or clear perception of Britain in many countries', the report proposes to create a 'British brand'. Part of this process of revisioning involved asking '80 of the UK's most prominent creative thinkers' to conceive of a single image to sum up the best of contemporary Britain (Myerson, 1998: 58). After participating in a workshop, design consultant John Williamson of the brand consultancy firm Wolff Olins presented three images of sheep to express the new Britain (Figure 3.2):

> Sheep 1: a sheep on the hillside, evocative of our natural heritage, traditions and landscape – our inherent strengths as a nation. Sheep 2: the Damien Hirst sheep pickled in a tank, showing the radical, avant-garde side of British culture and creativity. Sheep 3: the genetically engineered Dolly, symbolising British leadership in innovation, science and technology.
>
> (Myerson, 1998: 58, 60)

In this example, nature, culture and second nature are set alongside each other as optional sources for a new British national identity. As Strathern (1992a) remarks, however, what is reproduced by this and other examples of the conventions of choice are not persons or nations, but *auto-enabling choice itself*, a construct which is its own construction, an exemplary trope in the global imaginary.

What fuels this trope of self-construction or auto-generation are a set of animating processes, including the genetic code as it is being defined in the human genome project, the information codes that underpin demographic data-sets, the futures market on the stock exchange, and the notion of (life)style at work in decisions about art, health, leisure and consumption. As Strathern writes, 'Styles appear to imitate other styles, replicating them by an inner momentum that is contained in the very notion that style itself is an imitative act' (1992a: 171). Significantly, though, this is '[n]ot the imitation of nature or of more noble ages, as it might have been seen a century before, but imitation of versions of itself' (1992a: 171).

The animating techniques of life itself are the tightly regulated switching points, or, in Bruno Latour's phrase, 'obligatory passage points', necessary for access to planetary consciousness or entry to the global imaginary (Latour, 1987). At the same time, in a reciprocal legitimating process, the global itself provides a model and guarantor for the principle of auto-enablement that underpins many of these techniques. While Haraway argues that such switching points 'greatly increase the density of all kinds of other traffic on the bridge between what counts as nature and

Figure 3.2

A proposed rebranding of Britain by designer John Williamson of the consulting company Wolff Olins is represented here in this triple image of sheep on the hillside, Damien Hirst's pickled sheep in a tank, and the cloned sheep Dolly – evoking nature, culture and industry.

culture for my people' (1997: 56), Strathern (1995a) points out that globalising projects conceal the relational dimensions of social life on two counts. First, social relations vanish when the concept of culture is globalised on the presumption that cultures are manifestations of a universal self-consciousness about identity (in which the naturalness of choice described above is a key element). Second, they disappear when a distinctive instance of global culture (such as notions of choice and lifestyle, genetic information, codes and systems thinking more generally) is no longer contextualised by (first) nature, but by its 'own' forms, so that it seemingly creates (self-referentially, essentially) its own context. This is the basis of the new universalisms of global nature, global culture. As Strathern notes:

> Culture has become a global phenomenon. By that I mean that a Euro-American perception of the role of culture in human affairs can be summoned in almost any context, at almost any level of human interaction, a ubiquity seemingly underscored by the fact that it refers to what is taken as a universal condition of human interaction.
>
> (1995a: 2)

However, as Pollan and others point out, the use of patents and other forms of intellectual property such as trademarks are integral not only to the creation of what we have called the universalisms of global nature, global culture, but also to their private ownership. Companies such as Monsanto, he claims, are attempting 'to privatise one of the last great commons in nature – the genetics of the crop plants that civilisation has developed over the last 10,000 years' (Pollan, 1999: 12).

These shifts in cultural logic surrounding questions of animate systems with lives of their own, and the related questions of shifting meanings of genealogy, are explored further in the two icons below, the seed and the breed. Using contrasting examples of the uses of genealogy, origins and creation drawn from the ever-widening menagerie of reprogrammable life forms, we use this final set of icons to develop the contrasts and connections discussed earlier in relation to the foetus, the planet, the cell, the fossil, the pixel and the brand – asking again what forms of life have become possible in global nature, global culture.

● ◉   The Seed

To specify yet another of the ways ideas of the natural are reconstituted within global culture, we return briefly to the earliest, and what Raymond Williams describes as the primary, meaning of 'culture', in the sense of cultivation or husbandry (1976: 87). It is here that the culture that belongs, or tends, to nature overlaps with the nature that belongs to, or becomes, culture. As Williams notes, this is the sense of culture found in gardening, as in seed culture, or in biology, as in cultures of the petri dish. Significantly, we find in these examples a thickening of the sense of 'culture' more characteristic of what Williams describes as the distinctive feature of the word 'nature'. According to Williams, the complexity of the term 'nature' is composed of the many different meanings *simultaneously present* in any one utterance (1976: 222), while 'culture' is described as 'thick' in the sense of having many distinct meanings *across a range of uses* (1976: 92). We suggest the way culture has now become more like nature, in the sense of carrying several meanings simultaneously, is another instance of the way in which global nature and culture mimic each other while remaining distinct.

Numerous examples of this condensation of the culture concept could be drawn from the biosciences – in part due to the increasing reliance of molecular genetics on literary, textual, linguistic and informatic analogies. Through the following pair of icons we describe this process with reference to *biodiversity*, broadly described as the effort to preserve the world's genetic resources against the threat of their potential extinction. With the emergence of biodiversity as a cultural value definitive of a global worldview, both seed culture and petri culture carry what Williams describes as the oldest and most recent meanings of culture. The human genome diversity project (HGDP), for example, specifically seeks to preserve cultural uniqueness by sampling and preserving the endangered DNA of rare, indigenous peoples threatened with extinction. Haraway (1997) locates this potent turn-of-the-century project, funded by the National Science Foundation in the US and various European bodies, as heir to the traditions of genealogical mapping of universal human characterisitics, which began with the family trees of Darwin and Haeckel, and now continues as an effort to map human descent under the auspices of molecular biology. Of as yet untold potential value, the immortalised cell lines created from the germplasm of 'primitive' indigenous peoples are envisaged both as a 'multi-cultural' genomics and as a significant source of biowealth. In such an enterprise are thus united 'culture' in its classic anthropological sense (of 'other' cultures), the biological sense of culture (the culturing of the immortalised cell lines developed from the blood and saliva samples of isolated indigenous peoples) and culture in the sense of shared values (for example, the value of preserving biodiversity). To appreciate both the logic and the lexicon of the HGDP, therefore, involves understanding several different meanings of culture – including culture as nature, wealth, diversity, biological growth and information.

A more quotidian and literally backyard version of the human genome diversity project, and one which is marketed through a similar lexicon, is the new genre of heritage seed catalogues such as that distributed by the Santa Fe-based enterprise Seeds of Change, Inc. Such catalogues advertise native seeds for home-producers, with the added benefit that heritage seeds are not only organic, but ancient and rare. Seeds of Change thus not only offers organic variety and novelty, but assists in preserving the heritage of ancient cultures, as well as contributing to the biodiversity of the planet (Figure 3.3).

In this holistic ethos, good gardening is more than a means to grow healthier food. According to company founder Kenny Ausubel:

Figure 3.3

Company founder Kenny Ausubel describes heritage seed cultivation as a form of 'kinship gardening' in his book outlining the corporate philosophy of Seeds of Change, Inc., based in Santa Fe, New Mexico.

Figure 3.4

The use of seed banks to preserve botanical diversity enables the conservation of up to 10 per cent of living seeds on the planet.

Species can live for millennia in seed banks.

> Seeds of Change sees true wealth as the heritage we can all share in the form of a seed. . . . [Seeds] connect us to the past and to those that have maintained varieties for us to plant today, as well as to future generations as we preserve the germplasm for their use.
>
> (1994: 2)

Here, the anthropological sense of culture is explicitly merged with its older meaning of tending, cultivating or preserving, so that seeds become at once personal, political, ancient, natural and manufactured: icons of both global nature and global culture. To culture the seeds is to nurture them, while at the same time the seed is a naturalised repository of cultural heritage: seed cultures reproduce cultural difference as well as biologically valuable plants. The establishment of the millennium seed bank in Britain, and catalogues for heritage seeds, as well as heritage sites such as the Chelsea Botanic Garden in London, all express similar principles (Figures 3.4–3.6). A panhuman scale of benefit is appealed to at the level of both reducing potential risks (extinction of seeds and cultures through mono-cropping) and offering an improved future for the planet (new unities of humans and plants, past and present, across time and cross-culturally).[9]

Seeds of Change rhetoric relies heavily on traditional idioms of kinship and genealogy, describing 'kinship gardening' of 'heirloom-variety seeds' as a 'form of planetary gene-pool gardening' based on planting and tending 'living genealogies' that 'allow us to investigate evolution for ourselves' (Ausubel, 1994: 54). In this New Age vision, 'Life is a living, pulsing, vibrating plasmic mystery, a spontaneous improvisation linked through time by memory encoded in genes. The seeds that carry these genes are the regenerative life form' (1994: 20). More colloquially, another Seeds of Change activist asks: 'We're all kin, aren't we? Isn't that what biology is all about?' (1994: 19). In such claims, molecular genetic kinship is evoked as a fabric of interconnectedness, manifesting the biological imperative of diversity, and thus the basis of life itself. Genealogy is the master trope in this web of connections uniting ancient farmer-cultivators with their modern-day descendants, who are similarly engaged in the preservation of lineages of seed-value. In the heirloom-variety model of stewardship,

We're collecting for the sake of every species.

Over the next 50 years, a quarter of the world's seed-bearing plant species will face extinction. It's a terrifying

thought, especially when the future of every species will then be put at risk – including ours.

We simply can't survive without plants. We need them for the air we breathe, the food we eat, and the medicines we use to combat disease. Some give us natural insecticides, reducing the use of chemicals on crops; others have the ability to reclaim land lost to the desert.

In all, over 250,000 seed-bearing plants work together to make our world habitable and beautiful. With every species that disappears, part of the fabric of the planet crumbles; and priceless genetic information is lost forever.

Conservation saves lives.

An enormous seed collection programme has already begun. It's perhaps the most ambitious conservation project of its kind.

By the year 2000, we hope to have almost every native UK plant species safely stored in the Millennium Seed Bank, Kew – a specially designed facility at Wakehurst Place in West Sussex. By 2010, we aim to have conserved living seeds from 10% of all plant species for the benefit of future generations.

Initially, attention will be focused on plants growing in arid areas like Africa, India and Latin America. These are the species most at risk – those on which a quarter of the world's human population depends.

Once in the Seed Bank, species can be kept for centuries or even millennia. They can be studied to discover their hidden potential, and reintroduced into the wild at any time.

You can help us today.

From as little as £15 you can help sponsor a species – on your own behalf, or for a friend or relative. Your money will make a real difference, speeding the collection of these priceless seeds. In return, you'll receive a Certificate of Sponsorship, and regular updates on the progress of our vital mission.

Give £250 and we can claim your tax back from the Government through Gift Aid, so your donation will grow to £328.95. With £1,000 you'll become a Benefactor, and your name will be recorded in the Millennium Seed Book, on permanent display in the Seed Bank for posterity.

Please give as much as you can, so that our descendants will continue to enjoy the rich, diverse environment we inherited. All you need to do is complete and return the form or call us now on **0973 10 2000**.

But please send your money today.

Tomorrow could be too late.

Figure 3.5

As part of the millennium celebrations in Britain, Kew Gardens' seed bank appeal promotes sponsorship of botanical species as a form of charitable activity to protect 'the fabric of the planet'.

millennium
seed bank
appeal
kew

Yes, I want to help.

Call **0973 10 2000** to make an immediate credit card donation or fill in this coupon.

ROYAL
BOTANIC
GARDENS
KEW

I will help save the seeds that could save the world. I'd like to sponsor a species for:

£75 ☐   £50 ☐   £30 ☐   £15 ☐   Other amount £ ☐

To help keep costs down, please do not send me a Sponsorship Certificate. ☐

Gift aid
I would like to sponsor by Gift Aid and understand that with my payment
of £250, you will be able to collect an additional £78.95 in tax recovery. ☐

Benefactor
I am interested in becoming a Benefactor (£1,000), and having my name entered
into The Millennium Seed Book for posterity. Please send me more information. ☐

Legacy
I would like to support the work of the Millennium Seed Bank, Kew,
by remembering it in my Will. Please send me more information. ☐

Payment method
I enclose my cheque/PO
payable to The Millennium Seed Bank Appeal, Kew   for £ ☐

Please debit my: Visa ☐   Access ☐
                  Amex ☐   Mastercard ☐   CAFCard ☐   for £ ☐

Card No. ☐☐☐☐ - ☐☐☐☐ - ☐☐☐☐ - ☐☐☐☐

Expiry date ☐☐ - ☐☐

The Foundation and Friends of the Royal Botanic
Gardens, Kew is a registered charity No. 803428.   supported by Orange

(IN BLOCK CAPITALS)
Mr/Mrs/Miss/Ms _____   Initials _____

Address _____

_____

_____

_____   Postcode _____

Signature _____

Date _____

Name to appear
on Certificate
(if applicable) _____

Thank you. Now cut out and return this completed Sponsorship Form to:
The Millennium Seed Bank Appeal, P.O. BOX 4370, London SW15 2PF. Or call us
now on **0973 10 2000** to make an immediate credit card donation.

To raise vital funds we may allow other selected organisations to
write to you. If you would rather not receive such mailings, please
tick this box. ☐

orange

6789

Seeds like these can save the world.

Syrian Rue
*Helps treat asthma, encephalitis
and Parkinson's disease; also a
natural insecticide.*

Desert Date
*The fruits of this tree helped
thousands of Ethiopians survive
the 1980's famine.*

Horse-radish Tree
*Powdered seeds are used to
purify water to prevent diseases
like typhoid and cholera.*

Prickly Juniper
*A useful sand stabiliser
that can help reforest land
already lost to the desert.*

Will you help us save the seeds?

millennium
seed bank
appeal
kew

Figure 3.6
*Planetary survival is the theme of much
biodiversity activism linking seed cultures to
global futures.*

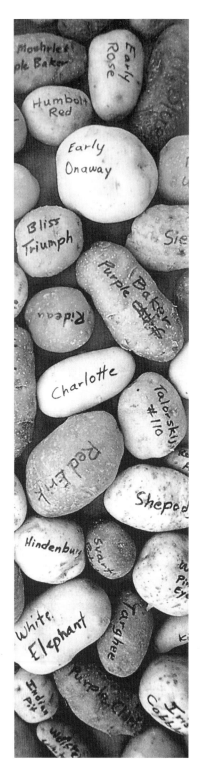

Figure 3.7

Heirloom varieties of domesticated plants preserved in seed banks enable the long-term storage of both genetic diversity and the (agri)cultural labour needed to cultivate specific strains of staple crops, such as potatoes (shown here).

the native seed becomes a germplasm repository of the end-products of both natural and cultural selection – preserving the agricultural labour of traditional seed-tending cultures as a source of future global biowealth (Figure 3.7). The uses of genealogy in this consumer appeal are of the most conventional kind, securing progeny to genitor, seed to wealth, and pasts to futures through the idiom of purity, discursively fusing progress, enterprise, consumption, green activism and public health.

Seeds of Change invokes both the cultural-as-the-natural and the global-as-the-personal, using the most traditional reproductive idiom of pure-bred inheritance to connect these threads. As we shall see, this usage is very much in contrast with much of the language associated with new breeds, such as Dolly the cloned sheep, and this disjuncture underscores an important point about our broader argument: that global nature and global culture are produced out of some of the oldest and most traditional cultural values *which are being used to signify transition and change*. As in our discussion of the global brand, genealogy performs traditional service here in the space of its own displacement, exemplifying the process we argue constitutes the distinctive power of global nature flexibly to reinvent itself. Biodiversity is precisely the kind of emergent cultural value by means of which it is possible to trace the paths of what we call new universalist essentialisms in the production of global nature, nature renaturalised, nature seconded into the service of culture – indeed nature as global culture. What is noticeable about the Seeds of Change appeal is the sequence of shifting frames, or contexts, through which familiar concepts are enabled to signify in new and different ways. Hence, Seeds of Change moves us from the naturalisation of cultural diversity as 'an endangered bio-resource', to the materialisation of this naturalisation in 'heirloom-variety' seeds, to the invitation to purchase such seeds as a form of politicised horticulture, to the commercialisation of this venture through the marketing of new commodities ('Seeds of Change, Inc.'), and to the packaging of this invitation as a contribution to global survival ('kinship gardening'). It is not insignificant, we suggest, that biodiversity discourse addresses reproduction, heredity and 'the facts of life' within a familiar historical, Darwinian, frame – achieved through specific practices such as selective breeding, pedigree-keeping, genealogical restriction, lineage preservation and seed purity. That commercial enterprises such as Seeds of Change are marketed through a procreative discourse of ensuring the survival not only of indigenous plants but also of indigenous knowledge (which 'authored' the seeds) and ancient cultures (whose seeds will continue into the future) exemplifies the connections between such diverse practices as breeding, branding and banking, and their relation to forms of subject formation through personal consumption and relations of belonging.

The emergence of the natural-as-the-global, or nature seconded, is literally reproduced in the iconic world of the heirloom-variety seed-commodity.[10] Historically, the seeds are naturalised within the fabric of life, as an expression of evolutionary variety. They are denaturalised by their enrolment within historical cultures, where they are artificially selected, bred, preserved, classified and tended, eventually to become the 'heirloom' varieties of seeds now marketed as native, ancient, indigenous and endangered. The heritage seeds, and the cultures who tended them, are in turn renaturalised within the idiom of 'kinship gardening', through which they are depicted as integral threads in the fabric of life itself. This renaturalisation is multiply extended through an evolutionary analogy: by culturing the seeds, kinship gardeners assist nature by restoring variety to the gene pool, thus aiding the future sustainability of the human species and the ecosystems on which its survival depends.

In the same way that seeds can be recontextualised as global, commercial, natural and cultural entities, through a series of frame shifts in which traditional idioms of kinship and genealogy perform familiar types of connection, so too with the emergence of new forms of breeding it is possible to illustrate the reverse. In the following section, which might be named 'breeds of change', the emergence of quite unfamiliar forms of kinship, genealogy and reproduction are also organised to produce global nature and global culture.

The Breed

In turning from the heirloom-variety seed to the manufacture of transgenic breeds, we invoke a contrasting context in which the uses of genealogy as seconded nature are reversed. Whereas the heirloom-variety seed indexes the most traditional uses of genealogy, mobilised to invite novel forms of personal consumption, self-health, political activism and environmental stewardship, the patented cloned and transgenic breeds manufactured by corporate agribusiness and pharmaceuticals signify the precise opposite to a wary public, both captivated and disturbed by their coming into being. In both their making and their marketing, the new breeds depart significantly from conventional models of genealogy. Breeds of cloned and transgenic sheep such as those produced by the Roslin Institute in Scotland in the 1990s raise significant questions not only about the ownership of particular animals, or animal reproduction techniques, but about the patenting of life itself – an increasingly significant futures market for world trade and venture capital (Franklin, 1997b). While celebrated as scientific break-throughs, new breeding techniques such as cloning by nuclear transfer challenge established beliefs about evolution, origins and the naturalness of 'the facts of life'. Complex reproductive and commercial futures are on offer through technological possibilities and imaginative speculations linking the birth of Dolly the sheep to the digital, virtual and artificial lifeworlds increasingly familiar to global audiences, and increasingly part of a shared sense of global interconnection.

We use the icon of the breed in this section as a noun, in the common sense of kind or sort, in part because it is, like the seed, already the object of a reproductive practice in which nature and culture are combined and yet remain distinct. The dictionary definition of 'breed' as a noun makes this point clear, stating that a 'breed' is both 'a group of organisms having common ancestors and certain distinguishing characteristics', and 'especially a group within a species developed by artificial selection and maintained by controlled propagation' (*American Heritage Dictionary*, 1992: 236). In other words, a breed is an exemplary case of artificial, or domesticated, nature – and an ancient one at that, the development of which is considered one of the definitive feats of human civilization. Categorially, a breed is both a sub-set of a species and its opposite: whereas a species is defined as a product of natural selection, the breed is forced into being and maintained by artificial means. These tensions are also evident in the definitions of 'breed' as a verb:

> **breed** *(tr. v.)* **1**. To produce (offspring); to give birth or hatch; **2**. To bring about; engender. **3**. a. To cause to reproduce; raise. b. To develop new or improved strains in (animals or plants). **4**. To rear or train; bring up; *(intr. v.)* **1**. To produce offspring. **2**. To gain origin and sustenance; be nurtured.
>
> (*American Heritage Dictionary*, 1992: 236)

The proximity of the notion of the breed to definitions of both nature and culture is quite literal: a breed is cultivated nature, nature shaped, selected and tended artificially. Plants and animals can be bred, and by this means can be domesticated and denaturalised. Breeding describes the creation of new kinds or types of animals, while it also refers to their training, and is, in this sense, synonymous with the narrow Arnoldian sense of 'culture' (to have 'good breeding'). The well-bred animal is the result of careful cultivation, selection and reproduction – the racehorse is a product of the improvement of nature in its physical capacities, its stature. As the history of animal breeding makes clear, however, the cultivation of nature is unevenly realised and often unsuccessful (Ritvo, 1995; Russell, 1986). Historians of animal husbandry depict a curious juxta-position between the evident success of breeders in producing a wide range of recognisably distinct breeds of sheep, horses, dogs, cats, cattle, pigs, pigeons, poultry and various other animal strains, and the lack of evidence of consistent principles by which this was achieved.[11] 'Selective breeding' reveals itself to be based on every possible constellation of practices, from cross-breeding, to in-and-in breeding, to serial hybridisation. That some breeds flourished and others disappeared is today attributed to the comparatively recent emergence of 'proper scientific management' of animal husbandry, and, in particular, the eventual application of techniques derived from botany and horticulture to the practice of animal breeding.

As demonstrated by its history, and its meanings as both a noun and a verb, breeding is, like kinship, a hybrid category, combining the natural and the cultural. In the very notion of the breed, nature becomes culture, and culture becomes nature, through a series of recontextualisations. Both seeds and breeds evince this capacity for dual signification, being both part of but more than nature, repositories of cultural knowledge but quite literally with lives of their own. What is notable about the new breeds, then, is the ways in which this recombinant feature of breeds and breeding is refigured.

The late twentieth century saw the introduction not only of new types of breeding, but of whole new understandings of breeds. This shift can be explored in terms of new uses and units of genealogy. The development of embryological tech-niques enables the introduction of DNA from other species, most notably humans, into an animal lineage. The inaugural higher mammal successfully marketed as a transgenic breed was Harvard/Dupont's OncoMouse[TM], bred to contain human DNA in the form of oncogenes which produced cancer in each individual in order to provide standard-ised animal models for the testing of pharmaceuticals. This controversial innovation made of the animal both a new transgenic life form and a new form of private property, which was marketed under patent as a form of laboratory apparatus – an animal model. Admittedly, this breed had in common with others, especially other mice, the fact of its commercial existence being driven by its utility for scientific experimentation. The novelty of the new transgenic animals lies in the form of intellectual property rights their creators are able to mobilise to protect their value as commodities, and in the techniques used to breed them. Unlike former animal models, the means of producing transgenics is not selective breeding, in the sense of selective mating of two individuals to produce desired traits in the offspring. Rather, transgenics could be said to be closer to the second definition of the verb 'to breed': 'to bring about; engender', for they are the product not of mere procreative activity, but of instrumental manufacture using techniques unknown to 'nature'.

Before transgenics, the reproductive model of the breed could be represented by direct analogy to life itself, in the form of natural selection, by which, according to modern evolutionary biology, all life forms have emerged. They embody this evolutionary principle in their manifestation as individuals with slight variations of genetic inheritance out of which different rates of reproductive success are determined, and in turn through which, over the course of time, some species survive and brachiate, and others become extinct. This genealogical model is well known: we are all related through shared ancestry, and all of life can be described as a family tree – the tree of life. Reproduction, in which the genetic material of two individuals is combined to produce distinctive offspring, is seen to be the engine of this process. Natural selection is the governor, the regulator, the invisible hand shaping life's progression into the spectacular variety that is now celebrated as biodiversity. Transgenic breeding departs from this familiar reproductive model, technologically assisting nature's own recombinant pathways by introducing new channels of genetic exchange: the human into the mouse, the fish into the strawberry, the protozoan into maize. The ensuing pedigrees for such life forms are unfamiliar genealogically and non-Darwinian. No longer bilateral and brachiating over time, no longer tree-like at all, the oncomouse's genealogy is polylineal – composed of multispecies parentage. For this recombinant assemblage, there is no readily available diagram to perform for transgenics what the tree provided for Darwin, in the form of a pre-existing biblical analogy which transferred happily into service as a linear representation of natural history. Technique replaces sex or genealogy for the Roslin animals, much as the patent has replaced their pedigree.

As Haraway (1997) has noted, a change of writing technologies has occurred in the denominations of transgenics under the signs of diacritical marks, such as those denoting a registered trademark. She suggests the transgenic breed emerges as a kind or sort marked no longer by genealogical continuity or lineage (that is, by the narratives of evolutionary time secured in the fossil's imprint) but by commercial ownership as intellectual property, that is, *as information*. To restate Haraway's thesis more formally, the shift is from kind:kindred to brand:commodities – a movement from one reproductive universe (of procreation) into another (of commerce), *but one that is also recalibrated in terms of how relations are defined*. The effects of this shift transform how forward movements in time are understood, as well as refiguring what descent lines can organise.

Previously regarded as a biological impossibility, the birth of a lamb cloned from an adult cell at the Roslin Institute, an animal research laboratory near Edinburgh, in 1996 precipitated yet another departure from familiar reproductive models. Dolly was cloned using an adult cell of a six-year-old Finn Dorset ewe, taken from a cryo-preserved cell line, and transferred to a denucleated ovum of another sheep (see Figure 3.8). The new cell was enabled to merge with the unfertilised ovum through mechanical insertion, accompanied by a metabolic slow-down of both parties, and finished off with a short electric shock to stimulate cell division. After several unsuccessful attempts, Dolly was born to a Blackface ewe, who served as surrogate to the technologically assisted embryo.

Dolly's birth, which was not announced until February 1997, was followed just under a year later by the birth of Polly, a cloned transgenic ewe carrying human genes. It is with Polly that another genealogical template emerges, whereby cloning preserves

Figure 3.8

The successful cloning of Dolly the sheep from an adult cell gave rise to extensive worldwide debate over the future of reproduction in the context of the rapid innovation characterising the global biotechnology industry.

the exact constitution of a transgenic animal (which could be lost through conventional mating). Polly's birth established a means of producing transgenics that is more reliable than any other method. Although Dolly marked the birth of a new kind of breeding, it is Polly that represents the birth of a new kind of breed altogether. Using the Polly technique, scientists will potentially be enabled to clone transgenics reliably and predictably as never before. The consequences of this shift in turn affect definitions both of genealogy and of property in the form of breedwealth (Franklin, 2001b).

The Roslin animals return us again to Williams' description of the earliest uses of the term 'culture' in English, to refer to the tending of nature, as in agriculture. In turn, as Marilyn Strathern has argued, nature comes to be understood as a separate domain, 'when the cultivation of nature was replaced by its own grounding naturalism, that is, by apprehension of nature as a natural system'. She continues:

> Given a concern with reproduction ('inheritance') of organisms, one might suggest that evolutionary thinking also facilitated the equation of procreation and biology. The 'natural facts' of life were natural in the sense of belonging to the biology of the species.
>
> (1992a: 119)

Today, the 'natural facts' of Dolly's existence, or coming into being, are 'natural' in the sense of belonging to embryology, genetics and reproductive biology – which deal with 'natural' processes such as reproduction. To speak, however, of cultivated nature in the case of Dolly is to become increasingly literal about a species of animal which began life in the pure culture of the petri dish.

Like 'heirloom-variety' seeds, the Roslin animals are assemblages of cultured nature. Yet it is not intact genealogy which is celebrated in the case of Dolly or Polly, but instead precisely the opposite: their recombinant impurity. Two poles of both stewardship and human health are sketched in such a contrast between the breed and the seed. At one extreme, the integrity of the germplasm is marketed and consumed as both a means and a symbolic expression of continuity with the past. At the other extreme of postmodern evolution, the milk of the transgenic dairy animal is heralded as the source of relief for human suffering, and the improvement of public health. While a genealogical rhetoric suffused in biblical imagery does service for an enterprised-up form of organic gardening, the enterprised-up genealogies of corporately owned and produced dairy ruminants secure a faith in scientific progress offering hope for human salvation. What is inevitably intriguing about the juxtaposition of these two primal scenes of recombinant genealogy is the number of places they intersect both compatibly and interchangeably. A testament to the accuracy of Raymond Williams' observations about the excessiveness of both nature and culture, and to Strathern's cogent exposition of their hybridity, what remains of interest are the pathways of the traffic though which both nature and culture continue to generate as idioms of what is innate and acquired, intimate and universal, personal and global, and in the future as well as the past.

● ●   **Figuring GlobalNatureCulture™**

As the last two pairs of icons have indicated, one way to think about contemporary forms of traffic in nature is in terms of the changing facts of life within global culture, that is, in relation to the many and varied forms of reproduction which have come to define turn-of-the-millennium life and its production, be it in the form of cloning, the patenting of immortalised cell lines, the development of artificial life and bioinformatics, or the corresponding set of changes in the industries of information, communication, animation and visual production. In the same way that the critical analysis of 'natural facts', the politics of biology and reproductive politics have long been central to the analysis of race, gender and sexuality, so we suggest an important dimension of understanding globalisation requires taking seriously its means of reproduction – cultural, 'natural', informatic and biotechnological.

In developing our concern with ideas of the natural in these first three chapters, we have often returned to the question of 'the facts of life' as a means of exploring global nature, global culture. More often than not, the semblance of vitality, or lifelikeness or animation which attaches to entities as diverse as planets and cells, fossils and pixels, seeds and breeds, turns on a relationship to reproduction – in its many and often overlapping senses. Hence, for instance, the example cited at the very beginning of Chapter 1 of the marketing of DNA perfume clearly turns on the importance of genetic material, in no small part because of the perceived importance of genes to the reproduction of life. And the success of Virtual Skin as a branded commodity is in part due to the reproducibility of its products across widely divergent international markets and audiences in the global cosmetics industry.

We mark the importance of *reproductive power* through an extension of Donna Haraway's argument concerning a 'shift from kind to brand'. In *Modest_ Witness@Second_Millennium*, Haraway develops her previous theorisation of gender as a device for producing kinds and types by introducing the anthropological concept of kinship to describe 'a technology for producing the material and semiotic effect of shared kind' (1997: 53). Kinship becomes a useful concept for Haraway to address 'the question of taxonomy, category and the natural status of artificial entities' (1997: 53), because 'establishing identities is kinship work in action' (1997: 67). Critical to Haraway's use of kinship in this way is her fascination with brands as a means of producing kinds through proprietary marking. In the same way that she describes brandnames as 'genders', so she suggests that for kinship also 'type has become brand', thus identifying the significance of the continuing movements between nature and culture for world-making.

Extending Haraway's argument about the shift from kind to brand, we suggest that at the same time that breeds have been partially denaturalised through biotechnology, *so brands have become renaturalisable in return* – for example, by being written into the animals' genome. This example of the germinal, innate or genetic brand effects a shift from branded literally to kindred. For both breeding and branding are seen to be reproductive, and genealogy now variously informs and is being redefined by branding power (the power to impose a mark of private ownership; to proliferate copies without recourse to an original; to create 'families' of products which both reproduce themselves through their confirmation of natural and non-natural family forms). One kind of lifelikeness, or animation, comes from reproduction in the biological or sexual sense. Another comes from the lifelikeness of informational and other systems in their capacity to become autogenerational, self-representational or autopoietic, with 'lives of their own'. We suggest, then, that breeding and branding strategies have become more interchangeable, as more means of reproduction, literally a wider selection of reproductive technologies, allow a switching back and forth.

A further way in which breeds and brands can be seen to exemplify contemporary understandings of nature and culture as distinct-but-isomorphic is in terms of their ability to revise understandings of context – of the relationship between figure and ground, matter and form, or of scale, horizon and perspective. As Marilyn Strathern points out, understandings of the global (both natural and cultural) conceal their dependence on relationality and on context (1995a). However, our analysis of the icons above led us to extend this argument too, by suggesting that specific understandings of both global nature and global culture now make use of a kind of *self-contextualisation*; indeed, this is precisely the basis of their claims to universalism, *as well as being what makes those claims distinctive*.

The breed operates in relation to a time made newly productive, that of the time of evolutionary crisis, a time of exposure in Virilio's sense, but, in this case, one which might otherwise lead to extinction of species. Evolution, the animating dynamic of modern understandings of natural history, is no longer the assumed context for the origin of species; indeed, it is now possible to suspend 'natural time', the time of genealogical descent, individual variation and species adaptation. In its place is a new time, the time of the laboratory, a time in which reproduction is reconstituted as production, in which there is no original and in which the breed is literally, biologically, its own context for (re)production. Such a transformation of 'the facts of life' brings into closer proximity the classically modern 'natural' identities of race, sex or nationality and their contemporary equivalents of race, sex or nationality as style, choice or commodity (see Chapter 5).

The global commercial brand also seeks to provide its own context through the ways in which the consumer's attention to products is anticipated through the production of standardised expectations. This occurs through the brand's occupation of the time of exposure as it is made visible by the new technologies of communication, the non-temporal rectangle of not only the computer screen, but also the television, the sponsored rectangles of sports courts, and the themed spaces of retail outlets such as Disney World. In these spaces, corporations can gain proprietary access to the time of exposure, making use of the brand to plan the creation, distribution and sale of products in relation to already anticipated expectations. This is a process in which the brand reproduces itself through a process of self-contextualisation, in which the legal power of the trademark to secure possession is tied to the pre-formed recognisability of the brand's products and the ability of its exploiters to protect the spaces and times in which it appears. The brand is thus an example of nature seconded, indicative of a process of denaturalisation, yet able to be renaturalised through its ability to provide it own context.

Notes

1   Haraway first draws attention to the ways in which various animals created by biotechnology occupy 'a new grammar' in her article 'When Man[TM] is on the Menu' (1992b). She develops this argument in more detail in relation to OncoMouse[TM] in *Modest_Witness@Second_Millennium* (1997).

2   This is the tradition of theorists such as Butler (1990), de Lauretis (1987), Haraway (1991) and Wittig (1992), outlined in the Introduction in terms of the use of gender as a 'technology' to produce and secure difference. It is paralleled in feminist anthropology by the work of many theorists of gender and kinship who have critiqued the 'grounding function' of 'the biological facts of sexual reproduction' which naturalises gender and genealogy as after the fact of biological sex (Collier and Yanagisako, 1987; MacCormack and Strathern, 1980; Ortner and Whitehead, 1981; Strathern, 1988; Yanagisako and Delaney, 1995a).

3   The original design for the Coca-Cola bottle was based on Marilyn Monroe's figure. The mid-1990s launch of Virgin Cola vaunted the fact that its bottle was based on Pamela Anderson's figure. The advertising trade journals made much of the 'joke' that the original version of the bottle was so 'top-heavy' as to fall over.

4   Such a relationship of the brand to the body of its founder is particularly relevant to the case of Anita Roddick, founder of the Body Shop, whose policy of not advertising their products has led to even greater identity between Body Shop products and the company founder (see Kaplan, 1995 and Chapter Four in this volume).

5   Ironically, the importance of policing the means of reproduction as a defence of property rights is itself signified by the use of the term 'clone' to describe an illegitimate product which is copied from a branded 'original' (such as Gucci luggage, or Donna Karan fashion). Similarly, the loss of brand identity is also described by this term, as in the use of 'PC clones' to describe the machines that became available in the wake of successful antitrust litigation against the computer giant IBM in the 1970s.

6   Schulman criticises what she describes as the glossy gay press or the 'gay management class' for misrepresenting gay people as consumers. She writes:

> There seems to be an unspoken strategy among certain sectors of the gay community based in the belief that corporations produce culture. Therefore, by positioning homosexuals as a consumer group to be niche-marketed to, corporations will be motivated to include gay images in advertising. This assures that, in the crassest American terms, we exist. And there is some truth to that line of thinking. But, the problem is that only the most palatable sector gets included, thereby obscuring the range of difference among gay people and how we really live.
>
> (1994: 3)

7   'Terminator' is not the denomination chosen by Monsanto for this technique, which the company sought to acquire in 1998, but instead the appellation coined and widely circulated by Canadian protest group RAFI (the Rural Advancement Foundation International), which vigorously opposes the use of this technology. For a full discussion of the Terminator technology, see Crouch (1998). In part due to the controversy surrounding various of its genetically engineered products, Monsanto's life sciences division was sold to Pharmacia-Upjohn in December 1999.

8   Interestingly evident in the debate about genetically modified foods in both Britain and the United States is the presence of the unmarked brand. In other words, yet another dimension of brand hygiene is the necessity for demonised brands, such as Monsanto's soy products, to be introduced by stealth. Deliberate mixing of GM and non-GM soy at source exists in tension with attempts by supermarket chains and product lines to reduce consumer anxiety by labelling foodstuffs which contain GM ingredients. Sometimes it turns out a brand needs a disguise to make its market, and, as in Monsanto's case, sometimes such strategies may be terminal for certain families of product.

9   In contrast, and direct competition in some cases, with their value as forms of corporate biowealth, the preservation of seeds used in the context of rural, subsistence agriculture is essential to the survival of many communities around the world, who fear their appropriation by industry. Seed banks thus serve quite divergent interests, marked by significant power imbalances (Shiva, 1989, 1991).

10   As Haraway notes:

> [A] seed contains inside its coat the history of practices such as collecting, breeding, marketing, taxonomizing, patenting, biochemically analyzing, advertising, eating, cultivating, harvesting, celebrating, starving. A seed produced in the biotechnological institutions now spread around the world contains the specifications of labor systems, planting calenders, pest control procedures, marketing, land-holding, and beliefs about hunger and well-being.
>
> (1997: 129)

11   For example, throughout much of the history of animal husbandry it was assumed only the male animal passed on traits, and that female animals changed the shape and colour of their offspring according to what they saw while pregnant.

Part Two / **Nature Seconded**

Chapter 4 / **The Global Within**
Consuming Nature, Embodying Health

Jackie Stacey

This chapter is specifically concerned with the embodiment of global cultures. How do we imagine the global within? What might be meant by the subjective embodiment of the global? I shall argue that 'the new universalisms of global culture' have particular subject effects and modes of embodiment that depend on seconding nature to secure their appeal, even as they simultaneously display its constructedness in so doing. I shall examine the place of global cultures in the West's bid to reinvent nature, even as it simultaneously declares its death, announces the assisted basis of its reproduction, and the cultural character of its commodification.[1] Indeed, I shall demonstrate not only that these apparent paradoxes are operating within the health practices of global culture, but that they lie at the heart of their appeal.

An increasing number of studies look at what have been called the cultural dimensions of globalisation,[2] and yet almost none of them examine the forms of embodiment, subjectivity, fantasy and desire invoked by such dimensions. One of the welcome exceptions to this[3] is Arjun Appadurai's argument that the intensification of

> electronic mediation and mass migration mark the world of the present not as technically new forces but as ones that seem to impel (and sometimes compel) the work of the imagination. Together they create specific irregularities because both viewers and images are in simultaneous circulation. Neither images or viewers fit into circuits or audiences that are easily bound within local, national or regional spaces.
>
> (1996: 4)

My own concern extends the remit of debates about imagined global communities and citizens (Anderson, 1983) and the work of the global imagination (Appadurai, 1996) to include an analysis of the modes of subjective embodiment they effect. I begin my discussion with the question of what the global means in consumer markets,[4] for contemporary consumer culture is one of the key sites in which we encounter the global on a day-to-day basis, and commodities get globalised in a number of very different ways.[5]

● ●   **Consuming the Global**

The range of products that now depend upon the marketability of 'the global' is ever more prevalent: food and wines, cosmetics, music, clothes, airlines and information technologies. A proliferation of companies now circulate the fantasy of global parti-cipation in their repertoire of marketing imagery, be it British Airways, IBM or the Body Shop.[6] More and more commodities invite us to take part in a global culture as we consume (see Myers, 1999a). But what exactly does the global signify in contem-porary consumer markets, and how might this relate to changing understandings of nature and culture?[7]

Apparently unifying a world otherwise growing in disparity and inequality, the global sign promises access and exchange across cultural difference and national boundaries.[8] One way in which certain brands achieve their global status is through the scale of their availability: McDonald's, Coca-Cola, Walt Disney, Nike or Levi's, for example, are seen as global insofar as their image is one of universal availability. Here the global appears as the marketplace which makes the world seem smaller. This version of the global is most closely associated with the continuing success of North American domination of world markets and of the intensification of the penetration of capitalist enterprises throughout the world. Not restricted entirely to North American companies, these global products nevertheless tend to be associated with the universal expansion of capitalist interests into markets beyond the United States. The impact of their global reach hits home when North American products reach pre-viously 'protected zones', especially communist, or post-communist, countries such as China, Hungary or Russia: Coca-Cola in Beijing, McDonald's in Budapest or the appearence of Gorbachev in a Pizza Hut advertisement.[9] Hence, 'McDonaldisation', 'Disneyfication' and even 'McDisneyisation' have become metonymic terms for the successful Americanisation of markets across the globe (see Ritzer, 1995 and Ritzer and Liska, 1997). This version of the global is one in which the increased reach of capitalist markets apparently brings us all closer together, uniting us through homogeneity and a familiarity with particular brands.

In the above cases, the global refers to brands which have achieved the reputation of universal availability. They need not necessarily deploy explicitly global imagery in their marketing strategies, for they rely upon a taken-for-granted global scale in the universal recognisability of their brands.[10] For many other companies a more explicit use of global imagery is incorporated into their marketing strategies (see Myers, 1999a: 61).[11] This second strategy involves the advertising of products through use of the globe icon, such as the front cover of the promotional booklet of the genetic engineering company Promega (see Figure 4.1).[12] In this example, the small blue globe is placed in front of the palm of the large human hand, and both are set against the background of four photographs of elemental, natural phenomena: windblown sand, ripples on water, a skeletal leaf and cracked, dried earth. Each of these four photographs (like the four corners of the Earth) depicts some aspect of change and transformation, suggesting both the wonder, but also the limits, of nature (and in turn, perhaps, the potential of science). The human hand (raised in the gesture appropriate to an oath or a blessing) is placed in between these images of natural processes and the blue globe; as the interface between the natural and the global, here the hand is positioned to offer reassuring protection to humanity. The hand and the blue globe are shot through by a white double helix sign that runs centrally from the top to the bottom of the image, connecting these universal icons with the company's logo. This double helix icon cuts through the heart of the Earth and the hand, like a vein sustaining this global tree of life. In the age of genetic engineering, when scientists are often accused of playing God by interfering with nature, this image shows 'man' rather than God cradling the Earth and offering hope for future genera-tions through science and technology not religion.[13] In other words, genetic engin-eering, widely perceived as an interference with nature, is thus renaturalised through its power to perform a global good. The icon of the globe holds together a vision of a natural world with the commodification of its scientific denaturalisation. Here nature guarantees a shared meaning to global life. The global gets within through a renaturalised nature which literally makes up our genetic systems of life, nutrition and consumption.

A third strategy for globalising products and companies is the use of global imagery without the actual presence of the globe itself. From Coca-Cola onwards, companies have deployed an iconography of diversity to signify a global scale of operations. For example, advertised as 'the world's favourite airline', British Airways was rebranded as a global service in 1997 when it deployed 'ethnic' imagery to rebrand itself within a world market ('a painter from the Kalahari Desert, a Polish folk artist and a hand weaver from the Scottish Highlands', reported the *Sunday Mirror*, 15 June 1997). Its £60 million pound image change was reported as: '[using] designs created by dozens of artists and craftspeople from around the world for the tails of its fleet of 300 aircraft, as well as passenger printed material such as ticket wallets and luggage tags' (*The Independent*, 15 June 1997).[14] The new designs were brightly coloured, bold abstract patterns and the artists' authenticity was guaranteed through the appearance of their signature on each aircraft (*The Independent*, 15 June 1997) (see Figure 4.2).[15]

In its bid to give customers a sense of belonging to a global community as they travel, British Airways has used icons of local diversity to construct a sense of universal belonging in its food packaging. The British Airways 'Time for a Snack' cardboard lunch-box-style package offers passengers light snacks in boxes decorated with a range of 'world images', including paper cut-outs from Central Poland, and

Figure 4.1

In this cover to the promotional catalogue for the genetic engineering company Promega, the hand is the interface between the natural and the global, offering a reassuring sign of the humanity of scientific intervention.

Figure 4.2

The bold, abstract patterns of global creativity replace the traditional Union Jack logo previously displayed on British Airways planes (photograph by Sarah Franklin).

abstract art from New York City. These decorative forms are accompanied by the personal details of the artisans and artists described on the side of the box. Inside the snack-box, sepia-style close-up photographs of a diverse range of people are located in time and space by the text explaining why it is 'Time for a Snack' (Figures 4.3 and 4.4): '3.30 p.m., Washington, United States of America. An elderly farmer takes a well earned break from tending his crops, before heading home at sunset'; '10.00 a.m., Britanny, France. English schoolgirl Emily, snacks on an apple while on a camping holiday with her family' (text also given in French). The farmer stands earnestly in front of his field of grain, the schoolgirl grins through her windswept hair on her campsite; both subjects are situated in the outdoors, both are connected to natural-grown food products shown in the photograph. Thus, the in-flight traveller removed from national time and space is invited to share a snack with imagined fellow-citizens, made familiar in these supposedly universally recognisable types (the old farmer, the young schoolgirl), temporally and spatially located in their local worlds.[16] Simple foods, straightforward people, natural surroundings: these are the players in this version of universal humanity – a panhumanity that transcends time and space and yet can be relocated in the moment of consumption within these global cultures. This third mode of globalising products thus works through an appeal to a transcendent panhumanity, expressed through local diversities which are recontextualised in this global branding exercise. The global gets inside us here through literal consumption and connects passengers to the new transcendent universalism of global culture.[17]

The final way in which products achieve global status is the one to which I shall primarily be referring in the rest of this chapter. It builds upon the previous mode insofar as it relies utterly on notions of the 'other' located in cultures elsewhere, and yet departs from it in important ways.[18] Here the global is reproduced through a process of reverse synecdoche; dropping the 'third' from 'third world', 'world'

Time for a snack

3.30 p.m.

Washington,
United States of America.

An elderly farmer takes a well earned break from tending his crops, before heading home at sunset.

Figures 4.3 and 4.4

The photographs on the inside covers of these British Airways lunch-box style packs invite the in-flight traveller to share a snack with imagined fellow-citizens across the globe.

Time for a snack

10.00 a.m.

Brittany,
France.

English schoolgirl Emily, snacks on an apple while on a camping holiday with her family.

La petite anglaise Emily croque dans une pomme pendant ses vacances en camping avec sa famille.

Figure 4.5

Costa Cookies bring exotic ingredients from Indonesia, Latin America and Africa into proximity with the western subject through consumption (reprinted with permission from Costa Ltd).

products place their claim on the global by drawing on non-western practices and ingredients that are commodified for the western consumer. Thus, for example, 'world music' or 'world food' typically refer to music and food from non-European and non-North American countries of origin (Africa or Asia, South Africa and South America). The global in these cases is typically effected not only through an association with the 'third world', but often through a particular hybrid combination of different cultural practices which are then recontextualised as global within western cultures. Notably, this version of the global product works especially effectively in respect of commodities associated with the body, with its adornment, its maintenance, its sustenance and its pleasures (and, as we shall see later, its health and well-being).

For example, a range of biscuits produced by Costa Coffee deploys global imagery to such effect (see Figure 4.5). The biscuits offered in the global range are: Indonesian Island Cookies, Los Americo Latinos Cookies and Kaffa Africa Cookies. Each tubular tin is decorated with icons that gesture towards the appropriate third world connections (the batik design including names of islands; the guitar, the cactus and the coffee pot; the jazzy bordered paintings of salamanders and coffee beans). The text on the tube describes the combination of ingredients from around the world: 'An exotic biscuit of macadamia nuts . . . with a hint of papaya'; 'a scrumptious biscuit . . . with a mixture of wild Brazil nuts and cashew nuts from Latin America'; 'finest arabica coffee . . . [with] a dash of smooth coffee liqueur'. The authentic regional ingredients are combined with abstracted icons of 'third worldness' to produce the sense of participation in the pleasures of 'exotic' other cultures through consumption.

The global works here to bring the strange or unfamiliar into the proximity of the western subject through consumption. Thus, the global gets inside us as we literally ingest 'otherness' in consuming these exotic products. As Sara Ahmed argues in her book *Strange Encounters*, in consumer culture, 'the commodity object, which is at once an image and a material thing, enables subjects to have a close encounter with a distant other (the one already recognised as a "stranger")' (2000: 114). For Ahmed, such patterns of consumption tie a form of 'stranger fetishism' into commodity fetishism: '[t]he stranger is precisely that which is *produced, marketed and sold in order to define the value of the commodity object* . . . through the commodity, the stranger becomes a fetish' (2000, 116). Through consuming these global products, western subjects take the other into themselves and thus, Ahmed suggests, consumption is a technique which confirms the 'subject's ability to "be oneself" by getting closer to, and incorporating the stranger (a form of proximity which produces the stranger as *that which can be taken in*)' (2000: 133).

The taking in of exotic others (by consuming them) has been extended by analogy to the ways in which white culture in general commodifies Black otherness. As bell hooks famously argued in her chapter 'Eating the Other', consumer culture exoticises difference as style: '[W]ithin commodity culture, ethnicity becomes spice, seasoning that can liven up a dull dish that is mainstream white culture' (1992: 21, quoted in Ahmed, 2000: 117). Such a reduction of difference to style, as Ahmed points out, 'can be linked to a shift from biological to cultural racism' (Balibar, 1991, quoted in Ahmed, 2000: 117). Indeed, as Celia Lury argues in this volume, the reduction of racial difference to a playful series of colourful variations is part of the growing cultural essentialisms of consumer society. The increasingly prevalent fantasy of getting closer to exotic others through consumption gestures towards a flexible and transformable western subject; and yet, as Ahmed argues, 'the flow of cultural images and objects . . . may serve to reproduce *as well as* threaten the imaginary boundaries between social or racial groups' (2000: 116). By consuming global products, the western subject and the exotic other are thus reaffirmed even as such a dichotomy is apparently transcended by the appeal to a universal global culture.

The incorporation of exotic otherness through the consumption of global products is nowhere more evident than in cosmetics and toiletries primarily aimed at female consumers. Here the other is not ingested in global food products but rather becomes part of the western body through touch: the object 'comes to stand for globality, *but a globality which touches the skin of the body-at-home through consumption*'

(Ahmed, 2000: 115, emphasis in original).[19] In the Boots 'Global Collection' of shampoos, soaps, bath foams, body sprays, lipbalms and perfumes, an intimate encounter with an 'eastern' culture is promised through physical proximity of western body to exotic ingredients.[20]

> Even if you don't have a magic carpet to transport you to the exotic east, you can enjoy a Turkish bath of your very own with this rich, luxurious cream bath. Enhanced with rose extract to soothe and silk protein to help moisturise, Turkish bath will leave your skin feeling soft and smooth. Massage not included.

> The people of Oshima are famed for having luxurious hair. Oshima, Japan, is the traditional source of natural camellia extract, renowned for its softening and cleansing benefits. The wonders of their world are now yours to enjoy.
> (Boots Global Collection, quoted in Ahmed, 2000: 114)

The Body Shop (whose title alone clearly has universal aspirations – *the* Body Shop for *the* body) is perhaps the most striking example of incorporation of the global in this field.[21] As Caren Kaplan argues, the Body Shop's publicity offers 'a generalised metropolitan or cosmopolitan site of consumption where "women" can "travel" in a world "without boundaries" through the practices of consumer culture' (1995: 52). For Kaplan, this version of globalisation through commodity culture requires an analysis of the complexities of the transnational: 'that is, the representation of the "world" in these forms of advertising signals a desire for a dissolution of boundaries to facilitate personal freedom and ease of trade, even as it articulates national and cultural characteristics as distinct, innate markers of difference' (1995: 49). In the vast number of publications that accompany and account for the Body Shop's products, the global is always the foundational discourse. We read, for example, that an essential shared femininity (established through women's natural inclinations towards mother-hood and narcissism) unites women everywhere in their need for these global products:

> One of the wonderful things about women . . . is that we are bonded by shared experiences – by babies and the rituals and problems of our bodies . . . a sense of camaraderie and mutual interest already exists between us. All women are interested in looking after their skin, for example, and that is why a woman can go up to another and ask, 'How come your skin's so soft?'
> (Roddick, 1991: 70)

Here the skin becomes the global sign for authentic female knowledge about the body: a panfemininity is invoked, apparently dissolving differences through consumption (see Figure 4.6).[22] Skin here is the outer covering of the body that unites women in the intimacy of touch. In contrast to the notion of skin as a marker of individuality (the boundary of the body), skin is the marker of global unity, or, indeed, of difference, a unity achieved through the use of natural ingredients that enable women worldwide

MAP OF THE FACE

WHAT SKIN TYPE ARE YOU?

DRY SKIN: Normally fair and sensitive, finely textured and often lined with a low level of sebum production. Can be attractive and delicately textured during youth but may develop wrinkles and lines at an early age if not kept supple. Increased by wind, extremes of temperature and air conditioning.

NORMAL SKIN: Clear, with a fine-grained texture, soft, supple with a smooth velvety feel. No areas of excess oiliness or dryness. Can become drier with age.

OILY SKIN: Sallow, looks shiny, greasy to touch, has a coarsely-grained texture with the pores often visible. Subject to infection because excess sebum clogs pores (blackheads and spots are common). Tends to develop wrinkles less readily than other types.

COMBINATION SKIN: Common skin type - oily central panel (forehead, nose and chin) with dry cheeks. Oily skins often become combination with age. To keep oiliness and dryness under control, the skin needs to be cared for as two distinct types - oily and dry.

T-ZONE The oiliest section - the central panel from the forehead down to the chin, where the sebaceous glands are concentrated. Combination skin means an oily T-zone and dry cheeks. Adapt your skin-care routine to cope with this.

WRINKLES Young skin is like a firm new mattress, plumped up with moisture and kept springy by collagen and elastin. As time passes, these substances lose their strength and skin surface becomes worn and irregular like an old mattress.

EYELASHES Your eyelashes protect eyes from dust particles and act as a frame for your eyes. Regular applications of castor oil will slowly improve lash condition. Curl clean lashes, before applying mascara.

EYEBROWS Keep eyebrows well defined and shapely to balance your face and give it character. Keep them neat by regular plucking. First cleanse, then brush brows up with an eyebrow brush or a toothbrush. Use clean tweezers and start from inner corner, following the shape of the brow and plucking from underneath only in the direction of hair growth. Taper the curve gradually, following the line of the brow to the other corner of the eye. Brush back into shape.

UNDER EYES The skin around the eyes is the thinnest and most delicate on the body - it has no sebaceous glands and is quick to show signs of stress and age. Gently cleanse the area, keep it properly moisturised and don't drag or pull the skin around the eyes - ever.

LIPS Lips need lots of protection - they are thin-skinned (the stratum corneum allows the capillaries in the dermis to show, creating their red colour) and have no melanin (protective tanning pigment). Protect them with a lip balm or lipstick during the day.

SKIN AGEING Up to 90 per cent of the changes in our skin that we think of as getting older - wrinkling, dryness, blotching etc - are in fact sun damage. It can be avoided.

Figure 4.6

In this 'map of the face' from The Body Shop Book, *knowledge about skin is offered to a universal female consumer, dissolving differences in the name of 'panfemininity'.*

to benefit from each other's (ancient) knowledge. Thus, as the skin unites as it divides, so too the globe sustains universality through difference, as illustrated by the following text from Anita Roddick's introduction to the *The Body Shop Book*:

> The skin of Tahitian women looked pretty good for all their regular cocoa butter massages. And fresh pineapple seemed to get skin clean and clear in Sri Lanka. Why not use the successful traditions of other people to develop new products back home in England? I found something very reassuring about ingredients that had been used safely by human beings for hundreds, even thousands of years.
>
> (1994: 9)

The global gestures here work in conjunction with notions of longevity and wisdom. It is the duration of the beliefs and practices of these 'third world' women that secures their place as valuable commodities in the global market (see Figure 4.7). Thus, as Ahmed (2000) argues, this bodily intimacy with strangers facilitates access to knowledge for the female consumer; such processes of commodification 'work to re-produce knowledge of "strangers", or, more accurately, to produce the figure of the stranger through the accumulation of knowledge'. Ancient practices thus tie 'woman' and 'nature' firmly together in these decontextualised feminine rituals of skin- and hair-care (see Figure 4.8 for the image accompanying this text).

> The Himba women of Namibia lengthen their hair with twists of sheep's wool, then set it in place with a mixture of mud, fat and ochre.
>
> (Body Shop Team, 1994: 80)

> For centuries the American Indians have used jojoba oil to care for their skin and hair. Its superb conditioning qualities leave hair soft and silky.
>
> (Body Shop Team, 1994: 87)

> Tahitian women traditionally washed their black hair daily with sandalwood-scented coconut oil to leave it soft and glossy.
>
> (Body Shop, Team 1994: 90)

Here global nature becomes global culture through western consumption of ancient 'third world' feminine body rituals. The consumption of western products containing ingredients from the ancient traditions of the 'third world' returns the western woman to a nature lost to her through modernity (see Figures 4.9 and 4.10).[23] Whilst apparently dissolving difference and identities, these global hybridities reconstitute them. For Kaplan, such a discourse establishes a 'complete dichotomy between developed and underdeveloped, between First and Third World, such that any complex distinctions and differentiations within those categories are conveniently suppressed. We're left in a vaguely postcolonial zone of vanishing natives who require managed altruism from a concerned source of capital develoment' (1995: 58). As Ahmed argues, '[T]he commodity is sold through the fixing of difference in a discourse of origins' (2000: 116); and yet, simultaneously, the global subject of a panfemininity promises to unite

Figure 4.7

The Body Shop Book's 'recipe for longevity' gives western readers hints about lifestyles from the 'longest-lived peoples in the world', from Southern Russia, the Ecuadorean Andes and Kashmir.

Figure 4.8

This close-up photograph accompanies accounts of ancient feminine body rituals in the third world which are the inspiration for western hair and beauty products detailed in The Body Shop Book.

women everywhere through their intimate sharing of the ancient wisdoms of bodily knowledge.

From the ubiquitous American cultural imperialism of the Coca-Cola bottle to the endless variations of exotic third world raw materials, like ochre, jojoba and coconut oil, the multiple and contradictory meanings of the global demonstrate the extent to which global culture is as much *an effect as a condition*: it is something which must be achieved and cannot be assumed to pre-exist. This is not to argue that it is illusory – far from it, global culture undoubtedly has a very tangible materiality; rather, it is to suggest that the meaning of globalisation does not have a singular meaning, indeed definitions of global products may pull in quite opposite directions. The constitution of global consumer culture operates through a series of paradoxes which might be crudely summed up as follows: the global *condenses* through *expansion*, *unites* through *diversity*, and *authenticates* through *hybridity*.[24]

● ● ● **The Nature Quest**

This investigation of the operations of the global within consumer culture shows that the dependence upon the sign 'nature' could not be more apparent: whether through the 'exotic' connections to third world practices or ingredients, or through the appeal to the universal human subject, the global is achieved through its connection to *the natural* in all these examples. Within global cultures, nature connects consumers, unites citizens and authenticates ingredients. It promises the reassurance of nostalgic certainties in the face of the dizzying and disorientating effects of global change. And yet its commodification is ever present, and highly visible, without detracting from its power to authorise continuity and preservation. The commodification of nature as a sign of global culture is thus a contemporary paradox that is able to draw attention to itself with the greatest of ease. Far from being the irreconcilable contradiction upon which its foundational power founders, seconded nature becomes precisely the opposite, ensuring its continuing power.

TEA TREE

The tea tree (Melaleuca) is found in parts of South East Asia, Australia and New Zealand. It is a tough little shrub that flourishes where other plants can't grow.

Australia's Aborigines have used tea tree oil for over 40,000 years.

When Captain Cook reached Australia on his exploration of the Pacific in 1768-79, his botanist Joseph Banks found the Aborigines using the leaves of the Melaleuca to make tea. That's how the plant got its English name.

In Australia, tea tree oil has a wide range of germicidal and fungicidal applications. It is used to treat burns, sunburns, pimples, boils, stings, toothache, gum infections, cuts, sore throats and athlete's foot.

There are over 180 species of tea tree but only the oil steam-distilled from the leaves of one particular species (Melaleuca alternifolia) is used commercially. It occurs naturally only in Northern New South Wales.

The Australian government was so impressed by the healing effects of tea tree oil that they made it standard issue to troops during World War Two to combat a number of skin complaints.

Tea tree oil has been called a first aid kit in a bottle.

Though tea tree oil is not a good moisturiser, its valuable properties as a deep cleanser and antiseptic make it especially good for oily or problem skins and irritated scalps.

Figure 4.9

The multiple qualities of the healing and medicinal properties of the tea tree grown in South East Asia, Australia and New Zealand are detailed in The Body Shop Book, *which states, 'Australia's Aborigines have used tea tree oil for over 40,000 years'.*

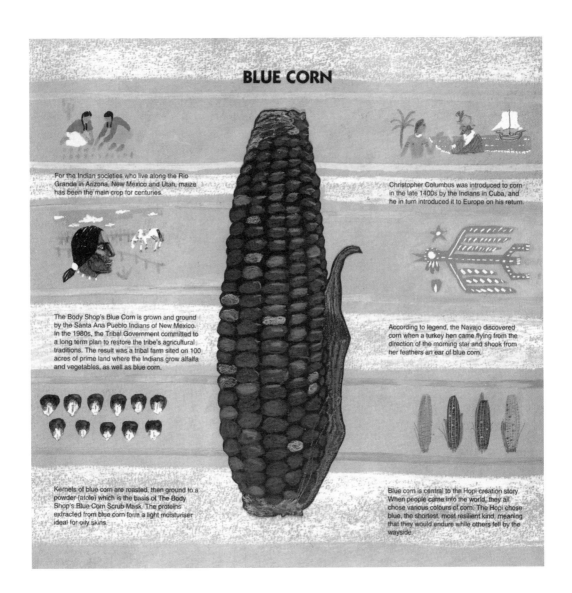

BLUE CORN

For the Indian societies who live along the Rio Grande in Arizona, New Mexico and Utah, maize has been the main crop for centuries.

The Body Shop's Blue Corn is grown and ground by the Santa Ana Pueblo Indians of New Mexico. In the 1980s, the Tribal Government committed to a long term plan to restore the tribe's agricultural traditions. The result was a tribal farm sited on 100 acres of prime land where the Indians grow alfalfa and vegetables, as well as blue corn.

Kernels of blue corn are roasted, then ground to a powder (atole) which is the basis of The Body Shop's Blue Corn Scrub Mask. The proteins extracted from blue corn form a light moisturiser ideal for oily skins.

Christopher Columbus was introduced to corn in the late 1400s by the Indians in Cuba, and he in turn introduced it to Europe on his return.

According to legend, the Navajo discovered corn when a turkey hen came flying from the direction of the morning star and shook from her feathers an ear of blue corn.

Blue corn is central to the Hopi creation story. When people came into the world, they all chose various colours of corn. The Hopi chose blue, the shortest, most resilient kind, meaning that they would endure while others fell by the wayside.

Figure 4.10

The symbolic and economic significance of corn is detailed here through the connections between the ancient agricultural traditions of 'Indian' societies and the Body Shop's blue corn products.

In his critical account of the 'Nature Company',[25] Neil Smith analyses the ways in which it thrives on successfully commodifying nature:

> The paradoxical hallmark of The Nature Company's vision is the simultaneous idolization and commodification of nature combined with an aggressive exaltation and effacement of any distinction between real and made natures. . . . *Virtual Nature* – the video – takes to the limits this genre of nature as psychic soporific. With appropriate New Age instrumental accompaniment, cascading waterfalls in verdant forests and soaring vistas of crystal white snowfields wash over the pacified viewer.
>
> (1996: 37)

For Smith, this contradiction between commodification and naturalness represents a glaring paradox of postmodern culture; however, considered within the context of global culture, such a paradox is less puzzling, indeed it increasingly appears as one of its obligatory characteristics. For if we consider the global as the recontextualisation of third world natures, such a move is integral to the successful commodification of nature in contemporary western culture. The technologisation of nature here is thus made compatible with mass reproduction and distribution of commodities through its recontextualisation in global consumption. As Smith himself highlights:

> Nature at The Nature Company includes natural objects, simulated nature, and representations of nature, either free-standing or emblazoned on everyday consumer objects. They sell fossils, gem stones and agates, all labelled with their precise countries of origin and global distribution – Brazil, Australia, South Africa. Their tree seed and plant kits beg you to grow your own nature on the window sill, while the precise Latin species labels and descriptions of ideal habitats and ecological requirements somehow guarantee a mainline to the ordered harmony of nature: everything has its place in nature, and The Nature Company is devoted to seeking out and celebrating the world's forgotten natural origins.
>
> (1996: 36)

In the case of the Nature Company, the global provides the means for the endless potentiality of recovering the lost origins of the natural; what the West has lost can be rediscovered elsewhere. And yet, obviously, such mass distribution of a global nature simultaneously decontextualises temporality and spatiality and threatens to render meaningless such claims to originality; for how can a nature from elsewhere, extracted from its context and commodified for western consumption, serve to reassure us of the authenticity of the natural? The answer to this question lies in the ways in which the global becomes the context for the natural and resolves the apparent contra-dictions between real and manufactured nature. 'Virtual Nature', far from being the contradiction in terms it might at first appear to be, thus becomes a logical paradox if and when it is recontextualised through the power of global cultures. It is this trafficking between nature and culture that is such a crucial, yet undertheorised, dimension to contemporary patterns of the global. The reinvention of nature could be said to lie at the heart of the appeal of the global in contemporary culture. Indeed, nature is one of the key ways the global gets inside us.

The quest to find nature has become inextricable from the currently popular search to 'find oneself'. In the thousands of books which invite readers to find themselves through journeys into global natures and global cultures, we find again what Ahmed refers to as the desire to 'be oneself' by getting closer to, and incorporating the stranger (2000).[26] For at least the last ten years, publishers' catalogues have been full of books which offer readers ways to reinvent themselves through an engagement with global nature. Through both literal and metaphorical journeys across the globe, (usually) western narrators tell stories of moving towards a more fulfilled lifestyle and of finding a more meaningful belief system in third world, indigenous or ancient cultures. For an audience to whom western modernity appears to have robbed us of our own authentic nature, these three routes (through third world, indigenous or ancient cultures) appear to be the only possible ways for us to retrieve it.

Marie Herbert's *Healing Quest: a journey of transformation* (1996), for example, offers 'vivid portraits of the shamans, master storytellers and medicine people' she met on her extraordinary inner and outer journeys in Native American cultures (back cover). This book typifies a more general trend towards the reclamation of non-western practices as the inspirational basis for a more natural way of life in the West, exemplified by books such as *The Ancient Wisdom of Egypt* (Hope, 1998), *The Tibetan Book of the Dead* (Thurman, 1998), *The Monk and the Philosopher: East meets West in a father–son dialogue* (Revel and Richard, 1998) or *In Search of the Divine Mother* (Goodman, 1998). A brief survey of the books in Thorsons catalogues between 1994 and 1998 (owned by HarperCollins, this is one of the leading 'Mind, Body, Spirit' book publishers in the UK) indicates the pervasiveness of the appeal of the global nature in contemporary cultures of self-management. These catalogues are full of books which narrate self-transformation by moving outside western models in order to discover a different and secure meaning to life.

Significantly, the fourth best-selling book for the whole of HarperCollins publishing house in 1998 was entitled *The Mystery of the Crystal Skulls*, a book about two independent television producers who visited thirteen sacred skulls that are to be found in different places across the globe.[27]

> The crystal skulls are a mystery as profound as the pyramids of Egypt, the Nazca Lines of Peru, or Stonehenge. Many indigenous people speak of their remarkable magical and healing properties, but nobody really knows where they came from.
> . . . Searching for the answers takes the authors on a fantastic odyssey . . . on a journey of discovery that takes them from the British Museum in London to the deserts of the United States, from the science labs of Hewlett Packard to the tropical jungles of Central America.
>
> (Morton and Thomas, 1998: back cover)

A 'global grail' was followed in order to pay homage at these locations, and, to enable others to witness the venture, a film was made about the pilgrimages. The success of *The Mystery of the Crystal Skulls* book is especially remarkable, bearing in mind that HarperCollins also publishes the best-selling novels of authors such as Jeffrey Archer and Barbara Taylor Bradford. The success of *The Mystery of the Crystal Skulls* is indicative of the current popularity of books which enable readers to participate in an imagined global culture. Numerous books of this genre offer a transcendent fantasy which reaches beyond national and indeed physical boundaries towards a new universal global subject informed by wisdom and knowledge.

The call upon nature to provide knowledge and wisdom, transformation and healing, and guidance and direction permeates not only the accounts of healing that turn away from the West for inspiration, but also those which look to 'civilisations' of the past. Alongside the 'global grail' books in Thorsons catalogues are numerous example of books about the natures of ancient cultures. These books are significant to a discussion of global culture not only because their move back in time matches the similar moves across space described above, but also because they index responses to the emptying out of contemporary western societies of meaningful, secure or resilient models of nature.

Books such as *The Modern Antiquarian: a field guide to over 300 prehistoric sites around Britain* (1998) by Julian Cope (of post-punk band The Teardrop Explodes fame), or *The Druid Renaissance* (1998) by Philip Carr-Gomm, for example, introduce today's readers to the lost traditions of western civilisation that have been obliterated by modernity. The former is advertised as taking us on 'an imaginative leap back to the dawn of civilisation, when our ancestors worshipped the Earth as Mother and erected great stones in her honour, and hills and rivers were seen as aspects of divinity' (Thorsons catalogue, December 1998: 14); the latter offers a 'celebration of the flowering of a tradition that is ancient yet ever-new', and claims that 'the Druid tradition lies at the heart of Western spirituality and today is experiencing a renaissance unprecedented in its long history. The Druids, like the Native Americans and Aborigines, revere and respect Earth. They see Nature as their teacher and mother' (Thorsons catalogue, January 1998: 19). The appeal of ancient cultures such as the Druids, it is claimed, lies in their reverence for nature: the worship of 'the Earth as Mother' and the regard for the hills and rivers 'as aspects of divinity'; or the 'reverence and respect for Earth' and nature as 'teacher and mother'. The inherent link here between the natural and the spiritual is implicitly contrasted with contemporary ways of life which have lost sight of the value of both. Connections to indigenous 'other' cultures that share the claim of ancientness (Native Americans and Aborigines) authenticate the return to nature as part of a broader project of 'retraditionalisation' (Heelas et al., 1996).

History appears here as the sign for nature. Emptied out of its foundational claims, nature in contemporary western culture struggles to signify through its traditional modes. But it all too often fails to reassure, to guarantee, to inspire or to transform at a time when its polluted contents and overdeveloped landscapes have become pervasive images. Assisted by the power of history here, however, its reinvention becomes possible. Just as our contemporary fascination with fossils is indicative of a particular postmodern investment in 'natural history', as we discussed in Chapter 2, so too is this worship of 'the ancient' indicative of a cultural nostalgia for something never experienced, driven perhaps by the same sense of loss, or remorse, about a broken connection to past ancestors and to divine natures (see Baudrillard, 1994b).

As Taussig (1993) has argued, 'the traditional', 'the primitive' and, indeed, 'the prehistoric' have been necessary counterpoints to the invention of the modern. The ancient is figured in these accounts as the new time of hope and salvation in a move to escape the ills of modernity. Druidism, like Native American and Aboriginal beliefs and practices, can be rediscovered by any reader willing to make the imaginative leap across temporal and cultural zones. Contemporary western readers and consumers can 'go native' and become 'a bit like the other' as a means of getting closer to nature, of finding a community and of achieving self-knowledge (see Ahmed, 2000). Time and space are re-imagined as holding vessels for essences that endure by virtue of their authenticity. New genealogies, new origins and new descent paths are mapped out here as the ancestral lineages connect contemporary readers to ancient knowledges. Indeed the transcendence of temporal and spatial boundaries becomes synonymous with a spiritual transcendence offered by such reclamation of ancient Natures. Thus, the apparent contradiction in terms of a 'decontextualised nature' is held up to confirm its power as a magical sign: nature is reinvented as history in a different place at a different time, thoroughly out of context, *and yet the very mutability that facilitates such a cultural change demonstrates its universality*.

In the above examples it is less a case of '*getting* the global within' as it is of '*finding* the global within' through a reconnection to a lost natural order to which we all inherently belong. According to these accounts, global culture already exists in the intimacies of the body, of memory and of the soul. Here an 'intimate global' supposedly waits to be found in the more natural ways of other cultures. The discovery of this lost nature, either in the elsewhere of other cultures, or in the pastness of traditional western cultures, reunites us with all living beings in a universal pan-humanity of global proportions.

Global Self-Health

In this section of the chapter, I consider such cultural shifts in relation to self-health books more specifically. By looking at the new market in self-health manuals (the 'how to' books on health and well-being) and the practices that accompany them, I examine the ways in which health is increasingly commodified in contemporary culture, and how such commodification produces fantasies of embodying the global through health practices.[28]

Self-health books are a hybrid genre of widely available accounts of ways of benefiting from better (more natural) ways of seeing, of feeling, of healing and of living (see Stacey, 1997). These self-health narratives crosscut a broader genre of books about the self (emotional, spiritual, physical) which are preoccupied with self-development, self-knowledge, self-control, self-improvement and self-healing. Along-side a host of more practical 'alternative lifestyle guides' on topics such as *How to Read Your Star Signs* (Fenton, 1998), *Herbal Defence to Illness* (Landis and Khalsa, 1998), *Coach Yourself to Success: how to overcome hurdles and free yourself from mind traps* (Rusk and Rusk, 1998), *Manifest Your Destiny: the 9 spiritual principles for getting everything you want* (Dyer, 1998) and *The 10 Minute Miracle: the quick fix survival guide for mind and body* (Rawson and Callinan, 1998), which are aimed at the more impatient and instrumental market, there are some examples of the 'transformative journey' genre in the Thorsons 'New Books List' for 1998 which remain within a western schema. Leslie Kenton's *Journey Into Freedom* by the ex-editor for *Harper's and Queen* (described as a 'one-woman Wall Street of well being'), for instance, is advertised as bringing 'to light natural methods of enhancing health and good looks that enable people to gain more control over their lives, and achieve a high degree of autonomy and better use of their personal creativity' (Thorsons catalogue, 1998: 16). Such role-model authors offer readers a new way of living and a new way of seeing, and yet do so within the recognisable metaphors of western individualism (control, autonomy and personal output).

Self-health books of all kinds can now be found in high-street bookstores, in health food shops and alternative health centres, and in their more popular forms in airports, stations, and so on. One marker of the significance of the expansion of this new market within publishing is the introduction of a new category of 'healing, self-improvement/awareness' books into the Book Marketing Limited 1995–6 survey of book sales in the United Kingdom.[29] This category was introduced into the 1995–6 survey to begin to track the success of this emergent market. The overall percentage of incidence of purchase appears at first glance to be relatively insubstantial, and yet as part of a broader changing cultural trend, such percentages are significant. As the statistics demonstrate, purchase varies according to geographical location, educational training and according to class and gender, being rather predictably more common amongst women and amongst higher income bracket middle-class consumers (see Tables 4.1 and 4.2).

More recent figures suggest that there has been an increase in book sales in this area even since the initial survey: sales of books under the category of 'Mind, Body, Spirit' (of which self-health forms a part) have increased from 2.5 million in 1997 to 2.6 million in 1998.[30] Another indicator of the increasing popularity of this type of material is the rise in the total UK sales of the books discussed in this chapter: between December 1996 and December 1997 total sales were 17,894, and between December 1998 and July 1999 total sales were 39,618.[31] The growth in the market for these books is especially significant when read alongside the general proliferation of activities and practices of self-health. This expanding market in publishing is indicative of a much more general intensification of interest in self-transformation and self-healing among readerships in western countries such as Britain.[32]

Table 4.1

	All adults	Profile of buyers of healing and self-improvement/awareness
Total	100%	100%
Gender		
M	48%	33%
F	52%	67%
Age		
15–24	15%	9%
25–34	22%	23%
35–44	16%	24%
45–54	15%	21%
55–64	13%	14%
65+	20%	7%
Social grade		
AB	18%	34%
C1	25%	31%
C2	27%	18%
DE	30%	16%
Terminal education age		
16 or under	63%	42%
17–18	16%	24%
19+	15%	30%
Still studying	7%	4%
Presence of children		
Any under 15	35%	37%
Any under 11	27%	27%
Any 11–14	15%	21%
None under 15	64%	61%
Region		
North	35%	21%
Midlands	27%	30%
South	38%	50%

Source: Books and the Consumer 1995–96, Book Marketing Limited

Table 4.2

**Incidence of purchase of healing
and self-improvement/awareness**

Total	4%

Sex

M	3%
F	5%

Age

15–24	2%
25–34	4%
35–44	6%
45–54	6%
55–64	4%
65+	1%

Social grade

AB	7%
C1	5%
C2	3%
DE	2%

Terminal education age

16 or under	3%
17–18	6%
19+	8%
Still studying	2%

Presence of children

Any under 15	4%
Any under 11	4%
Any 11–14	5%
None under 15	4%

Region

North	2%
Midlands	4%
South	5%

Source: Books and the Consumer 1995–96,
Book Marketing Limited

As these figures demonstrate, in many ways self-health books do not form a discrete generic category. To the extent that these books are concerned with self-development, they overlap with popular psychology 'self-help' books, such as those I mentioned above; to the extent that they combine mind/body/spirit philosophies and advocate a change in 'lifestyle', they overlap with New Age publications (see Heelas, 1996); and to the extent that they advocate self-healing, they also overlap with many books on alternative and complementary medicine (see Sharma, 1992). The expansion of many alternative health practices (such as acupuncture, or shiatsu massage) into western countries obviously informs the marketability of these ideas, since these contribute to the familiarity and credibility of non-western medical models. According to one study, as early as the mid-1980s (1984–7), 34 per cent of the population in Britain had tried at least one form of alternative therapy (Coward, 1989: 3). However, whilst some arguments presented here are pertinent in different ways to each of these intersecting areas, my discussion of these global self-health books should not be assumed to apply to all these other domains, whose specificity would need a con-textualised and thorough analysis of their own.

Here I examine the version of the global offered to readers in the form of self-health books in which they are invited to mix and match beliefs from non-western cultures, and to put together the particular combination that suits their individual project of self-transformation (see Giddens, 1991). In many self-health books, readers are offered hope for a healthier future through a borrowing of beliefs and practices about disease and healing from non-western cultures. These cultures appeal because of their more natural approaches and their appropriate reverence for nature. Having lost faith in nature in the West, these non-western cultures are mobilised to re-authenticate the subject and to invigorate the body, or, indeed, to return it to its original, more natural, state. Although these accounts construct non-western cultures in many different ways, the use of their more natural 'healing traditions' as a universal sign unites nutritional, psychotherapeutic and spiritual approaches. But how are the fantasies of bodily interiority that inform our understanding of disease connected to the effects of globalising cultures? What fantasies of 'other' bodies underpin emergent beliefs about health and healing in global culture? What kinds of desires inform the transcendent fantasies of these new healthy subjects of the global future?

In *Living, Loving and Healing: a guide to a fuller life, more love and greater health*, Bernie Siegel's advice to patients includes numerous references to the greater wisdom of non-western cultures, such as Buddhism and Native American culture. Interspersed with quotations from patients, poems and biblical parables are numerous gestures towards the wisdom of the East: for example, Siegel quotes from *The Joseph Campbell Companion: reflections on the art of living*: 'As you go the way of life, you will see a great chasm. Jump. It is not as wide as you think' (Campbell, cited in Siegel, 1993: 16). Similarly, in *An End to Cancer: the nutritional approach to its prevention and control*, Leon Chaitow's argument is typical of many other such books when he cites the lack of cancer among peoples of West Africa, Japan, Northern India, South America and Native American cultures; cancer, he suggests, is almost unknown amongst 'people living on natural (unprocessed) food' (1983: 46). Simonton et al. in their famous cancer self-help book *Getting Well Again* also reference Indian Yogis who are able to stick large needles into their bodies and not bleed, or walk over hot coals and not experience pain (1978: 29).

The contrast between western and eastern approaches to health and healing is central to another example of the self-health book: *Spontaneous Healing* by Andrew Weil (1997). Introducing himself as a 'dedicated follower of Hygeia', he states:

> In the West, a major focus of scientific medicine has been the identification of external agents of disease and the development of weapons against them. . . . In the East, especially in China, medicine has had quite a different focus. It has explored the ways of increasing internal resistance to disease so that, no matter what harmful influences you are exposed to, you can remain healthy – a Hygeian strategy.
>
> (1997: 4)

Hygeia (presumably from the Greek *hygieinos*, meaning healthful) promises a self-sufficient body if it is properly nurtured: 'The Eastern concept of strengthening internal defenses is Hygeian because it assumes that the body has a natural ability to resist and deal with agents of disease' (1997: 6). Weil continues to introduce the reader (by direct address) to his theory of 'spontaneous healing' (a man with terminal cancer and a diabetic woman with a severe heart attack are sent home to die and suddenly make an unexpected recovery – why?) in a chapter entitled 'Prologue in the Rain Forest', which begins:

> Let me take you with me to a faraway place I visited more than twenty years ago: the sandy bank of a wide river on a sultry afternoon in 1972. The river was a tributory of the Rio Caqueta in the northwest Amazon. . . .
>
> (1997: 11)

The hybrid 'best from East and West' approach is increasingly pervasive among these books, especially those relating to health and healing. According to the back cover of the book *Anatomy of the Spirit: the seven stages of power and healing* (1997), for example, the author, Caroline Myss, is described as presenting

> [a] long-awaited model of the body's seven centres of spiritual and physical power in which she synthesizes the ancient wisdom of three spiritual traditions – the Hindu chakras, the Christian sacraments and the Kabbalah's Tree of Life. With this model, Dr Myss shows how you can develop your latent power and spiritual maturity. As you begin to understand the anatomy of your spirit, you will discover the spiritual causes of illness, how to sense and correct energy imbalance before it expresses itself as physical illness, and how to recover emotionally and physically from any illness you may have.

Similarly, in *Ageless Body, Timeless Mind* (1993), Deepak Chopra, 'a world-class pioneer in mind/body medicine', offers a combination of ancient Hindu teachings on Ayurveda with contemporary research in quantum physics to 'demonstrate the innate intelligence of the mind/body processes and the extent to which sickness and aging are created by nothing more than gaps in our self-knowledge' (back cover). In both these examples, as in many others, proximity to the East authenticates the naturalness of select forms of western knowledge, marking them out as different from western approaches to health more generally.

Easternised Nature

The West's bid to reinvent nature for itself within global culture is achieved through the recontextualisation of practices, beliefs and commodities from non-western cultures. In many self-health books the alienation and loss of faith in the West are contrasted repeatedly with the solidity and longevity of cultural values in the East; the inhumanity and brutality of western approaches to health are endlessly compared unfavourably with the more holistic and natural healing systems of the East. The cultures typically presented as rich sources of more natural ways of healing associated with the 'East', are most notably India, Tibet, Japan and China, or those of the so-called 'indigenous' Native Americans and Aborigines.

The place of the East within the western imagination has long been the subject of academic and political debate. From Edward Said onwards, the place of 'orientalism' in the West's contempt, and yet desire, for the East has been thoroughly critiqued.[33] Said writes of the Orient as 'almost a European invention [that] had been since antiquity a place of romance, exotic beings, haunting memories and landscapes, remarkable experiences' (1978: 1).[34] The idealised eastern nature discussed so far in this chapter might be seen to extend the appropriative strategies of colonialism into postcolonialism. In his book *Green Imperialism*, historian Richard Grove, for example, argues that such fantasies belong to a much longer tradition within the colonial project. Indeed, some of these tendencies can be traced back several centuries, and are part of the history of green imperialism in which the fantasies of the East as closer to nature became part of the early colonial project. He writes:

> After the fifteenth century the emerging global framework of trade and travel provided the conditions for a process by which indigenous European notions about nature were gradually transformed or even submerged by a plethora of information, impressions and inspiration from the wider world. In this way the commercial and utilitarian purposes of European expansion produced a situation in which the tropical environment was increasingly utilised as the symbolic location for the idealised landscapes and aspirations of the western imagination.
> (1995: 3)

For Grove, the projection of a western search for an *innocent and Edenic* nature is intimately bound up with the history of imperialism: '[T]he whole tropical world became vulnerable to colonisation by an ever-expanding and ambitious imaginative symbolism.' He continues:

> Ultimately the search for an eastern-derived Eden provided much of the imaginative basis for early Romanticism, whose visual symbols were frequently located in the tropics, and for the late eighteenth-century Orientalism, for which the Edenic search was an essential precursor.
>
> (1995: 4)

As Grove suggests, knowledge of the natural was the respectable path to seeking knowledge of God in Calvinist seventeenth-century Europe (1995: 4). By the 1850s, he argues, early colonial conservationism amounted to a 'highly heterogeneous mixture of indigenous, Romantic, Orientalist and other elements' (1995: 12).

In contemporary global culture, the east continues to function as the source of potent fantasies of an Edenic nature. In the new markets of self-health, the mind–body–spirit axis depends upon a healing nature that is often borrowed from the East. Recontextualised and frequently hybridised within western practices of self-health, this eastern nature has come to promise a spirituality which many find lacking in the West. Easternised nature is fundamental to the reconceptualisation of the body and its relationship to its environment in the project of self-health. In this section of the chapter I suggest that increasing reliance upon an eastern nature, evident within self-health cultures, is part of a much broader transformation of western beliefs about the meaning of life, death and God, and that this is a crucial, and yet little-discussed, dimension of globalisation.

What figures so pervasively and so powerfully within global self-health cultures is a cluster of new beliefs that both draw upon and reinvent the religious philosophies of the East. Far from being the much-proclaimed godless materialisms of advanced western capitalism, global cultures might rather be seen as dependent upon new forms of spirituality. As Appadurai suggests: '[T]here is vast evidence in new religiosities of every sort that religion is not only not dead but that it may be more consequential than ever in today's highly mobile interconnected global politics' (1996: 7). These 'new religiosities' are drawn substantially from eastern religious philosophies and have profoundly shaped the contours of contemporary global health cultures. But what exactly is meant by 'easternised nature', and how does it play a part in how the global gets inside us in contemporary health cultures?

According to sociologist Colin Campbell, there has been a major shift in the ultimate religious belief paradigm in western cultures over the last thirty years which he calls a process of 'easternisation'. Whilst not losing sight of the processes of 'westernisation' through which the West has continued to dominate the so-called 'third world', and, more recently, the second (ex-communist) world, Campbell argues that easternisation is profoundly transforming western cultures. What might be said to characterise

such a process is a fundamental shift away from a 'transcendent' towards an 'immanent' conception of the divine, and from a dualistic to a monistic philosophy.[35] In
other words, whilst previously the divine was typically conceptualised as beyond the
limits of possible experience or knowledge (beyond the material), God is now more
commonly believed to pervade nature or the 'souls of man' (existing as an inner force);
and whilst a split between two guiding forces or principles ('man' and God, mind and
body, good and evil, for example) previously governed western philosophy, the move
now is towards a model of unity, of interconnectedness and interdependence (a complex entity, such as the universe, is basically simple and undifferentiated) (*Longman's
English Dictionary*, 1984). Campbell sums up this change thus:

> [T]hat dominant paradigm . . . which has served the West so effectively for 2,000
> years has finally lost its grip over the majority of the population in Western
> Europe and North America. They no longer hold to a view of the world as divided
> into matter and spirit, and governed by an all-powerful, personal creator God; one
> who has set his creatures above the rest of creation. *This vision has been cast aside
> and with it all justification for mankind's domination over nature.*
>
> (1999: 47, emphasis mine)

As Campbell states, it is not that these are entirely new beliefs, but rather that we are
seeing the widespread acceptance of ideas previously confined to the minority (1999:
37). Easternisation is not simply about the wholesale introjection of eastern beliefs and
practices (such as religions) into the West, but, rather, involves the intensification of
'easternised' paradigms and conceptualisations within western cultures in more diffuse,
and, at the same time, more profound, ways. Campbell cites as evidence of this shift the
growth in non-Judaeo-Christian religious beliefs (such as the impersonal nature of the
divine and reincarnation) and the displacement of the search for truth through religion
by a quest for enlightenment. In addition, Campbell argues, whilst traditional western
religions continue to decline, eastern ones (Hinduism and Buddhism, for example)
continue to thrive, as do 'westernised' forms of eastern religions (yoga and meditation,
for example). We might add to these the examples cited from the self-health literatures
above, which all conform to Campbell's easternised model of an immanent and
monistic spirituality conceptualised as a healing force within us all.

   But for Campbell, easternisation is not simply a question of 'the introduction
and spread within the West, of recognisable 'Eastern "imports"', whether these are
products, such as spices, yoghurt, and silks, and practices such as yoga and acupuncture, or complete religious systems such as Hinduism and Buddhism'. Rather it
suggests a more profound shift: '[T]he traditional Western cultural paradigm no longer
dominates in so-called "Western" societies, but has been replaced by an "Eastern"
one' (1999: 40–1). In place of the western paradigm, he claims,

> has been set the fundamentally Eastern vision of mankind as merely part of the
> great interconnected web of sentient life. For just as The Great Chain of Being was

the paradigm metaphor for the eighteenth century, so today there is emerging a similar overarching paradigmatic metaphor, one which represents all the earth's living creatures as interdependent, part of one natural-spiritual system. Its best expression to date has been in the Gaia theory – the Earth Mother. The Earth's living things are part of a great living being which regulates its own stability. . . .

(1999: 47)

This 'overarching paradigm metaphor' of all living things being connected within one 'natural-spiritual system' signals the emergence of *Life, rather than God, as the site of worship*. For Campbell, this shift explains the contradiction (in Britain at least) between the steady postwar decline in the percentage of the population who say they believe in God (from percentages in the low nineties in 1945 to those in the low sixties today), and the slight increase in the same period in the percentage of people who nevertheless believe in some sort of 'spirit or life force' (1999: 36).

Within the worldview described by Campbell, all creatures belong to a *divine nature*, and 'non-human animals should be considered to possess "rights" and . . . humans have a duty to see that these are respected' (1999: 37) The life force that is increasingly sacralised operates across the species, as a unifying force that links all humans to other animals; beliefs in reincarnation (which are increasing, especially in the young) extend further to a notion of natural life cycles in which spirits/souls move between human and non-human species. Vegetarianism, animal rights and environmentalism all find their place within this broad church of holism and interconnectedness.

The centrality of a *divine nature* to this notion of *sacred life* is the basis for its interconnectedness: all beings 'have their existence in God who is the ground or the soul, the "seed" or the "spark" of all creatures' (Campbell, 1999: 38). God here is transformed from a personified deity, separate from humanity, to one whose presence can be witnessed in the *life force and life cycle governing all living beings*. The generative metaphor of God as the seed or the spark, however, carries over the recognisable trace of his potency, his power and even his paternity from previous models. But this generative power becomes universally available to all those who participate in the transformative energies of universal life, and, consequently, self-development goes hand in hand with direct action to save the planet in some forms of this easternised nature (Campbell, 1999: 40). Inner and outer natures are seen to be part of the unifying system of the world's life-giving energies. Easternisation thus brings with it *an imperative* to individuals to recognise their own spiritual power within – what some have referred to as 'radical religious individualism' (Campbell, 1999: 39). Rather than relying on an external power elsewhere to offer absolution, the responsibility now rests on the shoulders of each individual: redemption lies within, and 'self-deification replaces the Western idea of salvation' (Campbell, 1999: 42).

But easternised nature has become inextricable from global culture in the present moment. For it is within the context of the global imagination that what Campbell describes as easternisation achieves such powerful and widespread appeal in the West. The trend to adopt more easternised worldviews may have a long and gradual history, but their appeal is amplified and diversified within the processes of contemporary global cultures. For the universalising power of such worldviews now belongs to the widespread effects of cultural formations which constitute subjects as part of a global order. The 'sacralisation of life', for example, is indicative of an emergent sense of planetary belonging that characterises a crucial dimension of global culture. What Paul Heelas (1996) has referred to as the 'cosmic self' of New Age philosophies might be conceptualised here as the global subject of an easternised nature whose citizenship is built upon a shared feeling of community within this new fantasy of a panhumanity. This belief in a life force within, by which humans are linked to each other and to all living beings on the planet, is a synecdochical relation in which the condensation of the whole planet within the whole self occurs in such a way as to preserve the conventions governing both.[36] This easternised version of life, death, nature and the planet places the subject firmly within the new universal processes of global culture. Read in this way, we might suggest that, according to an easternised version of nature, the global is already within.

Embodying the Global

If the global is implicitly within each of us in this easternised model of nature as life force, how might this affect our changing sense of interiority and of embodiment.[37] Within an easternised frame, the body is no longer thought of exclusively as physical matter, as organs, blood, bones and skin, but is reconceptualised as flows of life, systems of energy. An easternised spirituality transforms the substance and place of the body as a discrete, boundaried entity, which has important implications for how we think of health and healing in contemporary western cultures.

In *Changes: a guide to personal transformation and new ways of living in the next millennium*, for example, Soozi Holbeche offers the following meditative prayer in which the subject is connected first to the local, then to the global, as the power of inner light flows outwards towards others:

> Let us close our eyes for a moment, and imagine the flame of a candle inside our hearts. Let us feel it, imagine it getting bigger to fill our entire bodies. The flame of our hearts reaches out, threads and streams of light, filigree threads of light, stream out to members of our families, then into the hearts and minds of presidents and prime ministers, starving children of Africa and Bosnia, repressed people worldwide.
>
> Imagine the threads of light going out and out, connecting us with trees, flowers, the Earth, stones, valleys, seas, lakes, with oceans, suns and moons. . . . Imagine the whole planet suffused in the light of your love.
>
> Awakening to change means that now the human heart can go the length of God. We have that power.
>
> (1997: 212)

The power to heal is presented here through a notion of the panhuman interconnectedness of flows of energy and light. It is light that is given a textured figuration to enable its 'threads' to unite all people of the world with nature. Recognisable signs of global need (such as 'starving children') are combined with those of natural beauty (the flowers, trees and the moon and the sun) in a bid to empower people in this inclusive image. Light becomes love becomes power in this prayer through a belief in human consciousness and its capacity to heal. A hybrid model of healing emerges which combines western images of God's love as the healing light of Christ ('the light of the world') with an easternised attribution of this power to all human beings.[38] It is precisely by channelling our embodied natural energies that we can all now be seen to have the power to heal.

In numerous other examples, embodiment is figured through the combination of eastern mind/body/spirit connections and western information and communication systems. In *Anatomy of the Spirit: the seven stages of power and healing*, Caroline Myss asserts:

> Everything that is alive pulsates with energy and all of this energy contains information. While it is not surprising that practitioners of alternative and complementary medicine accept this concept, even some quantum physicists acknowledge the existence of an electromagnetic field generated by the body's biological processes . . .
>
> (1997: 33)

'Energy medicine' is consequently advocated by Myss as a way to rethink healing within this framework. According to this approach, each individual's energy is an emotional force that 'influences the physical tissue within our bodies. In this way, *your biography – that is, the experiences that make up your life – becomes your biology*' (1997: 34, my emphasis).

The conceptualisation of health and illness as *biographical biologies* is extensively elaborated throughout many approaches to self-health. One of its most renowned advocates, currently dominating the market of both workshops and publications in this area, is the New Age author and practitioner Deepak Chopra. For Chopra, 'quantum healing' combines the mind–body flows of eastern wisdom with the innovations of western science, especially quantum physics. This hybrid coupling is marketed as the bringing together of

> the current research of Western medicine, neuroscience, and physics with the insights of Ayurvedic theory to show that the human body is controlled by a 'network of intelligence', grounded in quantum reality. . . . [T]his intelligence lies deep enough to change the basic patterns that design our physiology – with the potential to defeat cancer, heart disease and even aging itself.
>
> (1989: back cover)

Authenticating this approach with reference to examples from across the world (but noticeably from the East), he claims that: 'India, China, Japan and to a lesser extent the Christian west have given birth to sages who realized their essential nature as a flow of intelligence. By preserving that flow and nurturing it year after year, they overcame entropy from a deeper level of Nature' (1993: 16).

In refiguring the body in *Ageless Body, Timeless Mind*, Chopra argues that 'in their essential state, our bodies are composed of energy and information, not solid matter. This information is an outcropping of infinite fields of energy and information spanning the universe . . .' (1993: 6). As such, bodies can be transformed, rejuvenated and reprogrammed. Rejecting the western medical paradigm, Chopra urges readers to adopt the quantum worldview, or new paradigm, which

> teaches us that we are constantly making and unmaking our bodies. Behind the illusion of its being a solid, stable object, the body is a process, and as long as that process is directed towards renewal, the cells of the body remain new, no matter how much time passes or how much entropy we are exposed to.
>
> (1993: 41)

Easternised natures, conceptualised here as interconnecting energy and information flows, thus locate the global within, even as they break down the dualism of inside and outside. The global gets inside us, not just because we consume it (eat it, drink it, rub it on our bodies, feel it on skins), but also as we imagine we embody it through our integration within the universal energy systems that characterise its power. According to these models, we embody it not in a fleshy or substantial way, but rather through the life force that connects us to each other and to nature. Within this emergent easternised cultural imaginary, the global within thus signifies less the introjection of an external object, commodity or belief, and more the *embodiment of flows that unite inner and outer within a set of mutually dependent systems.*

These ways of imagining health and illness draw upon eastern paradigms to reframe our relationships to each other and to nature. However, they also depend upon changing conceptualisations of the body *within* western science and medicine. Indeed, their current appeal arguably derives in part from their ability to recontextualise elements from both East and West and to enhance their claims to global status. It would be a mistake to posit these forms of global embodiment as entirely outside, or even in total opposition to, western models. For not only would this ignore the complexities of West–East appropriations within globalising cultures, but it would also underestimate how much self-health books incorporate aspects of western scientific knowledge within their so-called 'eastern' frames of reference. The books by both Myss and Chopra, discussed above, are typical of the more general trend within self-health that incorporates particular western scientific conceptualisations of the body's mechanisms for dealing with illness to serve the purposes of an easternised philosophy. Although such dependence upon western science is usually tolerated only insofar as it adheres to the reconceptualisation of flows of energy as healing sources and is utilised to argue against the more mechanical, biomedical explanations of illness, these borrowings nevertheless need further exploration. For it is only when the correspondence between an easternised model of energy flows and more recent western models of disease has been elaborated that the full impact and appeal of embodying global self-health can be understood.

● ● ● Informational Bodies

> Your physical body is surrounded by an energy field that extends as far out as your outstretched arm and the full length of your body. It is both an information center and a highly perceptual system. We are constantly 'in communication' with everything around us through this system, which is a kind of conscious electricity that transmits and receives messages to and from other people's bodies.
> (Myss, 1997: 33)

According to numerous self-health books, and increasingly within popular discourse, our 'ease' or 'dis-ease' depends upon our successful integration into systems of energy (see Coward, 1989). As I have illustrated, the suggestion is that we embody such systems as individuals, as well as being part of a universal system of energy: the life force.

Such representations draw directly upon a new scientific modality in which 'most systems in nature' are seen, as cultural theorist Manuel DeLanda puts its, as 'subject to the flows of the matter and energy that continuously move through them' (1992: 129). DeLanda's conceptualisation posits a new ideal of 'a *dynamic* equilibrium' to be achieved through the regulation of the body system (1992: 129). As the feminist historian of science Donna Haraway (1989c) has argued, such an ideal is part of the broader transformation of industrial society into an informational one. Haraway notes that:

> In communication sciences, the translation of the world into a problem of coding can be illustrated by looking at cybernetic (feedback controlled) systems theories applied to telephone technology, computer design, weapons deployment or data base construction and maintenance. In each case, the solution to the key questions rests on a theory of language and control; the key operation is determining the rates, directions and probabilities of flow, of a quantity called information. The world is subdivided by boundaries differentially permeable to information. Information is just that kind of quantifiable element (unit, basis of unity) which allows universal translation, and so unhindered instrumental power (called effective communication). The biggest threat to such power is interruption of communication. Any system breakdown is a function of stress. The fundamentals of this technology can be condensed into the metaphor C^3I, command–control–communication–intelligence, the military's symbol for its operations theory.
> (1989c: 188)

Within western biomedicine, we have seen a significant shift away from the mechanical body towards the informational body (Braidotti, 1994; Stacey, 1997). Our bodies, like other systems, are translated into codes, sequences and spelling errors, as art historian Barbara Stafford (1991) puts it. As Stafford argues, the increasing visualisability of our bodily interiors has a profound impact upon our understanding of disease and treatment: 'Computer tomography x-ray imaging (CT), positron emission tomography (PET), magnetic resonance imaging (MRI), and ultrasound now probe non-invasively, but publicly, formerly private regions and occluded and secluded recesses' (1991: 26). No longer viewed as a mechanism made up of relatively autonomous, yet interdependent, parts, the body has increasingly become systematised and is viewed as a network of information. Whilst both the mechanical and the informational continue to shape different aspects of biomedicine, the widespread conceptualisation of the body as an information system has now become fundamental to medical discourses of the body. Central to this transformation has been the emergence of immunology, in which the interconnectedness between the units of the body – the cells – is represented through notions of permeability, mutation and flows of information (See Chapter One in this volume.). The naming of AIDS as a disease of auto-immunity is part of this shift.[39] Together with an increased awareness of other diseases of the immune system, such as postviral syndrome, the AIDS epidemic has shifted public understandings of health and illness towards the direction of bodies as information systems.

Within contemporary self-health practices, systems discourse both constructs the bodily interior as a system (as Haraway [1989b] has detailed, in her analysis of auto-immunity) and locates the body within broader systems of global significance; furthermore, it posits a 'continuous' flow of informational and communicational energies between these interdependent systems. This model connects the individual to the global quite explicitly. Moreover, the embodiment of the global is imagined through a series of expanding but interlocking systems with ever-increasing remits. Thus the smallest unit of the body (here the cell) is but a microcosm of the earth in its entirety (here, the ecosystem and biosystem). For example, in *The Greening of Medicine* (1990), biomedical doctor and alternative practitioner Patrick Pietroni uses George Engel's models of the relationship between different systems: the cell system, the body system, the ecosystem and the biosystem. According to Pietroni, holistic medicine should be striven towards, not just in the sense of treating the person as a whole person, rather than just a collection of organs, cells and tissues, but in the sense of the place of the whole person in relation to the whole planet, vulnerably suspended in the silence of space, so we should care for ourselves, right down to the basic unit of our body's cells – and beyond. Supporting his argument with direct references to Lovelock's Gaia hypothesis and Weiss and von Bertanfly's systems theory, Pietroni suggests that holism necessarily depends upon a global perspective which situates the whole person within his or her environmental and planetary systems, as can be seen in Figure 4.11.

In such a model, the body is represented as a self-regulating system embedded within an ever-widening set of interconnected systems culminating in those of global proportions. In recognising our roles in the self-regulation of our mind/body systems,

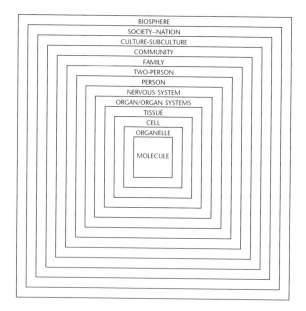

Figure 4.11

In the 'continuum of natural systems' the body is embedded within an ever-widening set of interconnected systems culminating in the 'biosphere' (Pietroni, 1990: 23).

we are also urged to recognise our role in the wider planetary systems of global well-being. We are invited to belong to an 'imagined global community' of healthy subjects through the construction of our inherent place within the global system (Anderson, 1983; Robertson, 1992).

The highly influential arguments about the causes of cancer made in *Getting Well Again* in the late 1970s have continued to shape current ways of understanding illness. The authors write:

> It is no longer possible to see the body as an object waiting for replacement parts from a factory. Instead we now view the mind and the body as an integrated *system* . . .
>
> The real issue is no longer whether the mind and emotions affect the course of treatment; the question is rather *how* to direct them most effectively in support of it.
>
> (Simonton et al., 1978: 31–2, 89)

As is clear in their 'mind/body model of cancer development', it is the immune system that is key to the successful regulation of a healthy body:

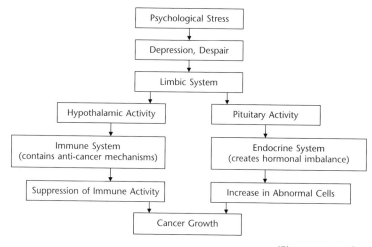

(Simonton et al., 1978: 92)

In this account, auto-immunity is constructed as a 'self-regulating system' of emotional/bodily integrity. Drawing on scientific knowledges which see, as DeLanda argues, 'matter as capable of self-organisation' (1992: 134), self-health books assure us that with the correct input, the system can be surveyed, refined and controlled by the patient.

In contemporary accounts of illness more generally there is a repeated correspondence between conceptualisations of the immune system defending the body through cell regulation and the autogenerative responsibilities of the individual. As shown by this example from feminist anthropologist Emily Martin's ethnographic study of people's understanding of the immune system, such a change in conceptualisations of health and illness has significant implications for people's understandings of causality and prevention:

> There is far more capacity to self regulate the physiological functions of the body than people imagined thirty or forty years ago. There's really enormous control that can be observed, much of which has been demonstrated through biofeedback. . . . So there's almost a re-owning of our own capacity to know our body, to experience it, to self-regulate it to train it.
>
> (Peter Boswell, quoted in Martin, 1994: 124)

The multiplicity of causal influences perceived to be at work within the immune system as a regulatory network has been widely translated into the obligation on the individual to monitor all aspects of lifestyle and activity. Within self-health practices, the equation between immune system regulation and individual responsibility is made quite explicit. In the following example from Rachel Charles' book *Mind, Body and Immunity*, such a correspondence is the basis of healing:

> What we so often fail to appreciate is that the body has a staggeringly complex system for healing and regulating itself . . . just as a delicately balanced system can be upset by poor diet, lack of exercise, long-term emotional problems and stress, so the opposite is true: it can be positively encouraged to operate more effectively, so that the body is able to function efficiently and remain healthy. If you are suffering from a serious disease, take heart in the knowledge that you can actively assist in your own healing.
>
> (1990: 5)

Such an emphasis on motivating readers to believe in their effect on their own health has become widely accepted within commonsense knowledge through an understanding of the immune system as a constant flow of information through the body. If the body is no longer perceived to be a purely mechanical entity, but rather an informational network, then its openness to transformation becomes much more feasible and the obligation on individuals to monitor the harmonious balance of their interconnecting systems becomes a stronger imperative. Participating in such a process connects people to each other and to broader systems. Thus, recognising one's part in the maintenance of one's own health becomes part of recognising everyone's part in the maintenance of the planet's health (as in the ecosystem). Embodying health means maintaining all the parts of oneself (mind, body, spirit) as a system, as well as, or rather, and *in so doing*, contributing to the stable functioning of the wider systems of which we are all part: micro systems here interlock with macro ones as individual well-being connects to planetary well-being. Global subjects are constituted through a sense of belonging which requires simultaneous monitoring of the body as an environment, and of the environment as embodied: interconnecting flows of energy and information.

Popular understandings of immunity to disease through a delicately balanced system of well-being are based on a notion of embodiment in which boundaries are mutable and states of health infinitely changeable. At the heart of such a discourse is the idea of the cell as the base unit of the body, a unit that stores and communicates information and that literally is the key to life and death. In his ten assumptions towards creating an 'ageless body and timeless mind', for example, Deepak Chopra suggests that these will 'give us the ability to rewrite the program of aging that now directs our cells'; he argues that

> The biochemistry of the body is a product of awareness. Beliefs, thoughts and emotions create the chemical reactions that uphold life in every cell. An aging cell is the end product of awareness that has forgotten how to remain new . . .
>
> Although each person seems separate and independent, all of us are connected to patterns of intelligence that govern the whole cosmos. Our bodies are part of a universal body, our minds aspects of a universal mind.
>
> (1993: 5–6)

This image of the cell as a unit in an information system is a way of thinking about the cell that has developed from the legacy of the history of immunology (see Haraway, 1989a; Martin, 1994). As Chopra's argument demonstrates, emergent models of global self-health such as those exemplified throughout this chapter not only draw on easternised natures to reframe the meaning of embodiment, but also depend heavily upon selected versions of western science to reconceptualise the meaning of disease.

● ●   **Managing Global Risks**

This model of 'self-organising processes' is not restricted to immune system discourse. Donna Haraway has argued that 'the analogous moves in ecology could be examined by probing the history and utility of the ecosystem' (1989c: 188); and, indeed, DeLanda details its take-up in ecosystems modelling and in debates about environmental change (1992: 158). Organic life is seen to behave according to new rules which govern both universal and particular systems; thus the genetic activity of an egg can be referred to as transferring information and as having a 'global dynamic' (DeLanda, 1992: 146). As Deleuze argues:

[T]his new style of disease is like global politics or strategy. They tell us the risk of war comes not only from a specific external potential aggressor, but from our defensive reactions going out of control or breaking down.

(1992: 292)

The power of contemporary self-health lies in part in its ability to represent disease through ideas about global risk management. In terms of health and illness the dynamic between local and global might be seen to be flows in opposite directions simultaneously: on the one hand, global disasters produce local health risks, the negotiation of which is achieved through new forms of identity; on the other hand, these draw upon discourses of universal healing systems and global consciousness.

Accompanying the construction of what Haraway has called variations on 'the defended self' (1989a: 18) is a requirement to negotiate constant global threats and risks. As we are increasingly exposed not only to iatrogenic disease caused by treatment 'effects' of biomedicine, but also to the harmful aspects of nature itself, the routine habits of today become the risk practices of tomorrow: sunbathing, eating, drinking, smoking and even breathing become potentially carcinogenic. In his chapter called 'The Planet Strikes Back', as well as detailing the risks of food and water consumption, Pietroni includes an analysis of numerous environmental health risks such as global warming, lead poisoning, acid rain, nuclear radiation, ozone depletion, air pollution and the greenhouse effect (1990: 58–66).

As sociologists such as Ulrich Beck (1992) and Anthony Giddens (1999) have argued, life in late modernity might be characterised by the negotiation of harms and dangers produced by technological processes. Indeed, Beck (1992) suggests that science is seen no longer as protecting people from risks, but rather as generating them. Technology in late modernity, it is claimed, is increasingly perceived to be proliferating potential physical harms, and the effects of many such harms are not restricted to local or even national boundaries but rather require risk management as a global issue (Giddens, 1999). Such perceptions are not restricted to sociologists; popular accounts of the risks of contemporary science and technology are also evidence of 'the risk society'. For example, disasters such as Chernobyl have local and global consequences. Jane Renouf cites Chernobyl as a possible factor in her son's illness and eventual death from leukaemia in north-west England, where the sheep still cannot be eaten because of their contamination with caesium 137 (1993: 25). Similarly, environmental problems such as ozone depletion, linked with skin cancer, are seen as global issues both in terms of the enormity of the threat (the escalating rates) and in terms of the dangerous impact of a set of practices in one part of the world on the environment of another. An icongraphy of global risk has solidified in our contemporary imaginations (see Toogood and Myers, 1999). For example, the poster for a conference organised by the pressure group Third World First places three photographs in a vertical line: the young black child against the sliced-through, ancient tree-trunk; the dolphins as the threatened species; and the indigenous people whose habitat and traditions are being undermined by western development (see

Figure 4.12). Here the global nature (the third world) is under threat by global culture (the West): the innocents (child, trees, dolphins, indigenous peoples) are at risk from the inhumanity of global capitalism.

The daily negotiation of such risks is central within the constitution of the global subjects of health management which populate contemporary health cultures. Flows of global risk might thus be added to Featherstone's conceptualisation of global culture in terms of the 'flows of goods, people, information, knowledge and images' (1990b: 1; see also Appadurai, 1996). As O'Neill has argued in relation to AIDS, a global panic, and desire to collaborate in the face of such a danger, might be accompanied by strategies of sealing off national boundaries against the threat of 'global viral flows' (O'Neill, 1990: 11). This anxiety about national and bodily boundaries is extended to include prevention, as well as treatment, of disease. As Rosalind Coward (1989) and Robert Crawford (1985) have demonstrated, ownership of health no longer means the absence of disease, but rather is achieved through hard work and self-discipline through the new emphasis on individual prevention. Indeed, anthroplogist Paul Rabinow argues that:

> Modern prevention is, above all, the tracking down of risks. . . . We are partially moving away from the older face-to-face surveillance of individuals and groups known to be dangerous or ill . . . toward projecting risk factors. . . . The nineties will be the decade of genetics, immunology and environmentalism, for clearly these are the leading vehicles for the infiltration of technoscience, capitalism and culture into what the moderns call nature.
>
> (1992: 242–5)

One way in which this intensification of risk perception might be explained is in relation to what sociologist Roland Robertson has called 'global uncertainty'. He argues that 'we have entered a phase of what appears to us . . . as great global uncertainty – so much so that the very idea of uncertainty promises to become globally institutionalised' (1990: 16). Robertson's argument is concerned with the reorganisation of alliances, borders and identities which produce a desire for some guarantees of global stability. The anxieties of the West, as its powers of global control are unsettled, and as the last remains of its empires collapse before it, are increasingly manifested in such a desire. Whilst there has arguably been global uncertainty for several centuries, there is a search for its institutionalised regulation under the banner of supposedly mutual interests of global 'security' now that western powers fear they may no longer be so securely in control of its direction. In this respect, it might not seem overly cynical to consider the category of the 'global' (and indeed the academic theorisation of 'globalisation') as a response from the West to the relativisation of its place in the world order.

The increasing emphasis on the management of the healthy body within western cultures is just such a response to these global uncertainties. Unable to protect the vulnerable blue planet, and yet ever more aware of its (and our) potential

Figure 4.12

In this vertical series of photographs advertising a conference on the 'Shared Planet', sponsored by the organisation Third World First and the New Internationalist *magazine, global nature is shown to be at risk from the inhumanity of global capitalism.*

destruction, our own bodies perhaps provide a more realistic, satisfying and literally manageable and limited project. In light of the threat from environmental risks, from nuclear weapons, from the break-up and relocation of familiar power blocs, the current western obsession with bodily management seems a far safer bet. Indeed, the regulation of our own embodied armies of good (white) blood cells and the invading (black knight) enemy cells, as referenced in one self-health account of the immune system fighting cancer (Simonton et al., 1978), looks remarkably like the relocation of colonial narratives, with their closures of global supremacy, to the bodily interior of the individual. As old systems of domination recede, and the West struggles to replace them with new ones, the maintenance of the purity of the body in the face of external dangers to it is represented as the new locus of fantasies of control.

● ● ● Grand Narratives of the Globality

There has been something of a generational shift in this period of global uncertainty from the 1960s to the present (Robertson, 1992), during which time, it is argued, the 'grand narratives' of science and technology have lost much of their credibility (Lyotard, 1984). Whereas people used to trust professional expertise and scientific progress, new generations, it is claimed, have become increasingly sceptical about the general benefits of innovation (as exemplified by the current controversies about genetically modified foods). Indeed, for many, scientific and technological 'progress' and medical developments are implicated in many of our current and future health problems. Following philosopher Jean François Lyotard's *The Postmodern Condition* (1984), which charts the changes in the status of knowledge which have occurred across the most 'developed' countries in the West, it has become a truism now to argue that science in general is suffering a 'crisis of legitimation'. Lyotard's argument maps the collapse of the legitimating meta-narratives of science which he considers to be at the heart of the 'postmodern condition', a condition within which knowledge has been relativised, moral certainties have been contextualised, and diversity and plurality have become the flagships of the future.

However, what Lyotard's account underestimates is the parallel rise in the authority of the individual to legitimate new forms of expertise located within the self. Anchored in the familiar stories of progress, of liberation and of the pursuit of knowledge, individualised accounts of global self-health condense the grand narratives of modernity, reconnecting subjects back into the universal narrative of modernity through their participation in the global: the 'I' of the individual story becomes the 'we' of the grand narrative of globality. The narrative of liberation may have become detached from the heroisation of science, but it has now been relocated within individual health biographies: the heroic subject of self-health now liberates him/herself from ignorance, fear and the general limits of the past, as in the following example from Rachel Charles' book *Mind, Body and Immunity*:

These [inner conflicts] involve feelings about ourselves, probably originating long ago in childhood, and beliefs we have held for many years. . . . [I]t takes great courage to make changes to oneself, but if glowing health and happiness are to be achieved, then some changes will almost certainly be necessary.

Repressed feelings

When you were small you learnt to behave in certain ways, so that you could win your parents' approval and ensure your own survival. You learnt it was right to express some feelings and not others. . . . As an adult, however, many of those childhood feelings, beliefs and behaviours are no longer valuable to you; indeed, they may be positively damaging and causing you unnecessary stress.

(1990: 108)

Similarly, the narrative of the pursuit of knowledge may have been separated from the modern scientific project, but has now been translated into the project of the self: knowledge for its own sake is legitimated in the pursuit of self-knowledge and a healthier and happier future, as exemplified in the following extract from *Living, Loving and Healing*.

I can't help thinking that if we had taken all the money we have spent on exploring outer space and used it for inner-space exploration, on knowing ourselves better, the world would be a better place, and we would be happier. I admire our curiosity about our inner systems and what lies within us.

Many of us are frightened to go into our inner space. Doing so may seem threatening, but I believe that going into that threat, that fear, is what life is about. I like to think there are five directions in which we can go: east, west, north, south and into our darkness. That fifth direction can be the source of great knowledge for us. Healing is a work of darkness. Think of the five dots on the dice. It is the fifth dot, at the center, that is the key.

(Siegel, 1993: 95)

Self-health books are overflowing with such examples. Addressed as the subject desiring change, readers are recruited to the project of self-transformation and self-improvement. Progress can be quickly achieved by the strategies laid out for the reader if they are willing to take the risk, face the truth, and understand themselves. These programmes typically lay out a plan for liberation from the follies of past lifestyles and habits through increasing self-knowledge and the wisdom that flows from it.

Contrary to Lyotard's claims, these models of self-knowledge within individual health biographies have proved highly compatible with so-called 'postmodern' information culture. For Lyotard, the move towards such a culture suggests not the end of knowledge, but rather its proliferation: '[D]ata banks are the encylopedia of tomorrow . . . they are "nature" for postmodern man [*sic*]', and that knowledge must now be translated into 'units of information' (1984: 51); however, what Lyotard did not anticipate is how these changes have been combined with the relocation of the macro-progress narratives of science within the micro-trajectories of the postmodern self. At a time when the informational body of immunology combines so comfortably with an easternised nature that connects these systems to the individual subject, the personalised story of progress towards global self-health relies heavily on the grand narratives of modernity that preceded it. Thus, the project of global self-health is not only heavily dependent upon western models of embodiment, such as immunology, but also reiterates and depends upon the power of some of the foundational structures of western modernity, such as the grand narratives of progress and liberation.

● ● ● **Self-contextualisation**

The balanced immune system, the perfectly toned body and the self-nurturing individual are all ideals widely reproduced within contemporary cultural discourses of health and illness. Self-health literature in general encourages the patient to aspire to some or all of these ideals. The patient is addressed within a consumer discourse as s/he is invited to assemble the new healthier identity according to his/her inner needs. Self-health philosophies introduce a new instrumentalism, making identity production into a project of the self. Within this framework, individuals are invited to reinvent themselves through whatever combination of mind/body/spirit practices suits them: the self becomes the context for authenticating appropriate knowledges and practices. Self-contextualisation now provides the guarantees previously secured by external belief systems.

For example, as Louise Hay assures us, we need to tap into the 'Divine Infinite Intelligence of the Universe' somehow; the important point is to get some spiritual ingredient into the recipe for your holistic lifestyle. For Hay, readers should choose a spiritual package that suits them, one which combines the elements which meet their individual needs. Thus the search for truth has been displaced by the quest to find what works for you:

> There are many spiritual groups. In addition to the Christian churches there are Metaphysical churches, like Religious Science and Unity. There are self-realization fellowships, M.S.I.A., Transcendental Meditation, the Rajneesh Foundation, the Siddha Foundation, etc. . . .
> I want you to know that there are many, many avenues you can explore. If one doesn't work for you, try another.
>
> (Hay, 1988: 88)

It is through our embodiment of nature that we imagine our unity within the global order. Hay's prayer below is indicative of this more general shift away from a Judaeo-Christian conception of a personal God towards a belief in a more generalised spirituality or life force which takes the self as the legitimating context for belief (Campbell, 1999: 3):

In the infinity of life where I am
all is perfect, whole and complete.
I am one with the Power that created me.
. . . My good comes from everywhere and everyone
All is well in my world.   (Hay, 1988: 126)

The instrumentalisation of identity through the relativisation of knowledge exemplified here corresponds precisely to the cultural change that concerned Lyotard in his study of postmodern culture discussed above. In this respect, the shift from universal rules to individual judgements coincides here with Lyotard's account of the crisis in legitimation occurring in western societies. Lyotard's reformulation of the question 'Is it true?' to 'Is it of use?' encapsulates Hay's philosophy perfectly. For Campbell, the loss of faith in western science is responsible for the growing appeal of an 'easternised' world-view which stresses repeatedly the introduction of relativity to people's religious beliefs in the West as we begin the twenty-first century. According to a growing religious mysticism that advocates a model of spirituality in which we are all part of the divine on earth, the particular form of belief is less significant than our acknowledgement of the divine generally. As Campbell states, this is a 'view which leads to an acceptance of religious relativity as far as all specific forms of belief are concerned and to the doctrine of polymorphism, in which the truth of all religions is recognised . . . and all forms of religion are regarded as identical' (1999: 8–9). However, when considered as part of global cultures, this move towards relativism and self-contextualisation is accompanied by the simultaneous reinstatement of particular universalisms. Indeed, as Campbell himself argues, such claims to accept religious relativity are based firmly within highly universalistic frameworks: '[T]his form of religion regards religious experience as a valid expression of that universal religious consciousness which is based in the ultimate divine ground' (1999: 8).

The instrumentalism of identity here can thus be seen as a form of post-modern humanism, reinstating authenticity through the work of imitation, choice and consumption through which the global is defined as a marketplace (see Heelas, 1996). In the contemporary enterprise culture which promotes ideas of individual choice and responsibility, 'non-western cultures' become identity resources which can be mixed and matched, and a global culture is constructed by the West to provide an endless source of personalised hybridity (Bhabha, 1994). Authenticity and originality are simultaneously decontextualised and recontextualised through individual health biographies within the new universalisms of global systems and energies. The discourses of self-health, whilst operating through a rhetoric of individuality, reproduce a form of the universal human subject through notions of planetary citizenship and global culture.

As numerous critics have asserted, the techniques of the body condense broader cultural values (Mauss, 1992; Scheper-Hughes and Lock, 1987). Part of the new health consciousness since the 1980s has been the explosion of popular fitness regimes. The shift in the cultural connotations of bodily fitness from either macho militarism (Gillick, 1984) or embarrassing keep-fit sessions for large middle-class ladies (Coward, 1989) to a desirable and, importantly, *responsible*, notion of self-health has led Rosalind Coward to the provocative conclusion that 'health has taken over from sex as the main area of self-determination' in contemporary culture (1989: 4). Indeed, Muriel Gillick, in her article 'Health Promotion, Jogging and the Pursuit of the Moral Life', suggests that the new imperative to health through exercise is 'about much more than physical fitness'; 'health', she argues, is a new 'form of national and global citizenship' (1984: 381). If health has become the new form of global citizenship, then self-health is its clearest example in the global cultures of the new millennium. And if 'become who you are' or 'become who you should be' are the imperatives that circulate in the world of self-health, then global culture appears to provide endless resources for the consumer in search of well-being. One consequence of the seemingly never-ending resources of health practices from the cultures of elsewhere is the apparent global mobility such a fantasy offers to the subject of health. Self-contextualisation is thus the necessary local counterpoint to global health cultures.

The Global Within

In the early part of this chapter I discussed three ways in which products achieve the status of the global: condensation through expansion, unity through diversity, and authenticity through hybridity. I argued that these apparent paradoxes, far from undercutting the powerful appeal of global culture, have become its trademark. The same claims have been made here about nature: to commodify nature is not to undermine its authority, but rather has quite the opposite effect. If, as Lyotard suggests, there has been a shift from the question 'Is it true?' to 'Is it of use?', then we might expect universal knowledge claims in general (including those based upon nature) to have been thoroughly destabilised. How can nature possibly remain a credible sign under such circumstances? And yet, throughout this chapter, denaturalisations have been shown quickly to transform into renaturalisations, and decontextualisations into recontextualisations. Thus, although the question is no longer 'Is nature real?', but, rather, 'Is nature of use?' (followed swiftly by 'Is nature saleable?' and 'Is nature efficient?', Lyotard, 1984: 51), the instrumentalisation of nature presents little threat to its continuing pervasiveness as authenticator. Indeed, as I have suggested, its endless adaptability has become evidence of its universality. Commodified to death, nature is reincarnated once more as the ultimate commodity.

What facilitate such immortality are the processes of globalising cultures. The power of nature as a magical sign has been rejuvenated in the service of the global that creates and often equates with a marketplace. Thus the global has reinvented nature; it has reinvigorated it by annexing it to a new set of resources. We can now say both 'How is nature of use to me?' and 'Nature connects me to the universe' because the individualised instrumentalisation of nature is accompanied by the simultaneous promise of belonging to a new global panhumanity. In utilising nature according to the needs of personalised identity narratives, we can also share in these new universalisms endowed by global culture. Indeed, we can become part of them in the most intimate of ways; in this sense, nature guarantees our intimacy with the global.

I have used the term 'the global' throughout to indicate its status both as resource and as effect. For the global provides ways of constituting new universalisms through a repertoire of images, products and practices that seem to come from elsewhere: third world icons, exotic ingredients, mystical practices. As western natures have become exhausted, global natures provide new ways of imaging health, beauty and fitness: energy medicine, cocoa butter, chakras. These 'other' natures are commodified with impunity within global culture. Manufactured, customised and digitalised, they form the consumable 'locals' of global culture that offer direct access to an authenticated nature. The global is also an achieved effect. Consumers are offered a sense of participating in this apparently endless choice of products, practices and beliefs. Global culture in this sense is an aspiration, a fantasy, a desire, as well as a marketplace and system of flows and exchanges. Global subjects are constituted through the promise of a transcendent mobility, allowing them to move freely across time and space, joining the transnational flows of other objects (images, information, products).

This global culture depends upon the ways in which easternisation has resurrected nature as a divine life force, a constant energy flow, a unifying system, an immanent and ubiquitous presence. This nature includes us all within its unifying principles: interconnection, interdependence and mutuality. Such a nature unites all beings on the planet and celebrates all life forms in their diversity. In this set of conceptualisations, nature is already global. Easternised nature is nature at its most expansive and universal; it is not the interface between 'man and his God', but rather it is that which incorporates both in a natural-spiritual system of Life. Self-health practices combine this easternised nature (with its philosophy of holistic healing and mind/body/spirit medicine) with its counterpart in western science: systems discourse. Compatible in all the ways I have shown, easternised nature, with its flows of energy, and western immunology, with its flows of information, fuse to underpin the basis of a new practice: 'global self-health'. In this sense, the powerful appeal of global self-health rests in its hybrid borrowings from East and West which conjoin to accommodate even the starkest of paradoxes. Given the hyperindividualism of the models of causation, prevention and cure within these philosophies, the self becomes the ultimate arbiter of appropriation: the answer is to know what we need to do for ourselves. Self-contextualisation here is not a contradiction in terms, as it might at first appear, but is the logical conclusion of health cultures with the inbuilt flexibility that global nature provides. Imagined as self-regulating environment, our own systems are the only necessary context for judging knowledge. Self-health is a form of global citizenship insofar as it facilitates participation at the universal level through the most local of practices; it is one way that the global gets inside us.

Globalising cultures effect their appeal to the universal not only through the breadth of their reach, but also through the depth of their permeation. Within the processes of globalising cultures, our bodies are now both inextricable from our global environment, and are themselves microcosmic environments indicative of our general physical, emotional and spiritual well-being. Systematised, yet flexible, boundaried, yet open, confected, yet natural, our bodies connect us to ourselves, to each other and to the global order.

● ● ●   **Notes**

1   See Edwards et al. (1999), Merchant (1980) and Part One of this volume, respectively.
2   The rapid rise in academic publications on the subject of globalisation is documented by Busch (1997), who notes that in 1995 alone over 100 books appeared with 'globalisation' in the title (quoted in Urry, 2000). Much of this work has had an economic or technological focus; for approaches to global culture, see, for example, Appadurai (1996); Bauman (1999); Beck (2000); Featherstone (1990a); Featherstone et al. (1995); Friedman (1994); Myers (1999a); Tomlinson (1999); and Urry (2000).
3   From a rather different angle, geographer Doreen Massey (1999) explores ways of 'imagining globalisation' in relation to power relations and changing conceptualisations of time and space. On the debates about the subjective dimensions of global culture, see Poppi (1997) and Robertson (1992).
4   The term 'banal globalism' has been used to describe the ways in which the global has become part of everyday life in contemporary culture (see Toogood and Myers, 1999). However, as Myers (1999b) has argued, whilst 'corporate leaders, advertisers, media professionals, policy-makers, academics and maybe footloose young people may talk about globalisation . . . what about shop owners, retired people, local government employees, or shop stewards?' Myers interrogates whether cosmopolitanism is a more appropriate term to describe people's everyday understandings of what academics have called globalisation. This work is part of the ESRC-funded research project on 'Global Citizenship and the Environment' based at Lancaster University (1996–9).
5   My reading of global products focusses exclusively on questions of how consumers are sold global culture in a number of different ways. This does not take into account the diversity of meanings people might associate with the global. For an analysis of the complex interaction between 'the development of global consumer culture, on the one hand, and the emergence of critical globalist values and movements, on the other' see Szerszynski and Toogood, 2000: 218). Here a more optimistic reading of globalisation and of people's resistance to its more dominant forms is offered through an argument about the emergence of 'a global civil society' as a 'conscious reaction and antidote to the growth of global corporate capitalism and environmental destruction' (Szerszynski and Toogood, 2000: 218)
6   For an attempt to classify the categories of 'global images' currently circulating within contemporary western cultures, see Toogood and Myers (1999). Here the authors identify three groups of global images (representations of the globe; specific places and environments; individual people as typifying 'peoples' or indeed the 'human race') and trace the visual conventions through which their globality is constituted.
7   For a discussion of the 'imaging of commodities', see Wernick (1991). For critical analysis of the consumer object of postmodern culture, see Baudrillard (1998).
8   There are numerous examples of research demonstrating that the division between rich and poor in the world has increased in the postwar period. Anthony Giddens (1999), for example, cites the following figures: 'The share of the poorest fifth of the world's population in global income has dropped from 2.3% to 1.4% over the past ten years.'
9   Coca-Cola's 'most populated operating group, the Middle and Far East Group, ranges from the Middle East to China, Japan and Australia', for details, see www.thecoca-colacompany.com/tccc/ profile.html. For further details of McDonald's franchised outlets worldwide, see their homepage: www.mcdonalds.com/corporate/corporate.html. Gorbachev appeared in Pizza Hut advertisements on US television in December 1997. www.ccnet.com/-funtzu75/gorb0013.html.

10   The categories I am using to describe how products are globalised inevitably overlap, and some products, such as Coca-Cola, are global in terms of both markets and iconography. Indeed, as Greg Myers demonstrates:

> The Coca-Cola Company was one of the first companies to build its marketing strategy on a single global product and brand image. It was also one of the first to use the globe itself and the ethnic and national diversity of consumers, as a sign of the brand's universal desirability and availability.
>
> (1999a: 55)

As Myers details:

> In 1971 The Coca-Cola Company produced a television commercial featuring 200 young people at sunrise on a hill, each dressed in national dress, each holding a distinctive bottle of Coke, and all singing along with the New Seekers:
>
> I'd like to teach the world to sing in perfect harmony
> I'd like to buy the world a Coke and keep it company
> It's the real thing . . .
>
> (1999a: 55)

Contributing to this reading of Coca-Cola as a global brand is the popular account of the shape of the Coca-Cola bottle having been modelled on the shape of another global icon: Marilyn Monroe. A recent Coca-Cola advertisement on British television shows polar bears drinking Coca-Cola, which might be read as an extension of the product's global appeal: it now even crosses species, and has reached the North Pole.

11   For an analysis of how images of particular kinds of local environments come to stand for global environments, see Szerszynski and Toogood, who argue that:

> Certain kinds of generic places can stand in for the global environment, such as deserts, beaches and rainforests. Local environments such as Chernobyl and Antarctica can also be typified by making them stand for the global environment as threatened, by radiation, global warming and other environmental risks.
>
> (2000: 224)

12   For a consideration of how the blue planet has become a foundational icon of global culture, see Part One of this book and also Cosgrove (1994) and Myers (1999a).

13   This image thus makes an implicit reference to the well-known gospel hymn 'He's got the whole world in his hands', but transfers the power of the hold from God to 'man'.

14   Ex-Prime Minister Baroness Margaret Thatcher famously placed her handkerchief over these new designs in a bid to demonstrate her disapproval of this move away from a more purely British brand image towards one of multicultural diversity. At the British Airways stand at the Blackpool conference hall in October 1997 she is reported as having 'handbagged the BA Director, David Holmes', as having 'draped her handkerchief over the offending aeroplane', and, 'before storming off in a huff', as having said: 'We fly the British flag, not these awful things you are putting on tails' (*The Times*, 10 October 1997).

15   In fact, the reversal of this branding strategy in 1999, in the face of competition with Virgin Atlantic and the perceived failure of the appeal of the global imagery, has now produced a mixture of Union Jacks with the ethnic designs: '[M]ore than half the 340 strong fleet are to carry a redesign involving the Union Jack, effectively halting BA's change to ethnic logos reflecting different countries' (*The Daily Telegraph*, 7 June 1999).

16   The idea behind these boxes was summed up by the designer as follows:

> to complement the global images by promoting exceptional artwork from around the world (different textures, media and cultures all represented) . . . with images on the inside of the boxes which were chosen from snapshots in time from people's lives around the world. . . . The ongoing theme was to surprise and delight people by giving them a glimpse of someone

else's 'perfect place to have a snack'. It's almost like these people are saying 'oh alright, I'll let you in on my secret, this is my favourite spot for my tea break'

(personal correspondence with Andrew Farish of Farish Associates, London)

17   This mode of globalising products and brands relies upon the visual iconography of 'the family of man' in which an underlying humanity unites people across different activities and diverse cultures and locations (see Szerszynski and Toogood, 2000: 224). For a discussion of Benetton's deployment of 'the family of man' iconography, see Celia Lury (1998) and Chapter 5 in this volume.

18   For a discussion of constructions of otherness in western consumer cultures, see Ahmed (2000), O'Barr (1994) and Lury, Chapter 5 in this volume.

19   However, as Ahmed notes, O'Barr has argued that 'the fascination with otherness within advertisements helps define the boundaries of a product's markets: that is, to define who is and is not the consumer audience' (O'Barr, 1994: 2, 12, quoted in Ahmed, 2000).

20   I am indebted to Sara Ahmed for drawing my attention to this material drawn from the work of her student, Jane Huntley (1996) on Boots' 'Global Collection' (see Ahmed, 2000). Notably, this collection of toiletries and cosmetics was discontinued in 1997 and was replaced by the 'Nature Collection' in 1998. The significance of the shift from the global to the natural as the signifier of desirable female bodycare will become clearer as the chapter demonstrates how nature gets the global inside us.

21   In this section I draw on the work of a Master's student, Marta Herrero, whose analysis of the Body Shop inspired the inclusion of Body Shop material in this chapter. The quotations from *The Body Shop Book* were first cited in her work (Herrero, 1996).

22   Again, I am grateful to Herrero's work for this insight.

23   For a discussion of the missionary discourse in the Body Shop's publicity material, see Ware (1992: 244).

24   For a discussion of hybridity in relation to globalisation see: Hall (1991a and b); Pieterse (1995); and Sum (1999). For more general discussions of the term 'hybridity', see Bhabha (1988, 1990, 1994); and Hall (1990). See also the special issue of *New Formations* on hybridity, no. 18, Winter 1992.

25   The Nature Company, which is a 'multi-national retail chain store that sells nature', is a 'global leader in world commerce' with outlets in the United States, Canada, Australia and Japan, with a share of more than '$200 of the $400 million in assets and $772 million' in sales of the CML conglomerate who own it (Smith, 1996: 36-7).

26   For a discussion of this simultaneous move back in time and across the globe, see McClintock (1995).

27   Thanks to Belinda Budge for providing me with materials from HarperCollins and drawing my attention to the significance of such a best-seller in the context of global culture.

28   A more ethnographic study of readers and users of self-health books and related practices would no doubt identify a number of ways in which people are partial subscribers to many of these philosophies, remaining critical of some elements and adopting others. Indeed, a number of people may be strategic or instrumental users who may try different health practices and continue with the ones that work, rather than the ones in which they profoundly believe (see Budd and Sharma, 1994; Sharma, 1992).

29   Book Marketing Limited is a market research company for and about the book trade.

30   This information was provided by Book Marketing Limited.

31   These figures were provided by Book Track in August 1999. The titles included in this survey were: Chopra (1989, 1993); Hay (1988, 1989); Herbert (1996); Holbeche (1997); Myss (1997); Siegel (1993); and Weil (1997).

32   For example, the Millennium Dome in Britain devotes a zone to each of the categories: mind, body, spirit. For more details see: http://greenwich2000.com/millenium/dome/zones/index.htm.

33   Said's work has been thoroughly critiqued by feminists for the ways in which it presents orientalism as a homogeneous discourse enunciated by a 'colonial subject that is unified, intentional and irredeemably male' (Lewis, 1996: 17).

34   For some of the more recent complications to this model of orientalism, see Jalan (1997) and Sum (1999).

35   For a full discussion of these changing belief systems in New Age philosophies, see Heelas (1996).

36   For a discussion of the place of synecdochical and analogous relations of nature and culture, see Strathern (1992a). Strathern herself uses the term 'merographic connection' to explore the part/whole relations of nature and culture:

> Culture and nature may be connected together as domains that run in analogous fashion insofar as each operates in a similar way according to laws of its own; at the same time, each is also connected to a whole range of phenomena which differentiate them. . . . This second connection makes the partial nature of the analogy obvious. It presupposes that one thing differs from another insofar as it belongs to or is part of something else. I call this kind of connection, link or relationship *merographic*.
>
> (1992a: 74, emphasis in original)

37   Colin Campbell's otherwise excellent argument ignores this and other feminist questions (such as those concerning sexuality, reproduction and gender), leaving his theory of easternisation strangely detached from the ways in which the East/West dichotomy has always been a gendered one.

38   This is not to deny that according to particular versions of Christianity, such as Quakerism, there has not also been a version of the light within all of us (see Heelas, 1996)

39   The full implications of the HIV/AIDS epidemic for the argument I am making here can only be gestured towards in this chapter. For further discussion of the cultural dimensions of this epidemic, see Carter and Watney (1989); Fee and Fox (1988); Patton (1990); Treichler (1988).

Chapter 5 /

The United Colors of Diversity
Essential and Inessential Culture

Celia Lury

In her 1994 presidential address to the American Anthropological Association, 'Culture and Our Discontents', Annette Weiner remarks,

> [U]nder the vast expansion of global capitalism and its accelerating volatility, culture has now become the contested focus of complex economic and political transformations. These shifts irrevocably alter the culture concept as anthropologists have used it in the past, and in less complex contexts.
>
> (1995: 18)

Weiner points out that 'the culture concept' now fits into global commodity production with ease: she notes that: 'Indiana Jones will soon meet Malinowski in the Trobiands on television, Balinese textiles are sold at Grateful Dead concerts, and The Dreaming becomes the new multicultural "high" gallery art,' adding that: 'Today most CEOs – many of whom probably learned about culture in our classes – know that to sell and produce globally, understanding culture is a priority.' She further argues that not only is culture now itself a commodity, but, 'in the vast circulation of goods and ideas where boundaries evaporate and space and time are electronically compressed, *things become different kinds of property*' (my emphasis). In this situation, she argues, anthropologists should not rely on 'the old appeal to the culture concept', but 're-think and reemphasize our long-established concern with difference and comparison' (1995: 19).

However, it is not only the culture concept that has been adopted and adapted by the 'manifold agents and interests' of globalising projects, but also the principles and practices of difference and comparison. As this book suggests, this is why the feminist analysis of gender as a principle of classification opens up new questions in the study of global nature, global culture. Consider the following claim: '[T]he differences between peoples and between individuals are humanity's most valuable resources. . . . Diversity is good' (*Colors* no. 4, spring/summer 1993). Diversity is invoked here by the fashion clothing company Benetton as the ultimate good in a global economy. In this chapter I will explore some of the ways in which the production of difference has become a means by which global companies such as Benetton can lay a proprietary claim to goodness itself. I will ask, can a fashion company really own the abstraction 'diversity'? And what is the nature of the relationality which this diversity encompasses? Is this an example of the move from kind to brand of which Donna Haraway (1997) speaks? And, if so, what are the implications of this for culture? Is it really the case that the culture concept has been irrevocably altered?

● ●   **Difference**

Benetton's claim to own goodness, if you believe their marketing personnel, has been accepted at face value by all of us: 'If you see five colours together and three different faces, you say "that's Benetton . . .", even if it really isn't' (Mattei, n.d.: 4) (Figure 5.1). However, it was not until 1984 that the imagery mentioned above, 'mainly colour and *joie de vivre*' (Mattei, n.d.: 4), first began to be used by Benetton to promote its clothing in international advertising campaigns; until then, the company's marketing had been primarily focussed on the representation of the products themselves. The press release accompanying the new campaign described the images as 'Groups of young people, of different races and sizes . . . photographed jumping and laughing' (quoted in Back and Quaade, 1993: 67). These images are still with us, although the slogan accompanying them changed from 'All the Colors of the World' to the now ubiquitous 'United Colors of Benetton' in 1985 (Figure 5.2). In these photographs, young people, sometimes waving national flags, or bedecked with national emblems such as stars and stripes, hammers and sickles, with accentuated, racially coded physical characteristics, parade in colourful clothes.

Unlike most other companies, Benetton produces its own advertising: the photographer Oliviero Toscani (himself the son of a photographer[1]) was, until recently, responsible both for Benetton's overall advertising strategy and for many specific images. Not only are all its campaigns made in-house, but there is also no market research done on new campaigns (O'Reilly, 1998: 4). Indeed, Toscani regards himself not as an advertiser, but as a journalist, a reporter/photographer. He says,

> I regard people not as consumers, but as human beings who live in a difficult world. So I have nothing in common with advertising people, whose job is to peddle happiness . . . .[2]
> I take pictures, I don't sell clothes.
>
> (1995: 20)

Toscani's avowed aim was to project a worldview through advertising: 'I am not here just to please my clients. To do that is a waste of everything. I don't want to have ideas: I have my own reality' (quoted in Back and Quaade, 1993: 66). The Benetton firm itself justifies its refusal to support charities on the grounds that its advertising promotes discussion of social issues.[3] What I will suggest here is that the 'reality' of a trained photographer should be a new humanity is not so surprising:

> Photography feeds back information about what it means to be a human being – not in this moment or in this time or among this class of people; it sweeps us up into its humanising grasp, leaving the viewer with a tentative and ambiguous understanding of the relations between the specific and the universal.
>
> (Rosenblum, 1991: 243)

Certainly Benetton's advertising is distinctive – at least in the UK – for its use of explicitly racially coded models: in general, advertising continues to be remarkably white.[4] In what ways, though, do Benetton's photographic images represent diversity? How do these pictures mediate the relations between the specific and the universal, the cultural and the natural? As Back and Quaade observe, the dominant theme of Benetton's campaign is 'the accentuation of difference coupled with a simple statement of transcendence and global unity' (1993: 68). Applying the work of Stuart Hall, Back and Quaade further argue that this accentuation of difference is generated within a grammar of race:

> [T]he overpowering reference point in their imagery is that *race is real*: racial archetypes provide the vehicle for their message, and racial common sense is overbearingly *present* in the 'United Colors' myth, such that the reality of race is legitimated in Benetton's discourse.
>
> (1993: 79, original emphasis)

However, while the legitimation of race in Benetton's campaigns seems beyond dispute, I want to suggest that the novel productivity of these images is missed if it is argued that racial difference is *naturalised'* here, if by that is meant that race is presented as an unchanging and eternal biological essence. 'Race', in this imagery, is not a matter of skin colour, of physical characteristics as the expression of a biological or natural essence, but rather of style, of the colour of skin, of colour itself as the medium of what might be called a second nature or, more provocatively, a *cultural essentialism*.

As noted above, 'The idea that's being sold is mainly colour and *joie de vivre* and can be recognised as such' (Mattei, n.d.: 4). So, for example, in Benetton promotional campaigns, young people are colour-coded: they are juxtaposed together to bring out colour contrasts as in Benetton outlets, in which stacks of jumpers are folded and piled up so as to seem as if they are paint colour charts (Figure 5.3). The overall effect of colour – not any particular colour but colour as such, colour as the medium of difference – is enhanced through the graduations in tone, the suggested compatibility of hues and contrasts in tints created by the endless repositioning of one shade against another. In the creation of this effect, the distinction between cloth and skin is eschewed (Figure 5.4). In a promotional illustration for tights (Figure 5.5), for example, the viewer is confronted by a series of legs in profile, each slightly different in shape ('different races and sizes'), completely encased in multi-coloured tights. Here, skin colour is not simply made invisible but displaced and reworked as a stylised act of choice: what colour is your skin going to be today? (The same choice was promoted by Crayola in the production of 'My World Colors', a box of sixteen crayons, supposedly representing the diversity of skin, hair and eye colours, from sepia to raw peach, of the peoples of a colouring-book world.) Similarly, in the publicity images adopted by Benetton of white and black faces daubed with brightly coloured sun-protection creams, the colour of skin is made up/out to be artificial. Race is not not 'real' here, but it is no longer founded in biology but in culture, that is, in culture as a second nature (despite or, rather, precisely because of the play on the white western depiction of 'primitive' tribes through the trope of face-painting).[5]

In yet another example, two eyes, of different colours, look out from a black face (Figure 5.6). The face is shot in such close-up that only the area surrounding the eyes is visible; the skin appears stretched to the edges of the image such that the contours of the face are flattened: its features and outline are hard to make out. Across this canvas is written, in white capitals, FABRICA, a word which, while taken from the Italian *fabbrica* (factory),[6] also draws on the idea of Andy Warhol's New York City Factory of the 1960s. It resonates with the association of fabrication for English speakers: skin is once again represented as cloth. The promotional slogan 'United Colors of Benetton' is attached, as always, to the side of the image, as if it were a label. This is, in Marilyn Strathern's phrase, nature 'enterprised up' (1992b): the natural, innate property and the artificial, cultural enhancement become one. Perusing Benetton's fashion catalogues, the viewer's gaze is drawn from shade to shade, obeying the textual laws of writing rather than the realist ones of verisimilitude, depth and figure. Biology is no longer a referent for race; rather, race is created in the colours constituted in the arbitrary relations between signifier and signified.

In fashion, what Walter Benjamin (1970) termed the phantasmagoria of commodities has always pressed close to the skin; clothing is quite literally at the borderline between subject and object, the cultural and the natural. Traversing this borderline is Benetton's problematic; indeed, it is the concern of a number of other fashion companies as well. For example, Moschino produced t-shirts with the slogan 'La nature c'est mieux que la couture'; while a brochure claims,

> In regards to prints we have chosen only nature themes taken photographically from scientific texts in an effort not to alter even in the slightest way the God-given details. It is a sign of respect for God that we enthusiastically have begun to show, and indeed, to stress, not only the conceptual and symbolic value of nature, but also to emphasize the incredible variety of shapes, designs, and arabesques . . . images that nature has always possessed.
>
> (Moschino promotional leaflet)

What distinguishes Benetton's iconography, however, is that it is explicitly concerned with a second nature, a nature that is a matter of choice.

● ●　**The Naturalness of Choice**

The representation of race as a choice (and of choice as a compulsory act) is central to Benetton's entire brand image and marketing strategy. This position is clearly elaborated in the fourth edition of *Colors*, a promotional magazine published by Benetton, the editor-in-chief of which was Toscani (although it is largely put together by the editor; in this case, Tibor Kalman). Here, the natural basis of race is both literally and figuratively deconstructed: photographic images of discrete parts of the bodies of people of different races – ears, noses, eyes, hair and blood – are juxtaposed, and the biological differences between different races are described and found to be either non-existent or unimportant (Figures 5.7 and 5.8). But this does not mean that race is done away with; rather, nature is enterprised up and skin colour, hair type and eye shape are represented as nothing more nor less than artifice, or the art of choice. Culture ('a few simple procedures') is represented as a natural extension of this artifice. There is, for example, a feature on,

> How to change your race. You mean you're not a round-eyed, blond haired, white skinned, perky nosed god or goddess? No problem. All you have to do is to undergo a few simple procedures.
>
> (*Colors* no. 4, spring/summer 1993)

Information, costings and advice on cosmetic surgery, make-up and hairstyling are provided, and there are photographic illustrations showing how a model, who is 'half black and half native American' can be made up/out to look realistically 'black', 'white' or 'oriental' (Figure 5.9). There are computer-generated images of a 'black' Queen Elizabeth II (Figure 5.10), a 'black' Arnold Schwarzenegger, a 'white' Spike Lee (Figure 5.11), an 'oriental' Pope John Paul II and a 'white' Michael Jackson (Figure 5.12).

This enterprising up is in part a consequence of the use of the cultural apparatus of photography. In her discussion *On Photography*, Susan Sontag notes that,

> according to one critic, the greatness of [the photographer] Paul Strand's pictures from the last period of his life . . . consists in the fact that 'his people, whether Bowery derelict, Mexican peon, New England farmer, Italian peasant, French artisan, Breton or Hebrides fisherman, Egyptian fellahoin, the village idiot or the great Picasso, are all touched by the same heroic quality – humanity.' What is this humanity? It is a quality things have in common when they are viewed as photographs.
>
> (1977: 110–11)

Figure 5.1

The text of this advertisement for Benetton asserts a parallel between a (Benetton) store and the world, while the image of racialised models presents this store/world in terms of diversity: a playful representation of difference.

Figure 5.2

A typical Benetton advertisement showing `Groups of young people, of different races and sizes. . . photographed jumping and laughing.'

Figure 5.3

Colours are continuously juxtaposed in Benetton iconography; in this photograph of Benetton clothing, colours and patterns cross-cut each other.

Figure 5.4

In this advertisement for swimsuits, the colours of the suits and the bodies that wear them are lined up with a formal symmetry. The black woman just to the left of the centre of the image is wearing a swimsuit whose multi-coloured stripes suggest that all colours – of both cloth and skin – could be displayed on one body.

5.1

5.2

5.4

5.3

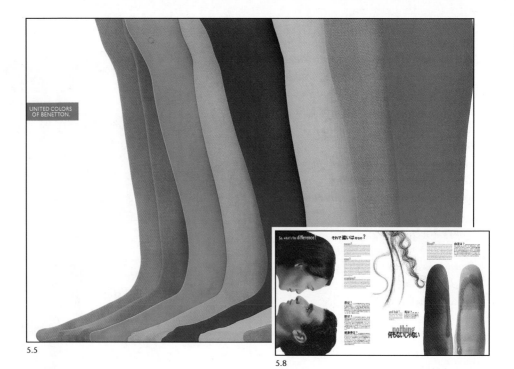

5.5

5.8

Figure 5.5

The use of multi-coloured legs standing in line in this advertisement for tights gives the impression that the colour of skin may not simply be hidden by clothes but revised, selected anew each morning.

Figure 5.8

The answer this article provides to its own question is `Nothing', yet the photographs of fingers, hair and heads suggest that there are visible differences.

Figure 5.6

In this advertisement, the analogy between skin and cloth which is the fashion manufacturing company Benetton's stock-in-trade is written across a black face in the word FABRICA, a reference to the English word `fabric' and the Italian word `fabbrica' (factory).

Figure 5.7

Juxtaposing a series of radically coded body-parts, an article in the promotional magazine Colors asks, `So, what's the difference?'

5.6

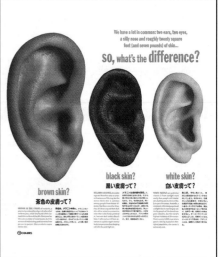

5.7

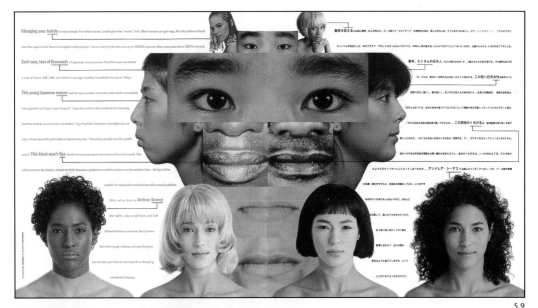

5.9

Figure 5.9

This double-page spread in Colors magazine offers advice on how to `change your race'. The layout makes use of symmetries and doublings to suggest the possibility of multiplying races.

Figure 5.10

A `black' Queen Elizabeth II provokes the viewer to consider the likelihood of black rule in the UK.

Figure 5.11

A `white' Spike Lee raises questions about racial politics.

Figure 5.12

A `white' Michael Jackson requires the viewer to do a double-take.

Figure 5.13

While the natural foundation of sex is typically effaced in the aesthetic equivalence of cloth and skin that is characteristic of Benetton iconography, it is reintroduced as a voluntaristic category of social being by means of the frisson associated with the representation of a `mixed-race' heterosexual coupling.

5.10

5.11

5.12

5.13

5.14

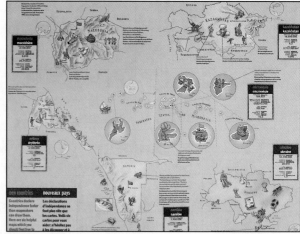

5.15

Figure 5.14

The use of a photograph of a Naked Neck chicken to illustrate the style of clothes designer Jean Paul Gaultier is a playful elaboration of the stylistic equivalence of cloth and skin (here, feathers) established in Benetton imagery.

Figure 5.15

This double-page spread in Colors magazine provides maps of `new countries' for the reader to `stick on out-dated atlases'. Benetton, a global company, must acknowledge national differences while seeking to transcend them.

Figure 5.16

This advertisement was one of a series which used photographs first used in photojournalism.

Figures 5.17, 5.18 and 5.19

In this tri-partite advertisement, Benetton positions itself as a kind of altruistic super-brand, capable of representing more important concerns than other, supposedly more sectarian, brands.

5.16

5.17

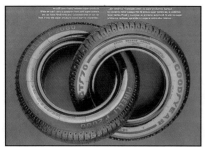

5.18

5.19

Benetton's advertising is self-consciously located in this photo-anthropological/ anthological tradition, an infamous example of which is 'The Family of Man', an exhibition created by Edward Steichen for the Museum of Modern Art in New York in 1955 (see Lury, 1998, for a detailed discussion of this exhibition and its relation to Benetton iconography). For example, one of Benetton's most widely discussed advertising images – that of a man dying of AIDS[7] – initially appeared in *Life*, while Benetton describes its promotional magazine *Colors* as 'a hipper *National Geographic*; an ironic *Life*; an amusing, irreverent, light-hearted, scholarly, over-the-top collection of off-beat and on-target stories about the people of the world' (Benetton press release, 1992, quoted in Back and Quaade, 1993: 78).[8] What is distinctive about the photography employed in the Benetton campaign, though, is that it proposes a panhumanity, a mix'n'match humanity which is animated by choice, the colourful play of difference.

'[C]olour and *joie de vivre*. . . . You like it because it reminds you of childhood, of well-defined, coloured pictures. Let us say that it is that type of style, more like printed paper, not necessarily real but neither totally unreal' (Mattei, n.d.: 4). In this not totally unreal reality, the aesthetic equivalence of cloth and skin as colours displaces not only the natural foundation of race, but also that of sex (Figure 5.13). This sidestepping is aided by the youthfulness of the models, one of the few constants in Benetton's universe of diversity, and a more general function of fashion itself. Of this function, Roland Barthes writes,

> Structurally, the junior is presented as the complex degree of the *feminine/ masculine*: it tends towards androgyny; but what is more remarkable in this new term is that it effaces sex to the advantage of age; this is, it seems, a profound process of fashion: it is age which is important not sex.
>
> (1985: 258)

At the same time that sex is displaced, however, just as with race, this categorial difference is also reworked and made newly productive. In the images which feature couples of both sexes many show individuals of visibly contrasting races. The *frisson* of a 'mixed-race', heterosexual coupling reintroduces sex as a voluntaristic category of social being. Fashion critics Evans and Thornton suggest that this tendency – submerging sexual difference to enable it to resurface as stylistic effect – was more generally visible in fashion imagery in the mid-1980s. They write,

> Much of the excitement of fashion imagery of this period, especially, . . . in those magazines aimed at both sexes, was achieved by the deployment of sexual difference as a pure signifier, detached from biological difference. In such images the play of clothing signifiers presented gender as just one term among many. However the *frisson* of excitement that accompanied these manipulations only existed because sexual difference waited in the wings, always ready to re-emerge as a 'naturalized' polarity – man or woman, precisely because sexual difference was construed as old-fashioned, it could be recycled in postmodern fashion.
>
> (1989: 64)

In later Benetton campaigns, the stylistic equivalence of skin and cloth as achieved in the photographic imagery of the fashion shots was extended to invert a whole series of natural relations and hierarchies. It lies behind the challenge to the biological basis of mothering in both the image of a black woman breast-feeding a white child, and in that of two women, one white, one black, holding an oriental child. It dissolves and reconstructs the natural distinction between animals and humans in the use of starkly black and starkly white animals – a white wolf 'kissing' a black sheep, a black horse mounting a white horse – as models, counterparts to the young people of different races in other images, and in the use of images of different breeds of chicken to illustrate the different styles of contemporary fashion designers. In the latter case, cloth and skin – or rather feathers – are represented as stylistically equivalent. Jean Paul Gaultier's designer style, for example, is represented by a Naked Neck chicken from Hungary: 'Modern yet nostalgic. Deliberate yet improvisational. Gaultier plays with contrasts in a peekaboo sable dress and thigh-high furry boots. The result is serious fun' (*Colors* no. 2, spring/summer 1992) (Figure 5.14).

The erasure of context in these pictures through the use of neutral colour backgrounds to the pages' ends is characteristic of Benetton iconography. This technique makes it difficult not only to contextualise the subjects of the photograph but also to identify their size, and the resulting effacement of scale and perspective reinforces the tendency for culture to displace nature, and for difference to be defined as a matter of choice. Toscani comments,

> I studied at the Zurich School of Applied Arts. They taught us the new photographic objectivity in the best Bauhaus tradition.
> . . . The white backgrounds of my photographs, the way the subjects all face the camera, the direct message, the strict objectivity – all that comes from Zurich.
> (1995: 20)

Through the consistent 'objectivity' of such stylistic devices, the context is represented as environment: the background is reduced to its capacity to act as a function of the subject, no more than a foil to give the subject its definition. In all these examples, then, the flattening of perspective and the playful juxtaposition of colour inverts and displaces the relations between figure and context, subject and object, culture and nature.

Diversity and Global Citizenship

And what of other forms of difference, the relations between the cultural and the social, the cultural and the political? National identity is subject to the same representational reconstruction as the categories of race, gender and species in Benetton advertising: it is accentuated, deconstructed and refigured. For example, in some of the early fashion brochures, caricatures of national costume are presented, national flags are waved, and campaigns allude to past and present national conflicts, including those between the USA and (what was then) the USSR, Germany and Israel, Greece and Turkey, Argentina and Britain. In such images, the tag-line 'United Colors of Benetton' symbolises the antithesis of conflict, and becomes the expression of unity and the nurturer of internationalism. Describing the Benetton philosophy, Toscani says,

> Our basic idea is always the same; we are all equal. There is no reason to slaughter each other, to fight, not even to hate each other. We can wear whatever we want, whatever colours we want – just live.
>
> (cited in Corrias, 1993: 16)

In a move paralleling the culturalisation of race, sex and species, social and political differences too are coloured: in a cartoon in *News* (another Benetton promotional magazine), Luciano Benetton, who was a member of the Italian parliament as republican senator for Treviso for a couple of years, remarks that: 'Basically, Parliament is like my advertising campaigns: there are reds, whites, greens, pinks, blacks.'

Clearly, Luciano lives on the blue planet discussed in Chapter 1, the world in which the elements of national cultures, including tradition, ritual and cuisine, can be recombined according to an aesthetics of pseudo-shock. In a feature on food, dishes from around the world are shown with insects (a source of protein described as 'nutritious' and 'plentiful') substituted for one of their traditional ingredients. Wax worms in mango salsa, crickets in bread or pecan pie, water bugs in paella, and agave worms in mescal are all illustrated. A featured letter from a reader of *Colors* renounces the redundant ties of nationality and expresses the principles of the new Benetton communities of taste: 'Hi, My father's Jamaican. My mother's Quebecois. I'm Canadian. I live in Japan. I'd like to live in a country of generous coffee cups.' The blue planet is a world in which 'everybody gets their own country' according to their taste: suggestions include, 'The country of people who squeeze toothpaste tubes from the middle? The country of people nostalgic for Communism?' One issue of *Colors* (no. 3, fall/winter, 1992), which describes itself as a 'global magazine about local cultures', comes complete with cut-out 'new' countries to stick on out-dated atlases, together with a guide to their national styles (Figure 5.15). The result is a new world, across the face of which Benetton outlets are scattered:

> [I]magine a life-size Risiko board, with an infinite series of little green flags stuck in all over the world. Or better, as suggested by the title [Under the sign of Benetton], of a sky full of stars linked in a secret drawing which, like an acrostic, form the four words UNITED COLORS OF BENETTON. Seen from below they certainly all seem the same, catapaulted by who knows what magic from a subterranean forge to the most remote corners of the sky. . . . Perhaps you have been into some, you certainly have stopped at other similar ones, while you knew nothing about the others, but you imagined their existence when buying a jacket or jumper, you had the strange sensation of not being alone: and perhaps at the same moment,

on the other side of the world, someone like you was buying the same jacket or jumper and, looking in the mirror to see how it looked, was smiling at you unseen. . . .

(*News*, undated, p. 8)

This is a planet in which 'the other side of the world' is just behind the mirror, in which, as Jean Baudrillard says, we have reached,

the last stage of the social relation . . . which is no longer one of persuasion (the classical age of propaganda, ideology, of publicity, etc.) but one of deterrence: 'YOU are information, you are the social, you are the event, you are involved, you have the word, etc.' An about-face through which it becomes impossible to locate one instance of the model, of power, of the gaze, of the medium itself, because you are always already on the other side. No more subject, no more focal point, no more center or periphery: pure flexion or circular inflexion.

(1994a: 29)

In a further campaign, in which images from photo-documentary and news genres are incorporated, life itself is culturalised. These now infamous images – a duck covered in oil, a dying AIDS patient, a burning car in a street, the shrouded body of a bloody corpse after a Mafia killing, and a black soldier holding a human femur behind his back with a Kalashnikov rifle hanging from his shoulder (Figure 5.16) – show images of life, animal and human, in situations of conflict, threat and disaster. Falk describes these images as operating 'primarily through non-sublimated shock-effects' (1996: 70) while Back and Quaade note, the 'over-riding theme is the fetishisation of images of abject catastrophe' (1993: 74). In these examples, the condensed-to-the-moment-of-catastrophe narrative space-time frame of these images disembeds them from specific historical, political and natural contexts (indeed, such contexts would appear parochial) and re-embeds them in apocalyptic time, in the photographic time of exposure of a planet facing global dangers.[9] These figures are out-contextualised representatives of life itself – how else to explain the image of a new-born baby in this series? – and only the United Colors of Benetton slogan offers millenarian hopes of new foundations in the face of impending disaster.

Difference and the Multicultural Planet

Sontag has suggested that, 'By disclosing the thingness of human beings, the human-ness of things, photography transforms reality into a tautology' (1977: 110–11). In Benetton's imagery, life itself is defined in terms of diversity: at the same time what all life has in common on the Benetton planet is diversity. This, I suggest, is the defining tautology of Benetton's photographic reality:

Wherever we go, we hope to find people and things we never even dreamed existed. We hope that diversity on this planet, whether cultural or biological, won't disappear before we (and you) (and everyone else) discover it and learn to appreciate and preserve it.

(Colors no. 4, spring/summer 1993)

The imagery of Benetton sets in motion a quest in search of a diverse reality, cultural and natural:

A guy sells incense, children beg, a parked car spills over with vegetables for sale, lovers kiss good-bye, a skinny man raves about salvation, a vendor serves steamed tripe to a hurried customer, someone sprawls face down on the sidewalk, a drug dealer chants 'loose joints' quietly to no one in particular, a woman floats by balancing a bag of clothing on her head, people bump, a little girl buys spices for her mother, activists clutching clipboards ask for signatures, a moto-taxi barely misses a distracted delivery boy, five kids play soccer and dodge cars, a wild-eyed girl tap dances for money, an old woman drags a shopping cart, a cat paces in search of something to eat, a baby stroller weaves its way through a crowd, three girls all dressed the same burst out laughing, a junk seller pushes his cart and sings of his wares, the wind lifts a swirl of dust, cigarette butts and newspaper, the smell of exhaust and roasted chestnuts rises with it. . . .

(Colors no. 5, autumn 1993)

This quest will simultaneously entail negotiating the 'simplifications' of reality and setting aside the false distinction between the real and the fake.

On the one hand, Benetton itself poses the question of whether the diversity it espouses exists in reality, whether the relations of equivalence it proposes between skin and cloth work in the real world. For example, the writers of *Colors* ask themselves, can 'the desire of Africans to look more European' be equated with 'the desire of Europeans to look more African'? The answer they give is,

Yes and no. Even if couture is sometimes inspired by third world styles, the rules about money and desirability are still made by first world media. The rules, in other words, are made by and for money, power (and, more often than not, white skin).

(Colors no. 4, spring/summer, 1993)

The problems of money, power and race, the editorial of *Colors* suggests, are a consequence of 'simplification', an anthropological constant of humankind, exemplified by nationalist movements and multinational corporations. The solution is to preserve diversity through the choice of identifying with Benetton's imagined reality, the diversity of colour.[10]

Yet, on the other hand, Benetton also asks how this reality is to be recognised when 'three percent of everything in the world is fake' and the brandname's fake counterpart is a 'sort of evil twin in the marketplace of fakes' (*Colors* no. 2, spring 1992). The answer it provides to its own question is that this distinction is itself false. Jean Baudrillard is introduced as 'the French philosopher' to support the view that '"The fake isn't fake anymore." What [Baudrillard's] also saying is that the real isn't real.' Counterfeit products, we are told, can give the same 'warm feeling' of prestige as the real ones: 'Which leads to the conclusion that only three percent of everything in the world is real. But who's to say which three percent that would be?'. Paradoxically, it is not Benetton's products that offer another, more real reality (they might as well be fake), but its advertising. It is no surprise then to hear one-time Chief Executive Officer, Aldo Palmeri, claim, 'Today our advertising can actually be considered a company product' (*News* undated: 3). Becoming your own unique self and thus being part of the creation of diversity is what you gain access to when you support Benetton advertising by buying its products. The products themselves are rendered transparent, invisible:

> [Y]ou're not what you wear but you wear what you are. If we really want to define the Benetton style we can say that it is a 'non-style'; a positive identification or, better, a 'clear' style. It doesn't hide you, it shows you off.
>
> (Mattei, n.d.: 4)

But what is the nature of this 'positive' identification? What kind of citizenship is on offer for the inhabitants of the blue planet?

In the place of the simplifications of reality, the arbitrary distinction between the fake and the real, Benetton proposes the positive principle of diversity. This principle makes possible a series of constantly changing analogies between the animate and inanimate, animal and human, the individual and the species: between the natural and the cultural; for example:

> The 12 million people of Bombay live and work in such close quarters that the whole city feels like one huge, vibrant living creature. . . .
>
> (*Colors* no. 4, spring/summer 1993)

> [The city of Bombay] is a bit like a forest; it appears to be wild and disorganised, but actually has a very complex ecology. . . .
>
> (*Colors* no. 4, spring/summer 1993)

> Of the estimated 10 million or more species on earth, we have identified 1.4 million. And every time we lose one, we lose its potential medicinal or nutritional value, and we lose the genetic information it contains. Every plant and animal on earth, no matter how small, is a text revealing some of the secrets of life. The earth's unnamed creatures are like a library of great books we haven't gotten around to reading yet. We need to value and protect biologically rich habitats. . . . The first step is to assign nicknames. Let's start with that copepod on the right; call her Teensy, Coco or Cipollina. . . .
>
> (*Colors* no. 4, spring/summer 1993)

At first glance, diversity is exemplified here by numbers, numbers of people, of species, but counting is simply one instance of coding difference, of making generic distinctions, just as numbering ('Of the estimated 10 million or more species on earth, we have identified 1.4 million'), naming ('The first step is to assign nicknames. Let's start with that copepod on the right; call her Teensy, Coco or Cipollina') and colouring ('The blue family') are other instances. Diversity, however, is a coding of these different orders or genres (painting by numbers, perhaps); this reflexivity upon difference is the animating principle of Benetton's technique of comparison.[11]

Indeed, reflexivity is an inevitable component of the writerly texts of Benetton promotions. Self-consciousness is, for example, evident in the publication of the magazines referred to earlier: *Colors* and *News*. The former, 'a magazine about the rest of the world', presents news value, information about the environment, teen idols, condoms, life forms under threat, computer sex, food, fat, marriage and 'tribes' of people from all over the globe as advertising for Benetton. Back and Quaade write,

> Unlike conventional newspapers, where advertising is carried as an income-generated appendix to the news, *Colors* uses its news as Benetton's advertising. The news stories are elided with the philosophy of the paper, which is, in turn, associated with the brand quality of its products.
>
> (1993: 77)

The latter, what Benetton calls *News*, contains information about its marketing strategy, including a catalogue of commentary, both critical and complimentary, about past advertising campaigns, cartoons, interviews with marketing personnel (cosmopolitan by 'bent' and 'necessity') and information about new products and sponsored sports personalities and teams. Such self-conscious generic transgression is also a part of some of its more recent advertising campaigns which incorporate images from photo-documentary and news media; this intertextuality is a logical part of the brand image of a self-conscious aesthetics. In some respects it can be seen as a radical move within advertising discourse, since advertisers have conventionally adopted an appeasing address to the consumer, although Falk (1996) suggests that this address is now being displaced by a more confrontational approach. Other parts of the media, however, have frequently taken some pleasure in reporting the problems raised by such a strategy. So, for example, a feature in the *Media Guardian* suggests that 'one could be forgiven for thinking that the whole ad industry was suffering from a mass outbreak of Tourette's syndrome, whereby those afflicted blurt out obscenities in public' (Bell, 1995: 13).

However, as a number of critics (Gaines, 1991; Mellencamp, 1990b) have argued, there is also a tendency in television to use tropes and modes of signification which make explicit the characteristic of generic transgression. From this point of view, the presentation by Benetton of advertising as information rather than entertainment is not surprising since, as Mary Ann Doane notes, 'Information, unlike narrative, is not chained to a particular organization of the signifier or a specific style of address. Antithetical modes reside side by side' (1990: 224). Reflexivity, then, is a mobilising technique which enables codes to be juxtaposed, compared and equalised, and for analogies to be drawn between codes across categories, for example between nature and culture. In this sense, reflexivity underpins a cartography that flattens differences between natural, social and political codes by removing what Marilyn Strathern calls the perspective of partiality. An example of culture as representation, the use of colour as the medium of this diversity does not seek to explain similarity and difference; rather, as Strathern writes, it gives a 'descriptive purchase on the way similarities and differences are made apparent' (1995b: 156). This purchase – this way of making comparisons, drawing resemblances and finding affinities – is what gives value to the brand.

Cultural Essentialism

What I have called cultural essentialism here is in many ways similar to other contemporary 'uses of culture'. Such uses, as Part One in this book argues, parallel many past uses of nature; they mimic the properties of nature while allowing a distinction to be drawn between nature and culture, thus distancing cultural essentialism from many of the social and political criticisms that biological essentialism has received. Nevertheless, the paradoxical implications of cultural essentialism for the fundamental categories, types or genres of national political life are beginning to emerge. In relation to race, for example, Martin Barker (1984) describes what he sees as the specifically cultural dimensions of racism in contemporary Britain, while Verena Stolcke suggests that an earlier nationalist version of racism is being displaced by xenophobia in many European countries today. She argues that,

> It may no longer be licit nor appropriate to categorize, bound and/or disqualify peoples or individual persons on purely racist grounds but there still remains cultural diversity as the raw material out of which a novel doctrine of exclusions can be construed by reifying culture in a new naturalistic ideological twist. In the global village disjointed by multiple national conflicts it is cultural identity and diversity which have become charged with new symbolic and natural meaning. Yet . . . cultural fundamentalism is not simply a new racism in disguise. Instead, cultural fundamentalism which is grounded in an essentialist notion of culture is a specific ideological response to a specific problem, namely that posed by foreigners 'in our midst'.

(1993: 8)

Similarly, Gayatri Spivak argues 'in the New World Order – or hot peace – the hyphen between nation and state comes looser than usual; and . . . in that gap fundamentalisms fester' (1999: 373).

In these analyses, culture is seen to be deployed as a fixed and fixing source of identity in ways which reproduce the previously naturalised hierarchies and exclusions of national citizenship and cross-national migration. However, other contemporary uses of the culture concept propose a more liberal tolerance of the differences that culture makes. A recent report from UNESCO, *The Multi-Cultural Planet*, insists that 'if culture is part of the problem, it is also our key to a solution' (1993: x).[12] The writers of the UNESCO report believe that recognising 'our shared vulnerability' will lead to a 'new historical beginning, a multicultural springtime, the humanist reflection of the movement from a bipolar world to a multipolar world' (1993: x, xi). The report suggests: 'The end of the Cold War has been interpreted by some as "the end of history", but the opposite may be true for culture' (1993: x–xi). The culture that is just beginning has much in common with nature, however: 'The destruction of one culture by another is just as undesirable as the extinction of a living species: both processes diminish the differentiation that, together with integration, is the precondition of all growth and development' (1993: 7).

In the opinion of the 'UNESCO international expert group', cultural development underpins both unity and diversity. The report's writers believe that '[t]he challenge of balancing the diversity of contemporary societies with a new level of unity is a cultural challenge *par excellence*' (1993: 5). Adopting the model of culture as a natural, organic system they argue that,

> If systems, whether natural or human, are to survive and develop, their interactions must be harmonized. If and when they are, a new level of order emerges. In nature, this is the cellular level for molecules, the organic level for cells, and the social and ecological level for organisms. In the human world the next level of order is the global. Unity on the global level need not diminish diversity on national, sub-national and regional levels. On the contrary, national, local and regional diversity is an enduring precondition of global-level integration.
>
> (1993: 2-3)

The report goes on to suggest that 'the search for peace, for understanding, for solidarity, for unity, is ultimately a search for the harmonious co-ordination of diversity'. UNESCO identifies its own role in this search in the following terms:

> UNESCO, the world body with a specific mandate to investigate and further the role of culture in human affairs, took a leading role. . . . Its principal objective, in addition to the stimulation of creative skills and culture in general, is to reinforce the emerging emphasis on culture in the processes of development.
>
> (1993: 6–7)

Here it becomes clear that this use of culture concept is intricately connected to the project of managing the global, and that this project is still sustained by what Spivak calls 'the great narrative of Development' (1999: 371):[13]

> On a crowded planet there is one future for all, or no future for any. The common future for humanity cannot be diverse without co-ordination, nor can it be united without diversity.
>
> (1993: 203)

However, although both UNESCO and Benetton assert the legitimacy of their own claims to create (cultural) order at the global level, they differ in the strategies they adopt to predict the future. While UNESCO believes that 'today the diversity of societies is insufficiently matched by their unity' and seeks to further unity by encouraging interaction, liberal tolerance and humanistic education, Benetton suggests that diversity is under threat. Moreover, the diversity Benetton seeks to preserve from extinction is not fixed, as are the uses of culture as difference identified by Barker and Stolcke; indeed, not only is it not fixed, it is, 'naturally', in flux. There is no essential stability or limit to this diversity; rather, its distinctive essence is reflexivity, constant movement and metamorphosis.

As noted above, the very goodness of the diversity of Benetton's second nature arises precisely from the fact that its differences are arbitrary (whereas those of reality or first nature are not). This arbitrariness enables Benetton to insist on the changeability of its colours, while standardising such changes transnationally. It is precisely this management of change through the ability to erase boundaries and draw them anew, to construct an ever-changing fixity, what has been called *generic estrangement* (Jameson, 1991), that characterises Benetton's use of the reflexive principles of difference and comparison. As such, the diversity that is the Benetton brand identity[14] is an exemplar of the move from kind to brand in the vampire culture of which Haraway (1997) speaks, for it is a product of the denaturalisation or estrangement of genre, kind or type.

The possibility of diversity being taken up as a form of (global) citizenship may be understood in the context of a history of consumer culture, in which, as Lauren Berlant argues is the case in the USA, product consciousness and brands became 'so crucial a part of national history and popular self-identity that the public's relation to business took on a patriotic value' (1993: 182). Berlant's argument hinges on the view that in US American culture legitimacy derives from the individual's privilege to suppress and deny the body, a convention that was initially instituted through the fetishisation of an abstract or 'artificial' person in constitutional law. This abstraction was the means by which whiteness and maleness were established as simultaneously 'nothing' and 'everything'. Since the commodity is the modern embodiment of the legitimate 'artificial person', US Americans, she argues, have now come to equate identification with the commodity as a form of citizenship, and it is this form which offers the most legitimate expression of the contemporary US American fantasy of bodily transformation. In brief:

> [I]n modern America, the artificial legitimacy of the citizen has merged with the commodity form: its autonomy, its phantasmatic freedom from its own history, seem to invest it with the power to transmit its aura, its body to consumers.
>
> (1993: 200)

Much of the discussion so far can be recast in these terms: the difference of diversity can be seen as the defining feature of the artificial personality that is the Benetton brand. As such, it offers what Berlant calls 'the corporeal logic of an other, or a fantasy of that logic, and [the possibility of] adopting it as a prosthesis' (1993: 200). The potentially hazardous entry into global public space, a time of exposure, is made safe by the prophylaxis of commodity citizenship. In this respect global brands such as Benetton contribute to what Wendy Brown has described as 'the renaturalization of capitalism that can be said to have marked progressive discourse since the 1970s' (1995: 60). Brown's argument here is that when not only the economic inequalities but also the 'other injuries to the human body and psyche enacted by capitalism . . . are discursively normalized and thus depoliticized, other markers of social difference may come to bear an inordinate weight' (1995: 60). In this respect, the iconography of the Benetton brand – with its explicit concern with markers of difference, and, as will be discussed later, its recognition of suffering and the offer of salvation – may share more than is easily acknowledged with contemporary political movements articulated in terms of politicised identity. For Brown, the enunciation of politicised identities through race, gender and sexuality involves a hidden reliance upon a white masculine, middle-class ideal. Non-class identities, she suggests, refer indirectly to this ideal for proof of their exclusion or injury; it provides the potency and poignancy of their claims. What this suggests for the argument being put forward here is that while the renaturalisation of capitalism as part of a global project may involve the denaturalisation of genre, kind or type by the brand Benetton, there remains an unacknowledged dependence upon class as an internal standard. This dependence is not completely invisible, however, for it re-emerges in the taken-for-grantedness of choice and self-making.

Thus it is important to remind ourselves here of the insistence on change-ability, the arbitrariness of difference, required by Benetton in the creation of its brand identity, for it relies on the operation of choice, of reflexivity, a self-conscious decision-making in which the global citizen's resolution is established. Indeed the importance of choice to the Benetton brand suggests that the renaturalisation of capitalism of which Brown speaks is more accurately understood in terms of its culturalisation. While in contrast with the unchosen, which both Benedict Anderson (1983) and Homi Bhabha (1993) argue underpins the naturalness of national identity, the label Benetton does not simply offer the chosen – or, rather, choice itself – as the origin of the imagined community of global citizenship, but renders choice itself a necessity. In other words, in place of the determining power of the indeterminate that Bhabha identifies in stories of national origins, Benetton insists upon the compulsion of choice or the voluntary as security for its global project. Nowhere is this more clear than in the images of catastrophe and disaster which Benetton has employed in its advertising.

Suffering and Salvation

In the emergence of global nature, global culture, the adoption of images of life and death, of suffering or 'catastrophe aesthetics' (Falk, 1996), has a special place. In establishing its brand identity, Benetton can be seen to call upon what Kleinman and Kleinman call 'a master subject of our mediatized times' (1996: 1). They write,

> Images of suffering are appropriated to appeal emotionally and morally both to global audiences and to local populations. Indeed, those images have become an important part of the media. As 'infotainment' on the nightly news, images of victims are commercialized; they are taken up into processes of global marketing and business competition. The existential appeal of human experiences, their potential to mobilize popular sentiment and collective action, and even their capability to witness or offer testimony are now available for gaining market share. Suffering, 'though at a distance,' as the French sociologist Luc Boltanski tellingly expresses it, is routinely appropriated in American popular culture, which is a leading edge of global popular culture.
>
> (1996: 1–2)

More succinctly, they note, 'Images of trauma are part of our political economy' (1996: 8), 'a postmodern hallmark' (1996: 10).[15] In a similar tone, Baudrillard declares: 'We must today denounce the moral and sentimental exploitation of . . . poverty – charity cannibalism being worse than oppressive violence' (1994b: 66). While Kleinman and Kleinman argue that we live in a world characterised by a mixture of 'moral failures and global commerce', a time which 'calls for images' (1996: 7), Baudrillard claims that the West needs 'the other half's human and natural catastrophes . . . which serve us as an aphrodisiac and hallucinogen' (1994b: 68). Indeed, so great is the West's need for catastrophe, he claims, that we manufacture our own.

Certainly, the use of such images by Benetton – presumably a prime instance of what Baudrillard calls the 'disaster show' – appears to resonate at all sorts of levels (producing strong reactions, both negative and positive), and thus can be seen as an effective attempt to undermine what Baudrillard calls the 'other half's . . . monopoly of the catastrophe weapon' and its potential to detonate the global project. The Benetton imagery is specifically addressed to the young people of that half of the world which has run 'out of emptiness', for whom 'the excess of means over ends' is producing a 'psychodrama of congestion, super-abundance, neurosis and the breaking of blood vessels' (Baudrillard, 1994b: 71); as such, it speaks to the desire both to be elsewhere, to leave one's family (perhaps even to leave 'the family of man'), and to do something, to make a difference. In Berlant's terms, Benetton's imagery offers the 'fantasies of disembodiment, self-abstraction, invisibility' (1993: 177) that appeal to those conventionally excluded from citizenship and national public space in the West. In this sense, it represents an instance of what Bronislaw Szerszynski (1996) tellingly calls the contemporary 'varieties of ecological piety' and is, as Michael Shapiro (1994) puts it, 'Benetton's ecumenical fantasy'.

In general terms, as Deirdre Boden remarks, the Benetton catastrophe images depict 'the intensity of immediate experience in the face of globalizing extensivity'.[16] The purchase of this intensity is tied not only to fears of suffering but also to changing understandings of life and death in the context of a globalising project. In an article written nearly thirty years ago, Parsons et al. argue that what appears as a denial of death in contemporary western societies is actually an indication 'of not knowing quite what to say or do and thus minimizing overt expression or action' (1972: 368). Benetton speaks to this growing uncertainty, setting itself up as one form of expression, and offering the possibility of solace. So, for example, Toscani asserts that to capture the death scene of a man suffering from AIDS is to show 'the real thing' and affirms the 'simple truth' that 'to die is to die' (quoted in Falk, 1996: 72), while the cover text to one edition of *Colors* reads: 'Let's talk about fashion – let's talk about sex – let's talk about death – let's talk about AIDS' (quoted in Falk, 1996: 76). In 'talking' in this way, Benetton, the fashion clothing company, is part of a growing industry of experts who, alongside the medical profession, are redefining life and death, speaking to 'the mediatized human victim we all are in different ways' (Massumi, cited in Shapiro, 1994: 451); like the ecological piety of which Szerszynski speaks, its imagery functions 'to stabilise self and society in a world understood as permeated with risk and hazard' (1996: 10).

Choose Life or Catastrophe as Progress

Writing in the early 1970s, Parsons et al. identified an 'evolution of medicine from an ethic based on the unconditional "sanctity of life" to one premised on the "quality of life"' (1972: 409); with this shift, they argue, goes a more 'operational view of death' (1972: 408). Other writers concur: we have now reached a situation in which, according to Zygmunt Bauman, '[d]eath as such is inevitable; but each specific instance of death is contingent' (1992: 5). An individual does not simply die, but rather dies 'because' of something, something that might be avoided, prevented or, at the very least, postponed. As a consequence, *life itself becomes a choice*. Bauman further identifies a range of techniques or policies of survivalism in Euro-American societies which draw on and extend the ways of understanding death identified by Parsons, Fox and Lidz (1972). These include: religious belief in the transcendence of the limitations imposed by the body; collective designs, such as nationalism, that contemplate the introduction and management of a total order in exchange for a guarantee of the propriety of individual death; the quest for a partner in love who, as a mirror, can offer a space of transcendence; and, most significantly for this discussion, contemporary techniques of self-care, lifestyle or experimentation.

Bauman further argues that salvation is now not to be arrived at through the 'entry' of death into an after-life, for death is no longer, as it was in more religious times, a sacrifice, an act of reciprocity for the gift of life, but only an 'exit'. Now, salvation is to be reached through strategies of survival, and what is significant about the contemporary notion of survival is that it is targeted on others, not on the self: 'We never live through our own death; but we do live through the death of others, and their death gives meaning to our success: we are *still* alive' (Bauman, 1992: 10, original emphasis). The personal achievement of self-preservation can be grasped only as a social relation of survival, and this, Bauman argues, is a social relation that is mediated by lifestyle, the choices of consumption and the instrumentalisation of identity. The gift of life is now a different kind of thing, more like a commodity. It is this shift that has made it possible for Benetton to insert itself in the chain of giving and taking (life), of credit and debt, of buying and selling.

More generally it has been suggested that self-preservation and consumption are now not merely linked for Euro-Americans, but operate in an analogous fashion. Thus, in an article discussing Andy Warhol's 'Disaster Series', Jonathan Flatley argues that the 'logic of disaster is a logic of consumption' (1996: 121) on the basis that disaster mediates between embodiment and abstraction in an analogous way to consumption. Both in witnessing the public spectacle of disaster and in the practices of consuming, Flatley suggests, the individual enters into a mournful fantasy of self-abstraction. Both sets of practices thus promise a limited possibility of managing one's embodiment, operating not only as prosthesis, enabling the individual to enter into the public sphere, but also as prophylaxis, separating the image from the body.

The survival policies that Bauman presents can be examined not only in terms of exchange, but also in terms of time and space. Indeed, he suggests that they can be ordered so as to expose 'the gradual shrinking of the space in which the thrust to immortality is vested'. However, the last strategy noted above – contemporary techniques of self-care, lifestyle or experimentation – shows 'an amazing capacity for expansion' (1992: 18). According to Bauman, what is involved here is,

> an attempt to belie the ultimate limits of the body by breaking, successively, its *currently* encountered, *specific* limitations. . . . By the same token, the impossible task of escaping the mortality of the body is never allowed to be encountered in its awesome totality, as it is split into a never-ending series of concrete challenges, reduced to a manageable, and hence realistic size. The time dimension of transcendence is turning here into a spatial issue: stretching the *span of life* is turned into the effort to stretch the *capacity to live*. Time all but disappears: it has been reduced and flattened out of existence. . . .
>
> (1992: 18–19, original emphasis)

In the terms of this last survival policy, the individual subject, forced by the fear of death to withdraw into itself, takes on the 'consuming task of transcending the technical capacity for living' (1992: 19); the individual is absorbed in the life-long labour of the defence of health, construing life as a process of self-constitution (see Chapter 4). He or she seeks to do so by stretching the capacity to live, expanding global nature, global culture, abolishing the future, which can no longer be colonised by planning, probability and responsibility and attempts to replace the time of social and political welfare with a multitude of individual occurrences, each with its own cause, the locus of personal experimentation or choice.

It is in relation to this last strategy that Benetton's iconography can be understood,[17] for it presents the compulsion to choose that underpins global citizenship: if the individual does not choose survival in the face of the free-floating anxiety which Benetton depicts, then he or she must face death as an exit alone. That Benetton's adoption of the survival strategy shows an 'amazing capacity for expansion' is indicated by the ways in which the caption 'United Colors of Benetton' can be illustrated by almost any image. Toscani himself argues that,

> today, language is dying and the language of images is the new language. There are things we can't talk about any more – it's like Babel, we are trying to explain ourselves constantly in language about a certain fact that we can't really explain until we have seen a picture. There is a reality, a truth in pictures that we don't get any more through the traditional language.
>
> (quoted in Popham, 1993: 26)

What I want to suggest, though, is that it is not simply 'pictures' in general that proffer this truth, but the photographic image in particular, for the photograph always operates through 'the narrowing down of the present'.

As Barthes (1981) and others have noted, the photograph 'takes' time, it declares, 'this will have been'. In the images of catastrophe, Benetton enters this time, the time of 'this will have been', and holds it open. This holding open occurs in what Paul Virilio (1994) calls the time of exposure, the time that had previously been so short that it seemed to be no time at all, the flash of an instant. However, in the Benetton images, the tense that defines the photograph, the future perfect is suspended; the instant is now made visible, and the viewer is offered the opportunity to participate in the perfection of the past. As Toscani remarks,

> [B]eing a photographer is not just pressing a shutter – it is much more complex. When you look in the viewfinder, you make a choice of space, dimension, perspective, colour and situation. Today I think you can also take a picture without having a camera, by putting together certain situations which become a picture.
>
> (quoted in Popham, 1993: 27)

As noted above, however, entry into the time of exposure is frightening as well as exhilarating: the global citizen may feel unable to face the exigencies of surviving in no/w/here alone (Friedland and Boden, 1994): as Bauman puts it, 'loneliness is frightening and unbearable, because of my uncertainty as to how adequate are the weapons I deploy to fight off the threats to my body' (1992: 20). In the images described here, though, Benetton is able to both represent and assuage this loneliness. In this way, the Benetton brand offers salvation.[18] While the future on offer here may be 'increasingly short-term' (Lowenthal, 1995: 391), the individual is offered membership of a collectivity on a global scale, and the flattening of existence is rendered manageable.

Once again, the powers of photography to intervene in time are important in securing this effect. The hypersemioticisation of the image that is an effect of the photograph's arrest of time holds the viewer in stasis, exposed to what might be, what is – both now and here and no/w/here. But more than this. Benetton's ability to stretch the capacity to live, to expand space, is in part effected by its adoption not simply of images of catastrophe, but of the temporality of catastrophe as its definitive mode of address. The claim here, then, is that Benetton's use of catastrophe is performing similar functions in relation to an imaginary global public or community to those performed by liberal notions of progress and development in relation to the imagined community of the nation.

For Walter Benjamin, that catastrophe is the culmination of progress is not surprising: 'The concept of progress is to be grounded in the idea of catastrophe. That things "just go on" *is* the catastrophe' (quoted in Buck-Morss, 1989: 228–9, original emphasis). However, what has changed in global nature, global culture is *how* things 'just go on'. What the contemporary uses of the notion of catastrophe make it possible to see are the previously unforeseen, unintended consequences of 'going on': the notion of catastrophe is deployed to describe 'jump behaviour', sudden discontinuities within a gradually changing system (Doane, 1990; Mellencamp, 1990b).[19] Indeed, catastrophe theory seeks to provide a means not just of seeing, but of mapping the discontinuous instance, the chance occurrence, *without reducing its arbitrariness or indeterminancy*. Mary Ann Doane writes,

> The etymological specification of catastrophe as the overturning of a given situation anticipates its more formal delineation by catastrophe theory. Here, catastrophe is defined as unexpected discontinuity in an otherwise continuous system.
>
> . . . [Catastrophe theory] confronts the indeterminable without attempting to reduce it to a set of determinations. . . . In this sense, television is a kind of catastrophic machine, continually corroborating its own signifying problematic – a problematic of discontinuity and indeterminancy . . . .
>
> (1990: 228, 234)

Benetton too can be seen as a catastrophic machine (a jump(er) machine) in that it too manufactures a problematic of discontinuity and indeterminancy. However, in doing so, it employs the still image, the photograph, and this in part explains the distinctiveness of Benetton's imagery, for this is what enables it to offer hope at the time of exposure, a time when there appears to be an infinite separation between present time and time to come.

Baudrillard asserts that:

> The South is a natural producer of raw materials, the latest of which is catastrophe. The North, for its part, specializes in the reprocessing of raw materials and hence also in the reprocessing of catastrophe.
>
> (1994b: 67)

Certainly the concern with catastrophe is not specific to Benetton, but is more widespread in Euro-American cultures. What I have suggested, however, is that, in not simply depicting or reprocessing catastrophe, but entering into it, occupying it, Benetton seizes the time of exposure, a moment of temporal transcendence, non-flowing time, time without continuation or consequence, as its own, transforming it into a global event, so giving it a spatial dimension in which private uncertainty may be lost in 'a shared audacity and temerity of numbers' (Bauman, 1992: 20–1). In the images described here, Benetton represents itself as the archangel of catastrophe, holding back the future until the past can be perfected, inviting the viewer to hold open the aperture of the camera by exercising his or her capacity to make survival a choice (and choice the only means of staying alive). As Bauman comments, 'Eschatology is dissolved into technology. It is "how to do it", not "what to do", on which survival concerns focus' (1992: 18–19). In its use of the catastrophic image, Benetton delays the closure of the moment in which the individual may be annihilated, offering salvation in the after-life of no/w/here.

● ● ● ● Brand Power

What underpins the power of the brand, of which the Benetton case is just one example, is the way in which it can recoup the effects of the subject or consumer's action, constituting these effects as the outcome of the brand's own powers through the repetitive assertion of its ability to motivate the branded object's meaning and uses. As noted in Chapter 3, this is achieved through the ways in which the brand as medium links the subject and object, making available for appropriation aspects of the experience of product use *as if they were effects of the brand*. In the creation of a logo, an image, a sign or an emblem which condenses the memory of a whole history of advertisements, packaging and promotion, the object is anticipated, brought into focus in relation to the logo; its properties reconstituted as the effects of the brand's repetition.

The capacity for the logo to act in these ways draws on long-established visual practices (although such visual practices are usually supplemented by marketing techniques). Consider, for example, the following comment from Siegfried Kracauer in a discussion of the rise of illustrated newspapers in the 1920s:

> Never before has an image been so informed about itself, if being informed means having an image of objects that resembles them in a photographic sense. . . . [Yet] the resemblance between the image and the object effaces the contours of the object's 'history'.
>
> (1995: 58)

Kracauer suggests here that since the beginning of the twentieth century we have seen an intensification of the imaging of the object. However, this has not contributed to the realisation of the object; rather, it has effaced 'the contours of the object's history', erasing the gradually accreted memory of its everyday or common uses, and replacing such memories with information, the technologically mediated resemblance or photographic likeness of the object. In this process, the established temporal horizons and habitual spaces of object use are displaced, and the hyper-semioticised product is replaced within a multiply mediated frame. Things no longer appear to the scale of perception as a series of given objects, with predictable and trustworthy properties, but rather as a continuum of possibilities defined by the brand. The argument put forward here, then, is that the brand – in Kracauer's examples, photographic likeness or the 'look' of an object – now subsumes objects in its own mediated superimpositions.

This subsumption is typically a consequence not only of the visual practices outlined above, but also those of marketing (that Benetton relies upon the former more or less exclusively is one of its distinctive characteristics and is one reason for the hyperbole of its visual rhetoric[20]). The over-riding assumption in contemporary marketing techniques is that objects are not adequately defined by their formal properties alone. Instead, it is the pattern of customers' needs that is seen to give an object its essential character, and objects are classified according to the way they are perceived, used and bought by consumers, resulting in product categories as 'convenience', 'speciality' and 'unsought'. Such product categories may then in turn become the basis of brand portfolios. In this way, the properties of objects are linked to their positioning relative to consumers' perceptions and needs, *but only as documented, interpreted and re-presented as information or brand image by the advertising and marketing industries*. Brands both negotiate and materialise these consumer connections to products as 'goods'. In these practices, not only do things become different kinds of property, but objects become artefacts:

> The artifact is something other than a controlled transformation of the object for the purposes of knowledge: it is a savage intervention in reality, at the end of which it is impossible to distinguish what in this reality arises out of objective knowledge and what results from the technical intervention (the medium).
>
> (Tort, quoted in Baudrillard, 1993: 64)

In sum, the brand reverses not only the relationship between the perceiver and the perceived, but also the relationship between product and image. In this reversal, subjective perception is anticipated and the object becomes artefactual. As a medium of exchange, the brand co-ordinates relations of production and consumption by controlling the translation from the two dimensions of representation to the three dimensions of the product and its presentation: if the brand is successful, as noted above, the individual supports the advertising by buying the product. Or to put this another way, *the object or product is now an effect of the brand*. '"First we sell the clothes, then we make them", runs a Benetton in-house joke' (Mantle, 1999: 145). As Virilio comments, 'the image is no longer solitary (subjective, elitist, artisanal); it is solidary (objective, democratic, industrial)' (1994: 52). Importantly, then, the power of the brand is not simply a matter of representation, it is a kind of reification, a technical intervention in the processes of objectification, what has been called here artefactualism.

The artefactualism of the contemporary commodity is further extended in the ways in which the brand is used to create and maintain links among product items, product lines and product assortments. This is typically achieved through the playing out of a theme across the articulations that comprise the brand as a material-semiotic practice, where thematisation is 'the moment at which an element, a component of a text is promoted to the status of official theme' (Jameson, 1991: 91). In the case of Benetton, the theme is that of generic estrangement itself; as Back and Quaade write,

> It is [Toscani's] preoccupation with boundaries which gives Benetton's campaigns a sense of thematic unity. He constructs, or invokes, a boundary in order to convey a message of its transcendence.
>
> (1993: 66)

Thus, across all its product ranges, clothes, perfume, accessories, the theme of the Benetton brand provides a unity in diversity, syncopating the moment of exposure (just or almost) in time for the production and consumption of a global panhumanity.

Practices of thematisation are extended and elaborated in the manipulation of the object's environment or temporal and spatial context; thus brand owners frequently present branded objects in theme-parks, -restaurants, -pubs and -shops or contribute to the elaboration of themed lifestyles through the sponsoring of events or activities. Consider, for example, the global brand Swatch, whose theme 'Time is what you make of it' is elaborated not only in the playful, plastic design of its watches, the colourful space of its retail outlets, and the marking of the time in which sponsored sporting events − such as the Olympics − occur, but also in its attempts to mark the time of one of the most important flows of the global economy, the Internet, as its own:

> Swatch has invented a new universal concept of time that eliminates time zones and geographical differences: the Swatch Internet Time. Swatch divides the 24 hours of the day into 1000 units. A unit is called a Beat.
>
> Each day has 000 to 999 Beats. Each Beat lasts 1 minute and 26.4 seconds. Internet time is displayed by @ and three digits and starts at midnight (winter-time) in Biel, the home of Swatch, with @000.
>
> Everybody all over the world then talks about time in Beats, no matter what actual time it may be in their time zone.
>
> (Publicity leaflet)

The Swatch theme, 'Time is what you make of it', is thus an example of the 'breaking down of rhythmicity, either biological or social, associated with the notion of a life cycle' (Castells, 1996: 446), and an attempted renarrativisation in no/w/here, what Manuel Castells (1996) describes as 'timeless time', the time of the flows of a global economy.

In the case of Benetton, the manipulation of time involved in the themat-isation of generic estrangement involves the creation of multiple fashion seasons. To synchronise these seasons globally, Benetton holds time still for agents and retailers by selling clothes – nine months in advance of the selling season – at exchange rates covered by Benetton's bankers (Mantle, 1999: 286). Indeed, generic estrangement or the arbitrariness of diversity that defines the Benetton brand image is highly com-patible with the production of commercially ordered change, that is, with novelty or fashion (rather than, for example, with the progressive narrative of history). As Toscani claims, 'Products change, images capitalize' (Rosen, quoted in Perry, 1998: 38). In this sense, Benetton's practices of thematisation are not only indicative of a shift in the representation of the categories of the genres or kinds of humanity, but are also integral to its economic policy, which some have held to be emblematic of the new global economic order.

Indeed, Manuel Castells (1996) describes the Benetton company as an ideal typical organisation in the emerging network society. The company is characterised by an intermediate form of organisation somewhere between a vertically disintegrated large firm and the horizontal networks of small businesses. 'It is a horizontal network, but based on a set of core–periphery relationships, both on the supply and on the demand side of the process' (Castells, 1996: 162). This form of organisation combines the benefits of new technology (especially information technology) and the cheaper labour costs of sub-contracting systems, while minimising (economic) risk and uncertainty by maintaining control of the production process overall (Phizacklea, 1990: 14–16). In the new global economic order of the networked firm, the sub-contracted workforce is typically either female, young or from the third world, or some combination of all three. In this sense too, then, the brand displaces – or renders invisible – whilst simultaneously sucking dry the categories of kind: of gender, age, race, nationality and class. Benetton's business practices distinguish it from some of its global competitors in that intensive automation of design, cutting, dyeing, packing and dispatching, together with the close regulation of a dense network of sub-contractors for assembly, ensure that much of its production continues to be carried out in Italy and other Mediterranean countries such as Turkey, rather than, as, for example, is the practice of the global company Nike, moving from one third world country to the next in search of the cheapest labour. Nevertheless, the workers who assemble Benetton clothes – employed by its many sub-contractors – are typically female, and are rendered invisible to the consumer.

Retail franchises within specific territories are co-ordinated by agents for Benetton who regularly visit the main Benetton site in Ponzano, Italy, to view and make selections from collections as they are displayed in an underground street, lit by artificial light and lined with a range of shops. All the shops along the street, known as Shopping Street, are Benetton shops (Mantle, 1999: 285). The co-ordination of franchises is further assisted by a 'fourth dimension . . . in the form of a virtual map that link[s] the operations of the company and its network around the world' (Mantle, 1999: 144): an information technology system that sends information about sales, styles and colours from key point-of-sale terminals to the design centre at Ponzano in Northern Italy, enabling Benetton to supplement its bi-annual seasonal sales with so-called 'flash' sales. In this way too, then, the theme of generic estrangement enables Benetton to operate in the time of exposure, approximating real time. It enables the company to map the discontinuous, the indeterminate, making progress out of the temporality of catastrophe.

Benetton may be further distinguished from other global companies such as McDonald's by the relatively unusual characteristics of its franchise arrangements: no written contracts; all clothes supplied exclusively by Benetton on a no-return basis; the full costs of setting up an outlet to be borne by the operator, although s/he must work within the rules of Benetton's shop organisation and adopt a particular style of interior design; no backroom stockholding; no royalties payable on profits or use of the brand name (Lash and Urry, 1994: 177). However, this is a strategic distribution of risk that is perfectly in accord with the brand as medium: the economic risks attached to the sale of *products* is allocated to franchisees, while both the risks and the rewards of *brand management* are absorbed by Benetton.[21] Moreover, the network of agents and franchise holders is subject to what the Benetton management describe as 'cleaning' (Mantle, 1999: 241), a process in which agents and shops are monitored and regularly visited by a core management team, and, if deemed necessary, their practices 'adjusted' or their contracts terminated.

Generic estrangement also describes the means by which the Benetton business operates self-consciously across the economic territories and politically defined borders of the nation. Thus, for example, Luciano Benetton justified the opening of a Benetton store in Myanmar, although it is currently run by a dictatorial military government, on the grounds that: 'Our relationship is with a local business-man who wants to do business with us and import our products. It is independent of everything else' (in Mantle, 1999: 281). Moreover, as Pasi Falk points out, the Benetton brand operates not only in advertising or the economic field, but also in 'other domains of public discourse on a scale which corresponds to its aim for global markets' (1996: 73). For instance, the advertising campaign which used images of children with Down's syndrome was launched with a press conference, an event more conventionally associated with news and public events. Toscani comments,

> You can see a news photo of the fighting in Saravejo, and it's in context; it conforms to your expectations. Shocking violence in the news is normal. But when you take the same photo out of the news and put a Benetton logo on it, people pause and reflect on their position on the problem.
>
> (in Mantle, 1999: 218)

In these and other practices, the brand can be seen as one of the most important factors in the organisation of the flows of the images, information, products, capital and people of the global economy (Castells, 1996). More precisely it is a medium of exchange, where medium is understood, as described by Fredric Jameson, as, a word which conjoins three relatively distinct signals: that of an artistic mode or specific form of aesthetic production; that of specific technology, generally organized around a central apparatus or machine; and that, finally, of a social institution.

(1991: 67)

However, the space of flows with which this medium merges are not easily navigated. As an editorial for *Colors* says, although it is 'a magazine about the rest of the world', even its producers are not sure what this means:

In theory, it means that we're as concerned with your culture as we are with ours. But because this magazine is produced by people from about 30 different countries, published in five bilingual editions, and distributed globally, we're not sure anymore which culture is ours. We have cultural vertigo, we feel dizzy.

(no. 3, fall/winter 1992)

Perhaps this is not so surprising, though, if, as Jameson defines it, a medium comprises a 'constant stream, or "total flow" of multiple materials, each of which can be seen as something like a shorthand signal for a distinct type of narrative or a specific narrative process' (1991: 86). Indeed, Jameson further believes that the intersections of such materials within the total flow cannot be understood by means of interpretation, for within this specific type of narrative,

no single sign ever retains priority as a topic of the operation; . . . the situation in which one sign functions as the interpretant of another is more than provisional, it is subject to change without notice. . . . [I]n [a] ceaselessly rotating momentum . . . signs occupy each other's position in a bewildering and well-nigh permanent exchange.

(1991: 87)[22]

The maintenance of the brand as medium of exchange involves the capture of one narrative signal by another: 'the rewriting of one form of narrativization in terms of a different, momentarily more powerful one, the ceaseless renarrativization of already existent narrative elements by each other'. Yet Jameson further notes that 'no product seems identifiable, nor even the range of generic products designated by the logo in its original sense, as the badge of a diversified multinational corporation'. For Jameson, this leads to a condition of Benjaminian distraction 'raised to a new and historically original power' (1991: 88). What is being suggested here is that the brand as medium is one of the disjunctive flows which characterise the fundamentally fractal forms of global nature, global culture (Appadurai, 1990).

Cultural Vertigo: From Here and Now to Now/Here and Back Again

Certainly Benetton seems to experience vertigo. Consider a further example. In the first of a series of images in one issue of *Colors* (no. 2, spring 1992), two children speak to each other through a home-made telephone of two cans and a piece of string: one can is Pepsi-Cola, the other is Coca-Cola (Figure 5.17). The text at the bottom reads, '(Pretend this is a message from Pepsi *and* Coke)'. The second image is of two inter-twined tyres: one is Pirelli, the other is Goodyear (Figure 5.18). The text at the bottom reads '(Pretend this is a message from Pirelli *and* Goodyear)'. The third and last image is of two televisions, side by side, out of the screen of each of which emerges a child; they are embracing (Figure 5.19). The text at the bottom reads, '(Pretend this is an image from Sony *and* Philips)'. The series of images invite you to move between each logo, interpreting neither as the sign of a referent, be it a soft drink, a tyre or a television, but rather as the arbitrary signifiers for the brand which is about not simply the movement between products, corporations or nations but also between logos, namely Benetton.

The broken text at the top of these images reads,

> Hello, Lola? Have you heard? The world's superpowers can't fight anymore. Now they have to work together. But don't worry competition isn't dead because. . . .

> . . . we still have rivalry beween super-products. While we can't carry a passport from both super-powers, we can have Pirelli tires and Goodyear tires on our car. Now, if only the super-products could learn to co-operate . . .

> . . . the superproducts could stop spending money (and talent and resources) on ads that tell people about products and spend it on ads that tell people about the world . . .

There is clearly here an attempt to position Benetton as a kind of super-brand or diacritical trademark, a grandmaster not only of generic estrangement but also of the alienation of logo-type, an exemplification of culture squared. What is interesting here, though, is that this positioning is achieved only by reinstating an opposition between nature – 'the world' – and culture – 'products'. Benetton has discovered, in its vertigo-inducing, hyper-stacking travels, that, as Strathern puts it, the ubiquity of culture becomes a problem as it 'ceases to work as a relational term' (1995b: 157), as it reproduces itself.

That Benetton is able to invoke a claim to the natural at all, however, is in part a distinctive feature of its use of photography. Toscani comments that his images 'speak to us of the spontaneity of nature, which is becoming more and more difficult to grasp in our artificial world, where nothing is what it appears to be' (in Mantle, 1999: 262). I argued earlier that Benetton occupies the time of exposure, holding open the aperture of the camera. It does so not through the use of computer-aided photography or the special effects made possible by digitalisation (see the discussion of the pixel in Chapter 2), but by continuing to insist upon the naturalness of its worldview. So important is this that Toscani introduced the use of images from newspapers in Benetton advertisements as a response to criticism of the staging of some of the early images. This is one means by which Benetton seeks to control what John Thompson calls 'the space of the visible': 'the non-localized, non-dialogical, open-ended space of the visible in which mediated symbolic forms can be expressed and received by a plurality of non-present others' (1995: 245). In mapping this space, the UNESCO report on the multicultural planet expresses the hope that 'new generations' can be taught 'not only to remember the past but above all to keep in mind that actions taken in the here and now form the conditions – the history – on which future generations will have to build' (1993: x). Commercial and public interests adopt a range of more concrete strategies to mobilise this hope.

So, for example, as is the case with a number of other brands, the promotion of Benetton operates at the level of person, product and company all at once (Falk, 1996), especially, but not exclusively, in its own national context, Italy. Indeed, the brand has a story or narrative of its own:

> It is post-war Italy and the four Benetton children, Giuliana, Luciano, Gilberto and Carlo, are struggling to find their way after the death of their father, Leone. The daughter, Giuliana, starts a cottage industry knitting business. Her brother Luciano sells his accordion to help the fledgling firm. By 1975 it has 200 shops in Italy.
>
> (Doward, 1999: 7)

As Jonathan Mantle (1999), shows, the inter-linkages between family, business and brand are complex. Thus, for example, not only the siblings mentioned above, but also some of their children occupy key positions in the business of Benetton. However, the business that is called Benetton (which includes a children's clothing company, 012) is only partly owned by the siblings, and is thus described by one of the senior executives as a 'public family company' (in Mantle, 1999: 289). Benetton Group is partly held for the siblings by another company, Edizione, which they wholly own, and which itself comprises a number – a family – of (part- and whole-owned) brands (including Nordica, Rollerblade, Prince and Kastle) and other properties, including a number of sheep and cattle ranches in Argentina. To enhance the performance of the latter, Edizione has invested millions of dollars in artificial insemination and improving breeding processes.

In other respects, too, the brand appears to rely upon insemination. The brand of Benetton is described by Mantle as the creation of the supremely patriarchal figures Luciano Benetton and Oliviero Toscani.[23] Thus, whilst the role of the only sister amongst the siblings, Guiliana, as designer and initially the actual maker of Benetton products, is acknowledged, she is not central to the process of brand-building which the book describes. Mantle further suggests that Luciano Benetton established Fabrica, an art and communication research centre, as the seed-bed for replacement(s) for Toscani in this creative partnership as and when it might become necessary (1999: 252). Here then the biological reproduction of the business is to be assisted by the cultural reproduction of the brand. At the same time, however, both (some members of) the Toscani and the Benetton family have been photographed by Oliviero Toscani as part of the advertising to support Benetton the brand. Finally, to further complicate the links between business, family and brand, the robots which co-ordinate the Benetton clothing and distribution plant at Castrette di Villorba are known by the Benetton siblings as 'the family'.

These familial practices of breeding, banking and branding can be seen as the creation of a second nature, and in this respect, it is interesting to note, as we do in Chapter 3 that integral to the power of many brands is the creation of so-called 'family 'resemblances among products, in which commodities sometimes come to be seen as lineage groups, with later generations of products descending from earlier generations. Benetton, for example, promotes one line of its clothing as 'The Blue Family'. Brand-name decisions, brand-family decisions, brand-extension strategies, multi-brand decisions and brand-repositioning decisions all variously associate a range of products with a brand as a source or origin, establishing a relation of ownership to the 'parent' company and a form of commodity affiliation among several generations and classes or categories of products. More generally, brand work may be seen to produce a form of commodity kinship. However, the argument being put forward here is that while the Benetton brand may sometimes secure its historical continuity by recourse to natural means of reproduction, it is principally through the elevation and protection of *cultural essentialism* that its reproduction in real time is being made good.[24]

Artefacts, Property and Essences

In this respect, the role of the law is of profound importance: it is one of the key mechanisms by which the brand as medium is not simply given shape but also legitimated and reproduced as a social institution. Indeed, the use of trademark legis-lation enables brand owners to assert a monopoly on the use of not simply particular icons and slogans, but specific colours, shapes and sounds. In this process, a search for cultural univerals is inaugurated, drawing on the subjective investments already made by mass culture in the imaginary of people belonging to different cultures (Mattelart, 1979). Trademark is the means by which the power of the brand can be harnessed, by which things can be turned into different kinds of property.

So, for example, the Lanham Act of 1946 has for a long time provided protection for a diverse range of symbols in the USA, including, among other things, sounds, fragrant scents, numeric radio frequencies and alpha-numeric telephone numbers, while in the UK the Trade Marks Act 1994[25] means that smells, sounds, gestures or movements, catchphrases, three-dimensional shapes and colours can now be registered as intellectual property. The extension of legal protection is thus apparently such as to include the object-ive or solidary capacities of the image, that is, those capacities which facilitate the movement of the brand from two dimensions to three and back again. According to a marketing trade press report,

> Boots the Chemist has made an application for 100% cyan, 100% yellow and 15% magenta for its artificial sweetener packaging. Meanwhile Mars has staked its claim for purple when applied to catfood.
>
> Reckitt and Coleman has applied for green in cleaning products, when covering the whole surface of a container, and Cadbury applied for purple in chocolate packaging. It then made a second broader application for purple alone.
>
> (Tutsell, 1995: 27)[26]

Marketeers themselves are not shy of asserting universalising claims, even without legal protection: a report in *Design Week* asserts,

> [A]s big brands become global, they become the new 'universal colour language'. Red has come to mean – to the tribesman as well as the tourist – the refreshment values of Coca-Cola rather than danger or rage, while yellow-and-black symbolises not 'radiant release' and death, but consistently successful photography courtesy of Kodak.
>
> (Sholl, 1996: 15)

As was widely reported at the time, Pepsi spent $500 million on advertising to publicise a change of dominant colour from red to blue in its promotional packaging.

> Liz Baker, image consultant at Colour Me Beautiful, reckons red and blue could not be more different in their meaning. 'Blue is more conservative and traditional. It's very reliable. It would give Pepsi a feeling of originality and does offer a clear point of difference from Coke,' she says. 'Coke's red, on the other hand, is passionate, impulsive and authoritative.'
>
> (Armstrong, 1996: 9)

And, at the same time as there has been this intensified interest in colour, there has also been a resurgence of interest in shape or form, as the Cola market once again shows. Coca-Cola, for example, has reintroduced its old hourglass shape:

> Coke believes that the icon may be a powerful and instantaneous way to stand out in a world of clutter. So it has reintroduced the contour bottle in plastic and glass. It has put a picture of it on the can and plans eventually to introduce a contour can. The company is also putting contour bottles without 'Coke' written on them on billboards that don't even identify the product. The aim: to generate near-instantaneous communication to consumers.
>
> (Morris, 1996: 36)

In the past, if a particular shape or colour had become distinctive in the eyes of consumers as indicating the goods of a particular trader, then the use of similar packaging would most likely be regarded as passing off and could be the subject of legal action as such. In this sense, the Trade Marks Act can be seen as merely pre-empting the necessity for such action by making registration of a distinctive shape or colour possible. However, it also widens infringement rights and, once a mark is registered, makes it easier to take action if the trademark is infringed. Furthermore, this Act also determines that if the mark is applied to goods and services that are 'confusingly similar', it is regarded as an infringement, whereas previously the goods or services had to be 'identical'. Taking all these changes into consideration, it can be argued that since the Act replaces the criterion of the centrality of use, and thus of consumer recognition and acceptance of distinctiveness, with registration and the economic power of large firms it indicates a shift in the legal regulation of producer–consumer relations (Slingsby, 1994: 40).

This shift moves logos and trademarks from an already closely regulated existence in the public domain further towards ownership by private corporations. It helps secure the producers' or brand owners' independence of the consumer, an independence which had been limited by the earlier legislation's emphasis on use and consumer recognition for the legal acceptance of a claim to the ownership of trade-marks. This shift thus confirms and consolidates the practices of brand managers who seek to own and control the new medium of the global economy.[27] More than this, in making it possible for brand owners to assert their ownership of not simply specific colours, shapes and sounds, but also the accumulation of sedimented subjective experiences associated with such object-ive properties, such legislation appears to establish a distinction between *essential and inessential culture and to make it possible to assert property rights in essential culture.*

This development has parallels in other areas of intellectual property law, including patent law. And what this legislation reveals is that just as commodity culture has made use of natural forms of reproduction, so the commercial appropriation of nature – in the form of 'products' of nature – makes use of cultural forms of reproduction. In a review article covering recent developments in intellectual property law, John Frow (1996) notes that the previously established distinction between inventions of industrial processes, which could be patented, and the discoveries of natural laws on which they are based, which could not be patented, is slowly being rewritten in terms of an emerging demarcation between 'natural' and 'artificial' forms of nature which parallels that between 'essential' and 'inessential' culture outlined above. The trend, Frow suggests, is to allow 'for "products of nature" so long as the inventor has changed the product to conform to the utility, novelty, and non-obviousness requirements of patent statute' (Greenfeld, quoted in Frow, 1996: 92–3). In this pro-cess, patent law 'has been shifting towards a more expansive definition of its proper subject matter' (1996: 93), thus extending 'the possibility of locking up aspects of "nature" itself' (1996: 92). So, for example, novelty may be defined here in the weak sense of 'not being previously available to the public' (Correa, quoted in Frow, 1996: 93).

These trends are closely tied, as noted in Part One, to recent developments in biotechnology and the global strategies of transnational companies that were consolidated by the Uruguay Round of GATT.[28] Frow comments,

> The genetic uniformity that has resulted from hybridization and crop-standardization has left First-World agriculture heavily dependent on importations from the Third World as a source of genetic variation. Yet this flow, which has enriched the corporate producers of hybrid varieties, has been almost entirely free of charge, since the model of knowledge as private intellectual property works to the disadvantage of the 'almost invisible, informal and collective innovation' characteristic of peasant communities. Patent law . . . favours innovation deriving from high-tech research rather than innovation by long-term breeding for genetic variety.
>
> (1996: 98)

Here, as in trademark law, there is not only a shift in the balance of power towards private corporations and away from both 'the public' and anonymous, informal, collective producers, but also a parasitic relationship between first and third worlds. What such laws make visible, however, is that natural forms of reproduction – such as breeding – rely upon and make use of cultural forms of reproduction – such as branding and banking. Yet just as the brand owners acknowledge this traffic only selectively in their use of techniques of inclusion and exclusion, so too is nature's debt to culture acknowledged only in very restricted terms.

In short, within the global imaginary as it is brought into being in intellectual property legislation, an emerging internal demarcation within both (essential and inessential) culture and (natural and artificial) nature enables an isomorphism to be established between the two, with each acquiring some of the other's powers, yet appearing to remain distinct. Indeed, while the emphasis so far in this chapter has been on the emergence of a cultural essentialism in the context of the global brand, the full implications of the analysis presented here are best appreciated by a consideration of the complex traffic between nature and culture. Thus, while unsettling inversions obscure continuing borrowings between nature and culture, their internal demarcations enable each to appear to contain the other within itself. Moreover, a further effect of the internal demarcations is that relationality in both domains is rendered a question of difference as it is recognised *within* either nature or culture – not as it is created in a relation of *criss-crossing* between the two. Consequently, each is able to appear self-reproducing. The effect of the internal demarcations is thus the creation of inverted yet parallel worlds: worlds in which difference is an internal relation, not a relation across or between, a relation producing substitute worlds with boundaries but without limits. As both this chapter and the rest of this volume demonstrate, the shift from kind to brand is an important part of the dynamic emergence of these substitute worlds, for the brand is one of the principal means by which the productive demarcations internal to global nature, global culture are established.

However, the further importance of the brand is that it is a generic *mark which insists on a property form of relationality* (Haraway, 1997). There are a number of points to be made here. First, as Marilyn Strathern points out, the brand, insofar as it is implemented as an *intellectual* property right, uses things to divide people (1999: 171). In other words, what is attributed to the thing is used to drive divisions between people. In this respect, as Strathern makes clear, intellectual property rights differ from many other property rights in Euro-American societies, which use (pre-existing distinctions between) people to divide things. Think, for example, of the property rights associated with acquisition and ownership by purchase, donation and inheritance: in these cases, people divide land, money and things. In the case of the brand, divisions are established not simply between producers and consumers, but also amongst producers and amongst consumers in particular ways, some of which have been described here.

Second, the brand is a mark of the increasing importance of rights not simply *in* but *to* relationality. As Strathern (1999) again makes clear, it can thus be seen, to mark a specific formation of what John Law (1994) calls relational materiality.[29] Or, to put this another way, insofar as the orderings of genre, type and kind are displaced by brand, the previously limited and not always saleable rights to nature and culture[30] may come to be replaced by virtually unlimited, saleable and 'absolute' rights in global nature, global culture. Thus the rise of brand power potentially has enormous significance for both nature and culture, insofar as both domains may be understood as primarily concerned with the production of relationality, with reproduction and the social relations of affinity and of difference. Indeed, this chapter suggests that the brand is not only an increasingly important property relation in the global economy but also likely to have disturbing implications for the (in)alienability of both culture and nature.

Elsewhere, No/w/here and Now and Here

However, the global condition is not yet an achievement. The absolute rights to relationality afforded by the brand outlined above are still only an aspiration. In the case of Benetton, the inability to secure absolute rights in relationality is especially clear in relation to the brand's complex co-ordination of relations of promotion, production, distribution and consumption. As noted above, the company feels dizzy. On the one hand, Benetton necessarily faces competition in its exploitation of the time of exposure that characterises the global economy. Indeed, it was overtaken in size of market share in 1995 by its American competitor Gap mainly because of its inability to match the latter's rapid turnover of 'seasons': it continued to rely on two each year – albeit supplemented by flash re-orders – rather than the six initiated by Gap (Castells, 1996). On the other, as Thompson notes, the space of the visible is open-ended, and 'the consequences of becoming visible cannot be fully anticipated or controlled' (1995: 247).[31] The implications of the rhetorical address in Benetton iconography described in the first half of this chapter are uneven, to say the least. The actions of franchise holders may undermine the position of the Benetton brand owners and vice versa. Consider, for example, the following account of shopping in New York provided by the American lawyer Patricia J. Williams:

> The installation of . . . buzzers happened swiftly in New York; stores that had always had their doors wide open suddenly became exclusive or received people by appointment only. I discovered them and their meaning one Saturday in 1986. I was shopping in Soho and saw in a store window a sweater that I wanted to buy for my mother. I pressed my round brown face to the window and my finger to the buzzer, seeking admittance. A narrow-eyed, white teenager wearing running shoes and feasting on bubble-gum glared out, evaluating me for signs that would pit me against the limits of his social understanding. After about five seconds, he mouthed 'We're closed,' and blew pink rubber at me. It was two Saturdays before Christmas, at one o'clock in the afternoon; there were several white people in the store who appeared to be shopping for things for *their* mothers.
>
> (1993: 45)

The store was a Benetton franchise. Or take another example: the charges made by retailers in France and Germany in 1994 and 1995 that they allegedly lost money because of the 'shock' advertising campaigns conducted by Benetton. According to newspaper accounts (Moir, 1995), retailers claimed to have mothers – the 'natural' guardians of the old reproductive order – on their side, as they reported that their children were ostracised by their friends if they wore Benetton clothes. While in some cases the retailers lost their case, others were settled out of court.

In discussing a prior controversy, Luciano Benetton asserts:

> Many people have asked why we didn't include a text that would explain the image. But we preferred not to because we think the image is understandable by itself.
>
> (quoted in Giroux, 1994: 16)

But this preference sidesteps the practices of seeing: although images do not require texts to be understandable, they are not understandable in themselves: the meaning of photographs resides in their uses in specific contexts. And certainly the uneven reception of Benetton imagery in different national contexts is testimony to this (the image of a nun and a priest kissing caused controversy in Italy, while the image of a black Queen Elizabeth II was considered 'beyond the pale' in the UK). Within the photograph itself the conditions of intelligibility may be implicit, but they are never fulfilled. A photograph may seem to insist upon its own intelligibility, but it is not (yet) a property of photographs in themselves; their meaning is realised only in specific circumstances or contexts of viewing. Insofar as a brand remains dependent upon acts of public recognition, it cannot yet reproduce itself. As Michael Shapiro notes, 'photographic meaning results not only from the codes the image deploys but also from "the stock of signs" belonging to the observer' (1994: 444); and that stock of signs has not yet been entirely subsumed in brand wealth. Meanings continue to be generated and transformed in social practices, confusing the demarcation between essential and inessential culture, and the equation of the media with culture (Coombe, 1998). As Gayatri Spivak puts it, as she attempts to reroute the traffic between nature and culture, 'culture alive is always on the run, always changeful' (1999: 355). In such movement, the diversity of cultural essentialism is recognised as a violent negation of the singular or general relations afforded by kinds.

While the phatic image may reverse the perceiver–perceived relation, while it may contain both 'a bit of the *present* and of the *immediate future*' (Virilio, 1994: 66), the future is not completely foreclosed. Indeed, adopting the view that the photographic image is an event (Solomon-Godeau, 1991) makes it possible to see that meanings are always an intervention in the narrativisation of time, and thus that the photographic image may both smooth and disrupt the speed of linkage between modalities in the flexible economies of global nature, global culture. Moreover, such an understanding of a photograph as an image-event points to the necessity of recognising that while many observers are already in the moment of exposure, not outside global nature, global culture, but in its very unfolding, their inhabitation of this time is insecure and uneven. As Spivak (1999) reminds us, we are teetering on the edge of the 'vanishing present'. This means that the moment of exposure may not be 'just in time' for production but may, rather, be disturbed by the time of the in-between.

Moreover, while the global brand of Benetton may appear to come into being by displacing kind, type or genre, this shift is neither complete nor secure. So, for example, as described in some detail above, the company continues to rely, in part at least, upon natural forms of reproduction, including the biological reproduction of the Benetton family, for its continuity. In addition, in many respects, brands are not safe from the continuing counter-claims of genre. In an attempt to intervene in the legal regulation of trademarks in a manner that recognizes the potential of such claims, Rochelle Dreyfuss suggests that if the use of a mark is the most economical way to refer to a set of connotations, it should be permitted as an example of 'generic expressivity' (1990, quoted in Coombe, 1998). She thus attempts to secure legal recognition of the radical heterogeneity of categories in use. Moreover, in a rule often referred to as genericide, it is legally established that if a trademark becomes the generic name for the thing itself, then the trademark owner loses exclusive rights to the mark (Coombe, 1998; see also Gaines, 1990). As a consequence, trademark owners must continually watch to ensure that brand and genre remain distinct, and that generic types continue to exist. So, for instance, in an example which nicely captures the paradoxes of reproduction in global nature, global culture, Rosemary Coombe notes, 'Xerox . . . promotes the concept of the photocopy so that its own trademark does not substitute either for the noun or the verb' (1998: 79). In short, common usage or inessential culture has the potential to undermine the power of the brand, its ability to draw comparisons and establish differences.

● ● ● **Coda**

The argument put forward here, then, has been that the brand is a defining medium of exchange in global nature, global culture: that it is a medium or organisation of flow in which relationality, the question of origins, of connection and disconnection and relations to time and space, is being refigured in the global imaginary. However, this chapter does not assume that the brand is successful in this respect; rather, the aim has been to show the potential implications of its aspirations. Perhaps the most important of these implications is that, in the navigation of the disjunctive flow of the brand, the essentials of culture may come to be identified.

On the one hand, as a consequence of the brand's intervention, the object is rendered artefactual, its properties the outcome of the repetition of what Virilio (1994) calls the phatic image. At the same time, the elements of the image are being defined in such a way as to make them available for (exclusive) ownership. In this process, then, they become essential. On the other hand, the brand promises to make the reproduction of the social and political categories of genre, kind and type a matter of choice. So, for example, while the reproductive techniques that underpin brand family values are often understood in terms of generation and family resemblance, biological generations reproduce themselves in terms of brand names, such as, for example, the Pepsi or the Prozac generation. In this sense too, culture is rendered as essence. Here, then, culture comes to display the overdetermined essentialism identified by Raymond Williams (1976) in his discussion of nature: as the essences of culture/nature describe the constitution of the (global) world, so they also describe the principles through which it is ordered.

This chapter further suggests that through its role in the creation of an internal demarcation between essential and inessential culture, natural and artificial nature, the brand has the potential to contribute to the fantasy of a self-reproducing global nature, global culture. Indeed, the notion of reproduction associated with the cultural essentialism of the brand is not to be understood in relation to genealogical time, nor in relation to a fixed origin. There is no attempt to fix a single point of creation and tie reproduction to this moment; rather, creation is multiple, constituted within the many and various re-formations of objects that arise in the medium of the brand's development and use. Nevertheless, ownership of the brand continues to be asserted through the ways in which the changing uses and meanings of a product are refigured as attributes of the brand, and are protected as such by intellectual property legislation. Central to this process of attribution is strategic intervention in the time of exposure for, as Castells suggests, it enables the global economy 'to escape the contexts of its existence, and to appropriate selectively any value each context could offer to the ever-present' (1996: 433).

The argument put forward here, then, is that the brand is part of a conception of a culture which has become 'superorganic', as Jonathan Friedman (1994) puts it; and, one might also add, super-territorial. This is a culture which is no longer clearly rooted in a place or in history, and neither is it the outgrowth of a people. It is not after nature; rather, it is in the same 'real time' as nature. Moreover, while it is object-ive and 'arbitrary with respect to those who possess it' (Friedman, 1994: 67), it is inherently restless. This culture is reproduced in the strategic, technically mediated couplings of objects with environments made possible by the transfer of information across the internal boundary between what is inessential and what is essential. Indeed, as Marilyn Strathern puts it, 'This is not a new essentialism but a collapse of the difference between the essential and the superadded' (1992b: 39). The brand emerges as the mark of this transfer of information; it is the identifying property of this complex system.

All this, however, is not to suggest a complete displacement of the relationships established between culture, place and property in the period sometimes described in terms of cultural nationalism – in which there was an evolutionary, hierarchically ordered, plural placing of cultures – but rather to emphasise the significance of the brand as a medium or migratory image (Quinn, 1994). It is to suggest that the brand is the means by which it has become possible to acquire the (exclusive) right to ask, 'Where do you want to go today?'[TM] while going no/w/here. It is also to propose that the brand is contributing to a shift in relations between (and within) nature and culture, in relations between people and things, and helping consolidate a property form of relationality. The argument, in short, then, is that the brand is contributing to the violent erasure of historical links between people, products, places and practices that is part of a shift from natural and historical understandings of the nation-state to the expansionist, mediated and market-led notions of global nature, global culture.

As Donna Haraway writes, 'The globalization of the world, of "planet earth", is a precise semiotic-material production of some forms of life rather than others' (1997: 12). The cultural essentialism identified here in Benetton marketing and UNESCO thinking and the cultural fundamentalism discussed by Stolcke and others are inter-linked examples of this global production. However, while cultural fundamentalism insists upon the naturalness of xenophobia as a human universal and assumes the inevitable incommensurability of different cultures, what I have called cultural essentialism insists upon the naturalness of choice as a human universal and assumes diversity, the constantly dynamic, infinitely changeable and combinable character of cultures. In both cases, the new universalisms they propose seem likely to occlude not only the partiality of the globalising processes they constitute but also their potential to create new forms of hierarchy, property and division while pulling wool(ly jumpers) over our eyes. Haraway's (1997) formula, Nature[TM] + Culture[TM] = The New World Order, Inc. thus seems likely to add up. At the same time, however, people will continue to combine nature and culture in ways other than addition, by doing inessential things, shifting contexts, pulling the world from under each other's feet.

● ● ● **Notes**

Many thanks to the following: Sara Ahmed, Les Back, Deirdre Boden, Susan Condor, Jeanette Edwards, Mike Featherstone, Sarah Franklin, Mariam Fraser, Elizabeth Greenhalgh, Penny Harvey, Scott Lash, Adam Lury, Giles Lury, Karen Lury, Greg Myers, Lynne Pearce, Stephen Pope, Beverley Skeggs, Jackie Stacey, Bron Szerszynski, John Urry, Sylvia Walby, Brian Wynne and Alison Young.

1   In an interview, Toscani recalls: 'Every morning [my father] would give me his still dripping prints to take to the paper [where his father worked] before I went to school' (1995: 20). A newspaper feature by Peter Popham (1993) reports that Toscani's father was responsible for the famous photograph of Mussolini's corpse suspended upside-down from a meat hook. Toscani junior studied photography in Zurich art school in the early sixties before going on to work for *Vogue*, *Elle* and *GQ*. While in New York in the 1960s and 1970s he spent time with Andy Warhol. In interview he remarked that while Warhol moved from commercial art to art, he has moved in the opposite direction (O'Reilly, 1998: 4). He ended his partnership with Luciano Benetton in April, 2000. At the time of writing, it is unclear what the implications of this will be for Benetton.

2   As Pasi Falk (1996) points out, advertisers have historically tended to avoid the use of a negative register in their advertising strategies, emphasising the 'positive' or 'happiness', as Toscani describes it. However, Falk further argues that some genres of advertising underwent a process of aestheticisation and spectacularisation during the 1980s and 1990s, suggesting that this has widened 'the range of representation beyond the conventional (narrowly defined) positive register' (1996: 70).

3   In a letter to the *Independent* newspaper in 1993, a representative of the Benetton Communications Department suggested that,

> It is extraordinary that Benetton, one of the very few companies that has devoted its advertising budget to communicate on issues of global concern instead of making self-serving product claims, gets accused of cynicism because it does not do more.
>
> Up to 30 per cent of most charities' budgets go into communication. Giving global problems a platform in more than 100 countries *is* doing something about them. We believe communication is more effective than cash hand-outs (and more expensive, incidentally) and hope that as more and more people understand our position and the urgency of these issues, we will become a vehicle for discussion and not its focus.
>
> (Galanti, 1993)

4   In a feature on the advertising industry, the advertising director Tony Kaye reported on his difficulties in getting acceptance for multi-ethnic casting:

> Kaye was at the centre of the last big row over using minorities in commercials a year ago when he was in dispute with Saatchi and Saatchi over payment for an aborted commercial for British Airways expected to be one of the most expensive ever made. Kaye claimed that BA instructed him not to use so many black, Asian, oriental and Jewish actors. 'Every time I showed them a black face or someone with dark hair or an olive complexion, they would say, "too dark, Tony" or "too ethnic".' They wanted to portray the face of British Airways as white with a cheesy expression.
>
> . . . He recalls bitterly how one of his British Rail commercials ended with a black child drawing with crayons, the drawing mutating into the logo. 'They made me re-shoot with a white boy,' he says. (Popham, 1996: 15)

5   In this context, W.F. Haug's description of the trademark as a 'second skin' (1986) seems especially apposite.

6   Fabrica is also the name of the arts and communication centre of the Benetton group.

7   Benetton's use of the image of the dying, emaciated AIDS activist David Kirkby in an advertising campaign in 1992 was approved by his family but caused considerable controversy.

8   The first editions of *Colors*, on which this analysis is largely based, were edited by Tibor Kalman, who had previously worked for the magazine *Interview*. In interview, he says, 'My lifelong

obsession was *Life* – the version that existed before 1965 – which to me was the most inspiring thing a magazine could be' (1996: 12).

9   Toscani describes his work as developing from the 'starting point' of 'a detail or fragment I find in a newspaper' (1995: 20).

10 In their study of the style magazine *i-D*, Evans and Thornton argue that it endorses a do-it-yourself-ethic in fashion as an expression of diversity:

> We believe in the individual
> in variety
> individuals produce variety.
>
> (*i-D*, 2, 1980, quoted in Evans and Thornton, 1989: 66)

11 For a related discussion of the uses of reflexivity in advertising see Cronin (1999).

12 One account suggests that the tag-line 'United Colors of Benetton' derives from a comment made by a UNESCO official visiting Toscani's Paris studio in 1984: 'My God . . . it's the united colors we're seeing here!' (cited in Mantle, 1999: 131).

13 She writes,

> The phrase 'sustainable development' has entered the discourse of all the bodies that manage globality. Development to sustain what? The general ideology of global development is racist paternalism (and alas, increasingly, sororalism); its general economics capital-intensive investment; its broad politics the silencing of resistance and of the subaltern as the rhetoric of their protest is constantly appropriated.
>
> (1999: 372–3)

14 See my *Cultural Rights* (1993) for a discussion of the importance of trademark in the contemporary culture industry.

15 Falk (1996) provides some indication of the mediascape that characterises this political economy.

16 Personal communication.

17 Indeed, it provides a basis for a comparison between Benetton and campaigning organisations such as Greenpeace, as the following letter to *The Independent* indicates:

> Sir: I find the 'Shetland' Benetton advertisement challenging and inspiring in the way it pushes the boundaries of advertising, a sterile and vacuous profession at the best of times. What I do find offensive is that charities such as Greenpeace and the Royal Society for the Protection of Birds are using the issue as a cynical recruitment campaign. Are they being any less exploitative?
>
> (Barnes, 1993)

18 It is not the only commercial contender here. Other advertising campaigns have been successful in securing trust. According to recent market research findings, both the giant M (or golden arches) symbol of McDonald's and the Shell symbol are more widely recognised globally than the Christian cross; and in the UK more people trust the brands of Kellogg's, Cadbury's and Heinz than trust either the church or the police (see Giles Lury, 1998). However, Nick Perry suggest that Benetton's claims to offer salvation draw on a specifically Italian tradition. He builds on Umberto Eco's discussion of the literally millions of magazines which are sent free of charge by orphanages, missionary societies and sanctuaries and circulate throughout Italy. '[D]espite differences in approach', says Eco,

> all these publications have one thing in common: the publication is a kind of outer wrapping for the payments slip. . . . The mediated objective is the support of orphans, the acquisition of an altar for a mission in the Congo and so on. The immediate objective is the future attainment of grace or recompense for grace received.
>
> (Eco, quoted in Perry, 1998: 41)

As Perry comments,

> This is just the kind of milieu out of which a Benetton style advertising campaign might be expected to emerge. But whereas Eco's analysis is designed to reveal the commercialization of the supernatural, the movement of Benetton's social issues campaigns is towards the sanctification of consumption.
>
> (1998: 41)

19   It is based on a theorem in topology discovered by the French mathematician René Thom in 1968 (Mellencamp, 1990b: 244–5).

20   Michael Shapiro too notes, 'Benetton's success is more a function of representational than political technologies' (1994: 438).

21   US retailers who believed that this kind of franchise arrangement was unfair – selling the Benetton brand name too cheaply, without risking the Benetton business's own money – were unable to find redress through the courts (Mantle, 1999: 161). However, as part of its decision to enter the cost-conscious mass market, Benetton has recently entered into a partnership with Sears, a nationwide chain of department stories in the USA: 'As of July 1999, in 450 Sears stories across America, there would be 1,800 "Benetton USA" corners selling a new, basic clothing brand designed for the American market' (Mantle, 1999: 303).

22   Toscani condones this provisonality:

> Today's culture is images, and I don't draw any distinctions between them. . . . Pasta advertising or tampon advertising or Red Cross information or reports from a war, for me they are all the same.
>
> (Popham, 1993: 26)

23   Certainly, as Michael Shapiro notes, 'Biographemes abound in the Benetton story, for Luciano Benetton has thrust his life into the center of his representational strategies' (1994: 441), while Toscani is clearly adept at self-promotion.

24   In this respect, the emphasis of my argument differs from that put forward by Rosemary Coombe. In her discussion of *The Cultural Life of Intellectual Properties*, she asserts that 'the legal recognition that trademark owners have a proprietary interest in marketing signs increasingly relies upon a reenactment of the author-function as described by Foucault' (1998: 61). While I concur with this statement at the level of law, I would suggest that if the *cultural life* of trademarks is indeed the primary focus of analysis – as, for example, in a discussion of brands such as that put forward here or in terms of the notion of a regime of rights elaborated in my earlier book (Lury, 1993) – the importance of the author-function is fading in contemporary society rather than increasing. Although, as Coombe notes, trademark law may recognise the trademark owner as the originator of a mark (Luciano Benetton in this case), I do not believe that this is to ascribe them the function of authorship. Brands in use are recognised to have multiple origins, to exist in a discontinuous time and an indefinite space.

25   This Act updated the then-existing Trade Marks Act, which was more than fifty years old. The update was instigated by the European Union to bring the UK in line with other European legislation (Slingsby, 1994).

26   While it is not clear how successful such claims will be, it appears that firms will be able to register ownership of colours at least in relation to specific classes of goods through the registration of trademarks.

27   See Rosemary Coombe (1998) for a more detailed discussion of this shift in the USA. She proposes that the focus of trademark law has been progressively inverted over the last century: the previous rationale of preventing consumer confusion has yielded to the current concern to protect the mark from dilution or misappropriation. Put crudely, in this process, the law has shifted its emphasis from protecting the consumer to protecting the producer.

28   The Uruguay Round of the General Agreement on Tariffs and Trade was concluded on 15 December 1993 and ratified by over 120 countries in Marrakesh on 12 April 1994. One of its principal objectives was the extension of patent enforcement to certain key industries such as

pharmaceuticals and agrochemicals which in many countries were exempt from patent protection. The failure of the following round of talks at the end of 1999, now under the auspices of the World Trade Organisation, indicates a growing recognition of the political importance of these talks for the development of a 'global' economy.

29   By using this term, Law means to draw attention to the ways in which the social world 'is told, performed, embodied and represented – for the verb will vary – in materials that are partly but only partly social in the narrow, usual, sociological sense of the term. Or, to put this another way, I assume that the social world is materially heterogeneous' (1994: 23). Moreover, he further argues that materials – amongst which he explicitly includes machines, animals and architectures – are effects, rather than having properties that are given in the order of things.

30   In the case of culture, such limits have historically been established through the counter-claims of inherited traditions, public goods and common usage.

31   Rosemary Coombe (1998) suggests that rumour is especially effective in undermining the reputation of the brand.

Chapter 6 / **Life Itself**
Global Nature and the Genetic Imaginary

Sarah Franklin

A defining feature of the present moment is our ambivalent encounter with biotechnology – a discomfort future analysts are likely to interpret as more than millennial nostalgia for the passing of long-established certainties. As the daily news can no longer be read without encountering some new disquieting biotechnological enablement, so also can be witnessed a process of cultural redefinition whereby foundational understandings of the human, the body, reproduction and the future are being transformed. This process of cultural redefinition accounts in no small part for the anxiety produced in relation to the technologisation of life itself.

These changes are both intimate and remote, global and personal, celebrated and feared. Public unease in relation to the reproduction of 'unnatural kinds' is increasingly evident in relation to the genetic alteration of animals, plants and micro-organisms. Worldwide public debate surrounded the birth of Dolly the sheep, the first higher vertebrate cloned from an adult cell. The introduction of genetically modified foods has proven an equally controversial issue, bringing to public attention complex questions of risk and regulation concerning the future of world agriculture.[1] While such developments have been widely debated in terms of law, ethics, public health and world trade, there remains the broad Foucauldian question of how they can be understood as part of an ongoing re-alignment of life, labour and language. We are currently witnessing the emergence of a new genomic governmentality – the regulation and surveillance of technologically assisted genealogy. This is necessitated by the removal of the genomes of plants, animals and humans from the template of natural history that once secured their borders, and their re-animation as forms of corporate capital, in the context of a legal vacuum. This dual imperative, to take evolution in one hand and to govern it with the other, is a defining paradox of global nature, global culture.

The major shifts inaugurating the genomic era can be restated schematically. Nature, in the sense of natural facts, such as 'the facts of life', has in the modern era been biologised, so that, for example, the beginnings of life are represented as an evolutionary narrative of natural selection. Similarly, the origin of each individual is explained in terms of a conception narrative referring to eggs and sperm and their union leading on to subsequent embryonic and foetal development, manifesting the unique genetic blueprint that creates diverse individuals. In referring to the natural facts of human variation, the facts of life, or the evolution of *Homo sapiens*, the discursive frame is biology.

In turn, biology has been increasingly geneticised, and this marks the second transformation of concepts of the natural to emerge out of the latter half of the twentieth century. The geneticisation and individualisation of pathology, behaviour and identity at the turn of the millennium is exemplary of the kind of risk assessment which belongs *to a nature at once globalised and personalised*. It is increasingly common to make reference to the genetic parent, to genetic relatedness, genetic risk, genetic identity or to human genetic variation. The public is increasingly aware of genetically inherited diseases, genetic screening programmes, the human genome project and human gene therapy. In sum, the discourses of genetics have become an increasingly important language to describe the human condition, the effects of environmental change, and the future of reproduction (Nelkin and Lindee, 1995).

Crucially, the geneticisation of nature and the facts of life is inseparable from their instrumentalisation (Rabinow, 1996a and b), which is the third major transformation of ideas of the natural within global culture I explore here. Genes have become an increasingly prominent iconic vocabulary in turn-of-the-millennium public culture *because there is a rapidly expanding range of things that can be done to them*. There is increasing public awareness of genetic disease because there are more and more diseases which are seen to be genetic in origin, and a corresponding number of screening technologies to detect them. This instrumentalisation has become inseparable from the capitalisation of life itself, and the commodification of genomics is the force driving intense international scientific competition to claim biotechnological market share. The management of genetic risk, through mapping and sequencing the genomes of humans, plants, animals and micro-organisms, is similarly one of the driving forces behind twenty-first-century medicine, and has become a motor of wealth generation in the effort to secure new forms of genetic capital in the form of genetically modified and patented food and pharmaceutical products. Emergent definitions of genetic risk, and their attendant techniques of detection and intervention, are indexical of changing relationships between health and pathology, disease and cure, technoscience and the body, humans and animals, and the regulation of public health. In turn, such altered understandings contextualise the ways in which life itself can be owned, capitalised and patented.

As Edward Yoxen (1981) presciently noted in the early 1980s, these shifts in the definition of life itself have both institutional and conceptual roots in the history of modern biology, and he points in particular to the emergence of a new definition of *life as information*. Describing the rise of molecular biology, he suggests 'we could describe it as a kind of meta-biology, as a reductive, information-theoretical idiom' which 'has created a new language for analysing nature' (1981: 70). He dates the beginnings of this change back to the work of the Marxist-inspired American geneticist Herman Müller, who, in writing on gene structure as early as 1924, could already confidently claim that 'the gene, then, arose coincidentally with growth and "life" itself' (Müller, cited in Yoxen, 1981: 71). A consequence of this reductionism, of life to the gene, and of the gene to information, was not only the displacement of a view of natural history organised in relation to more holistic units, such as species, populations or ecosytems; the information analogy also enabled the literal and metaphorical prospect of *reprogramming biology*.[2] Chronicling the intensification of financial, institutional and international competition to stake proprietary claims in the New World of the new biology, Yoxen concludes that biotechnology is 'not simply a way of using living things that can be traced back to the Neolithic origins of fermentation and agriculture. As a technology controlled by capital, it is a specific mode of the appropriation of living nature – literally capitalising life' (1981: 112).

Another way to describe the consequences of molecular genomic prowess is that they entail *a respatialisation of genealogy*, so that genetic information no longer necessarily passes in a one-way, linear path of descent from one generation to the next. Rewritten as information, message, code or sequence, the gene becomes newly flexible as it also becomes differently (re)productive. The ability to recombine genes from different species has detonated the formerly rigid conduits of DNA transmission, enabling mice and goats to express human genes, plants to express genes from fish, and sheep to produce human proteins because they have been equipped with the missing parts of the human genome lacking in sufferers of rare inherited diseases, such as cystic fibrosis.[3] Just as the human genome project represents a *molecular globalisation* of human kinship, so the transgenic industry has created postmodern genealogy, shorn of the very limits by which consanguinity was once defined – the slow, predictable and regular brachiations of the familiar family tree now superseded by more flexible dimensions of genealogical time (as speed) and space (which is post-arboreal).[4] The neat genealogical system that Darwin described as natural history is no longer closed, tree-like or unified. Even death no longer poses an obstacle to inter-generational transmission, as immortal cell lines can preserve DNA in perpetuity.[5] There is no reason not to assume that existing collections of dead botanical and zoological materials already comprise a kind of genetic bank, or perpetual genetic capital, for which the exact means of extracting animate expression will soon be developed, if it has not been already, as the blur of genetic innovation is another of its characteristically postmodern traits.[6]

In sum, we arrive at a simple sequence: nature becomes biology becomes genetics, through which life itself becomes reprogrammable information. This sequence proceeds along a path of increasing instrumentalisation, driven by commerce, legitimated in the name of public health, and regulated by the nation-state. The twentieth-century transformation of life itself has had the consequence that the grounding or foundational function of nature as a limit or force in itself has become problematic and lost its axiomatic, *a priori* value as a referent or authority, becoming instead a receding horizon. Nature, we might say, has been de-traditionalised. It has been antiquated, displaced and superseded, and now it is only a trope – a mere shadow of the referent it used to signify. That does not mean it is less useful, as we have already argued, but nature is in a spin. In the place formerly occupied by 'natural facts' is a new frame of reference, an offspring of the genomic era, which is life itself – now orphaned from natural history but full of dazzling promise.

In this chapter, I examine transformations in the definition of 'life', which has literally been unzipped in the context of its highly visible instrumentalisation, to become life itself, which has both displaced traditional ideas about the domain of the natural, and become the locus, and means of expression, for new forms of cultural production (including biological ones). This chapter extends a genealogy of critical attention to changing definitions of 'life' which begins with the work of Georges Canguilhem and moves through the work of Foucault, in order to introduce more recent critical accounts of 'life itself'. I pursue these claims further in relation to the genetic imaginary, illustrated by numerous examples which take as their figurative subtext the popular Hollywood film *Jurassic Park*. In this film, new genetic technologies are both narrativised and animated, and I explore how these generic forms travel back into the heart of natural history, specifically into the American Natural History Museum, where sober scientific professionalism merges with spectacular cinematic promise in an exchange that exemplifies the hybridities constitutive of global culture, global nature. In other words, by using an analysis of the production and consumption of *Jurassic Park*, I generate a set of interpretive perspectives I then borrow to fold back on themselves. Throughout these discussions, I ask not only how particular entities are born, bred or made, *but how they are imagined*. As José Van Dijck argues:

> The dissemination of genetic knowledge is not uniquely contingent on the advance-ment of science and technology, but is equally dependent on the development of images and imaginations. 'Imaginary tools' are crucial assets in the dissemination of genetic knowledge, as they are used to shape this science's public face.
>
> (1998: 2–3)

Both images and imaginations shape the directions of genetic science, as is made particularly evident in the case of *Jurassic Park*. Like Van Dijck, I am exploring the inextricability of the genome from its imagined future promises, hopes and dangers.[7] What are the fantasies and fears catalysed within the new genetics as a domain of millennial cultural practice? What are the forms of recognition, identification and imagination brought into being in response to new genetic technology? What are the pasts, futures and presents of genomic temporality?

The History of Life Itself

Many of these questions have already been the subject of considerable debate, spanning a range of disciplinary contexts from the history of the human sciences, to the cultural analysis of science, to the analysis of kinship in the context of new reproductive and genetic technology. Feminist scholars, science studies researchers and cultural theorists from a number of different countries and backgrounds have already begun to exploit the 'de-familiarising lens' of the technological to reconsider elementary dimensions of cultural practice and social organisation informing the quest to unlock the secrets of life itself.

Notable for his early researches into this field is the French historian Georges Canguilhem, whose prescient 1966 essay 'Le Concept et la Vie' inaugurated the cultural analysis of 'life as a productive force'. In his tracing of the concept of life from antiquity to the present, Canguilhem (1994) emphasised the specificity of the contemporary understanding of life itself derived from molecular biology. Like Yoxen, Canguilhem emphasises the significance of the modern biological model of life being based on *an informational model*, and notes certain similarities to Aristotelian notions of form. As Paul Rabinow notes of Canguilhem's contribution:

> This historical reconstruction provides the groundwork for our contemporary conceptualization of life. Canguilhem frames James D. Watson's and Francis Crick's discovery of the structure of the double helix as an information system. . . . The new understanding of life lies not in the structuring of matter and the regulation of functions, but in *a shift of scale and location* – from mechanics to information and communication theory. In an important sense, the new under-standing of life as information rejoins Aristotle insofar as it posits life as a logos 'inscribed, converted and transmitted' within living matter.
>
> (1994: 20, emphasis added)

Canguilhem himself rejected the implied *telos* of life as an informational force unto itself, as well as the fetishism of 'living codes' as synonymous with a *telos* driven by the necessity of their own reproduction and survival (as is claimed by contemporary 'selfish gene' theorists inspired by Richard Dawkins). Canguilhem viewed the history of science not as a history of the elimination of errors in the refinement of accurate scientific knowledge, but as an epistemological project which, like the life forms described by biology, always exists in relation to a wider historical and cultural environment.

Strongly influenced by Canguilhem's researches is the most significant contemporary historian of life itself, Michel Foucault, who first provides an exposition of this topic in *The Order of Things* (1970). Whereas Canguilhem is concerned with the *discontinuity* produced by an informational concept of life, Foucault is concerned with an earlier epistemic rupture – that of the late eighteenth century, when models of nature began to depart from their 'non-temporal rectangle'[8] and move into a genea-logical frame. He too is concerned with a representational shift effecting the emergence of the modern category of life itself, though in his case as an exemplary parable in his attempt to develop a method appropriate to the historiography of the human sciences – a method he describes as archaeological (Foucault, 1970).

Foucault's attention focusses on the shift from natural history to the life sciences in the broadest sense, asking how categories come to cohere within a social and historical frame, in order to document the forms of biopower brought about through fundamental transformations and re-alignments of life, labour and language. Foucault magnifies the emergence of the modern concept of life to comprise part of a larger thesis about the emergence of modernity and what he calls its power/ knowledges. Whereas eighteenth-century natural history was concerned to classify the diversity of living and non-living things within a static, non-temporal frame, it had no unifying concept of life itself. Until the advent of modern biology, Foucault claims, life 'itself' did not exist. He writes:

> Historians want to write histories of biology in the nineteenth century; but they do not realise that biology did not exist then, and that the pattern of knowledge that has been familiar to us for a hundred and fifty years is not valid for a previous period. And that, if biology was unknown, there was a very simple reason for it: that life itself did not exist. All that existed was living beings, which were viewed through a grid of knowledge constituted by natural history.
>
> (1970: 128)

It is the study of geology and change, so central to the emergence of the concept of evolution, which results in the production of an epistemic system focussed upon the underlying connectedness of all living things. These connections, envisaged as a system of genealogy, in turn produce the conditions enabling the emergence of a concept of life itself.[9]

However, neither Foucault nor Canguilhem was concerned merely to map the historical breakages and conjunctures out of which the modern category of life emerged as a composite of genealogy and information. Foucault's enduring concern with knowledge as a form of power builds on Canguilhem's insistence that all epistemological projects (*projets de savoir*) have consequences for the relationship of life to truth. As François Delaporte points out, Canguilhem's definition of science as historical epistemology, and his consequent insistence that for the life sciences the philosophical problem of truth can be understood only in relation to the living of life, was described by Foucault as 'one of the crucial events in the history of modern philosophy' (Delaporte, 1994: 10). Foucault's subsequent insistence that the history of the definition of life itself cannot be separated from biopolitics develops on this relation of epistemological systems to the human subjects they literally in-form and shape. The description of modern genetics as a form of biopolitics, or power/ knowledge, stems from the assumption that epistemology is never disembodied, is inevitably political, and is equally manifest in the shapes of buildings and institutions as in the epistemic categories of modern knowledge practices. All of these are shaped by the same grammar or syntax. As Canguilhem himself predicted:

> The science of life no longer resembles a portrait of life, as it could when it consisted in the description and classification of species; and it no longer

resembles architecture or mechanics, as it could when it was simply anatomy and macroscopic physiology. But it does resemble grammar, semantics and the theory of syntax. If we are to understand life, its message must be decoded before it can be read. This will no doubt have a number of revolutionary consequences, and it would take many chapters to explain not what they are but what they are in the process of becoming. To define life as a meaning inscribed in matter is to acknowledge the existence of an *a priori* objective that is inherently material and not merely formal.

(1994: 317)

Canguilhem's prediction that 'if we are to understand life, its message must be decoded before it can be read' could hardly have proven a more literal description of the 'revolutionary consequences' of twenty-first-century genetics. The project to map the human genome, that is, to decode or 'read' the entire sequence of human DNA, is an exact fulfilment of the imperatives built into the concept of life first described by Canguilhem, and later elaborated by Foucault. DNA is itself a condensed signifier of 'meaning inscribed in matter', as is the concept of 'genetic information' – both of which represent life as defined by 'an *a priori* objective that is inherently material'.

In the very concept of 'genetic information' is a collapse of matter and message at the heart of the contemporary life sciences. The Human Genome Initiative is the largest research project ever undertaken in the history of the life sciences. It is also the most global project in the history of biology, aimed at sequencing all the DNA not only in humans, but in a myriad other species, with the goal of controlling their genetic substance. Utilising a combination of state-of-the-art information and bio-technology to render binary the 'essence of humanity', the 'code of codes', the 'secret of life', the Human Genome Initiative is described by anthropologist Paul Rabinow as the apotheosis of the very definition of modern rationality. He writes: 'Representing and intervening, knowledge and power, understanding and reform, are built in, from the start, as simultaneous goals and means' (1992: 236). Yet, though he describes the Human Genome Initiative as exemplary of the modernist ethos, Rabinow also predicts it will inevitably produce a collapse of certain categories intrinsic to modernity. 'In the future', he writes,

the new genetics will cease to be a biological metaphor for modern society and will become instead a circulation network of identity terms and restriction loci, around and through which a truly new type of autoproduction will emerge which I call biosociality. If sociobiology is culture constructed on the basis of a metaphor of nature, then in biosociality, nature will be modelled on culture understood as practice. Nature will be known and remade through technique and will finally become artificial, just as culture becomes natural.

(1992: 241–2)

For Rabinow, then, nature and culture do not 'implode' or 'collapse' so much as their relations are inverted: culture becomes the model for nature instead of being 'after nature', as if a kind of successor project or evolutionary development. This new nature that is 'known and remade through technique' will be modelled on the new culture, 'known as practice', and both are defined as 'technique'. According to Rabinow, both culture and nature come to be defined in terms of *doing* rather than *being*, in a shift that directly parallels that described earlier by Butler in terms of gender performativity (1990). Context is also transformed in Rabinow's account, whereby a 'truly new form of autoproduction will emerge' out of precisely *the isomorphism between nature and culture*, which are now defined much more by similarity than by antithesis. In turn, this removal of the nature–culture axis from linear time, from the chronology of natural history with its temporal insistence upon genealogical succession, means that neither nature nor culture is a successor project: both exist in the same timeframe as part of 'a circulation network' in which they co-produce one another.

In contrast to the postmodernist view of culture becoming 'everything', as Jameson (1991) and Baudrillard (1994a, 1998) suggest, Rabinow retains a concept of the natural, only in inverted relation to the cultural – a nature that is 'after' culture, in both senses of the term. This, like Strathern's view, accords with what we are calling 'global nature', which retains an enormous power to signify *in spite of the very conditions under which it might be seen to disappear or collapse*. The rider to the view put forward by Rabinow, by feminists such as José Van Dijck (1998) or Valerie Hartouni (1997), is that while certain modernist definitions of nature or the natural are seemingly undone by techniques to assist them, these occasions *also provide the context in which familiar modernist categories can be reinforced and restaged*. As Van Dijck notes: 'While the new genetics, and especially genomics, is motivating an implosion of categories at various levels, [and] even though new concepts of genomics orient themselves towards the constitution of a new order – a cyber culture or technoculture – *they are cemented in the well-known matrices of modernity*' (1998: 194, emphasis added).

Life as a Public Sacrum

The feminist historian Barbara Duden has also explored the changing contours of the contemporary definition of life, and, like Foucault, has posed this as a question of historical epistemology. Duden's context for examining life itself is the controversy concerning abortion in Germany in the 1990s, where, as in both Britain and the United States, the idea of 'the protection of life' became a powerful anti-abortion slogan. Analysing the transformation of life itself into a public sacrum, or object of worship, Duden charts the emergence of the unborn foetus as a visible public entity, iconising the hitherto unknown of dark gestational space as a figure in need of protection, and thus instantiating what she describes as *the sacralisation of life itself*. She writes in her introduction:

> Politicians and jurists, theologians and physicians, are engaged in a major enterprise of social creation whose object is 'life'. . . . Concurrently, the term *life*

> (and *a life*) has become an idol, and controversy has attached a halo to this idol that precludes its dispassionate use in ordinary discourse. . . . I want to examine the conditions under which, in the course of one generation, technology along with a new discourse has transformed pregnancy into a process to be managed, the expected child into a fetus, the mother into an ecosystem, the unborn into a life, and life into a supreme value.
>
> (1993: 2)

Duden's compelling account of the emergence of the foetus as a *public sacrum*, a worship-object for life itself, underscores the point of many cultural historians of science that in much of its imagery and narrative, science closely imitates the familiar generic devices of Christianity. Like religion, science is a system of belief, of reverence, awe, worship and faith. Especially in their contemporary magnificence and grandeur, the life sciences evoke a distinctly worshipful aura that to many resembles idolatry.

Nowhere is this more evident than in the context of the Human Genome Initiative, which is replete with metaphors of creation. Self-declaredly a search for the secrets of life, a quest to unlock the mysteries of creation, an attempt to rewrite the blueprint of humanity – Man's Second Genesis, it is the modern Holy Grail of science. As Haraway notes, 'the discourses of genetics and information sciences are especially replete with instances of barely secularised Christian figurative realism at work' (1997: 10). Caught up in both secular and sacred discourse, and often condensing the two, life itself is also the site of an intense commodification at the turn of the millennium. This raises questions not only about historical epistemology and capital accumulation strategies, but about forms of popular relationships to the idea of life, including the witnessing and testimonial cultures of both science and religion. Life itself, in all of these senses, emerges as a powerful conversion mechanism, employed by funda-mentalist Christians, venture capitalists and molecular biologists to engender a sense of awe and to evoke resurrection and salvation.

Widening Duden's characterisation of the exposure of the foetus to public view as a new definition of 'life', feminist visual historian Lisa Cartwright examines 'the ascendancy of this term "life" as a core object of epistemological conquest in science, and the optical dissection and penetration of the human body that accompanied the popularization of this term throughout medical science, public health, and public culture generally' (1995: xi). Arguing that 'the cinema [is] an institution and an apparatus for monitoring, regulating, and ultimately building "life" in the modernist culture of Western medical science', Cartwright documents how 'the cinema, a technology designed to record and reproduce movement, was deeply indebted to physiology, both practically and ideologically' (1995: xi–xii). Thus linking the animations of cinema and screening technologies, such as X-rays, to both popular spectacles and expert discourses on 'life' – and demonstrating the inseparability of such framings to the emergence of the category 'life' as the object of both popular and professional fascination – Cartwright resituates the arguments of Foucault and Canguilhem within the theatre of contemporary spectacle, in which not only art and science, but *movement and epistemology* are merged. By 'implanting cinema in nature', and relocating the epistemological project of discerning life itself as one that belongs to a visual register, Cartwright articulates a crucial link for the analysis offered here. Using film as literal 'biography', or inscription of life, another link connecting life not only to labour and language, but also to spectacle and animation, allows the question of life itself to be reframed.

In the film *Jurassic Park*, all of the features of life itself discussed above are replayed as a major Hollywood motion picture, replete with state-of-the-art special effects and the magical allure of cinematic spectacle. Both the film itself and the enormous publicity surrounding its production, release and worldwide success as an entertainment phenomenon provide means to explore the layeredness of public fascination with new genetic technologies, the commodification of life forms, and the power to create life through the storyline of resurrecting extinct dinosaurs using the most advanced molecular and informatic techniques. At once a book, a film, a theme park and a global brand, *Jurassic Park* is an ideal theatre in which to observe the new genetics as performance.

Life Itself and the Genetic Imaginary

> The narratives of the world are numberless. . . . [U]nder this almost infinite diversity of forms, narrative is present in every age, in every place, in every society; it begins with the very history of mankind and there nowhere is nor has been a people without narrative. All classes, all human groups, have their narratives, enjoyment of which is very often shared by men with different, even opposing, cultural backgrounds. . . . [N]arrative is international, transhistorical, transcultural: it is simply there, like life itself.
>
> (Barthes, 1977: 79)

> To raise the question of the nature of narrative is to invite reflection on the very nature of culture and, possibly, even on the nature of humanity itself. . . . Considered as panglobal facts of culture, narrative and narration are less problems than simply data. . . . This suggests that far from being one code among many that a culture may utilize for endowing experience with meaning, narrative is a meta-code, a human universal on the basis of which shared messages about the nature of reality can be transmitted.
>
> (White, 1987: 1)

A genealogy seems unthinkable without an order of succession, as a sequence does not signify without a syntax, and as development is meaningful only as a progression. So too it appears life itself has always been inextricable from its invocation as a story, if not *the* story, be it Genesis, *The Origin of Species*, *The Double Helix* or the 'Book of Man'. Like the 'panglobal facts of narrative and narration', the power of stories about life itself and its Creation lies in their invocation of a global reach, a universal essence of humanity, a shared, primordial ontology. The storiedness of life itself is thus one place to explore its syntactical power. If part of the way life itself, as a discursive condition, or as historical epistemology, calibrates its syntax is at the level of politics, truth or liberation, another level of this syntax can be defined as an *imaginary*. Not in the technical sense of a psychoanalytic pre-symbolic realm of undifferentiated toti-potency, but in the more quotidian sense of a realm of imagining the future, and re-imagining the borders of the real, life itself is dense with the possibility of both salvation and catastrophe. This imaginary dimension of life itself is most evident in relation to the new genetics, and so I refer to it here as *the genetic imaginary*. As the genetic diversity now seen to comprise a vital source of survival-value is debated as a form of patentable, private property; as the spectacle of life as a 'public sacrum' mobilises campaigns to rescue frozen embryos and transgenic 'geep'; and as the borders of the undead and the unborn recede into an indeterminate horizon of enhanced technoscientific potency, the challenges to the imagination beckon irresistibly, uncannily, hopefully, and with an enormous popular appeal.

● ● ●   *Jurassic Park*: **The Film**

Released in 1993 to a rapturous public and commercial welcome, *Jurassic Park* has since emerged as one of the most popular Hollywood films ever produced (Figure 6.1).[10] The Steven Spielberg film of a Michael Crichton novel concerning the use of genetic engineering to bring dinosaurs to life for a theme park on an island off the coast of South America was rapidly promoted to become a highly successful and profitable global spectacle. The film opened as a record-breaking box-office earner in June 1993, having received lavish and adoring media attention ever since its pro-duction was first announced exactly three years previously, in June 1990.[11] Its popularity upon release surpassed all expectations, and the film is notable not only for its unique visual effects, but for the commercial infrastructures through which it was marketed, brandnamed, packaged and consumed.

Both the original novel and the film are set just before the park is scheduled to open, during the final risk-assessment period, with the island fully populated by resurrected dinosauria, and their keepers. These are joined by a cast of characters including a lawyer, three scientists (two palaeontologists and a chaos theorist), the entrepreneur Park owner John Hammond (played by Richard Attenborough), and his two grandchildren, Alexis and Tim. Consistent with the prediction of the chaos theorist Ian Malcolm (Jeff Goldblum), the life force on the island proves uncontain-able and uncontrollable, resulting in carnage and destruction, thus providing both the message of the film (that life itself is a force which will find its way out of any system designed to contain it) and its moral (that just because scientists *can* do something doesn't mean they *should*).

Described as 'the film that makes extinction a thing of the past', *Jurassic Park*'s celebration (and punishment) of the power to create life is heavily overdetermined. The

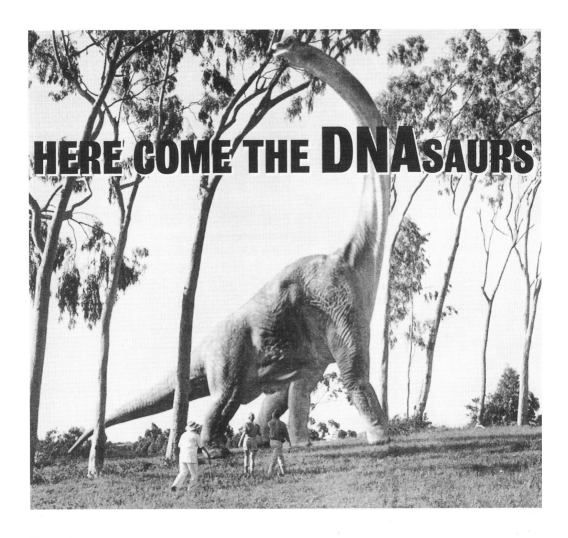

Figure 6.1

*Advertised as 'a film that makes extinction a thing of the past', *Jurassic Park* opened to a rapturous public reception in June 1993. It received extensive media publicity (such as the Newsweek *feature shown here) and remains a popular point of reference in discussions of the new genetics.*

narrative, concerning the successful resurrection of extinct dinosaurs by genetic engineers using fossilised DNA, is reproduced in the visual promise of the cinematic spectacle, which offers state-of-the-art special effects technology to animate the extinct dinosaurs – to make them move, breathe, eat, fight and reproduce, and to achieve this using the maximum visual enhancement attainable. As the film's narrative content is by this means collapsed with its cinematic realisation – both highly technologised attempts to bring dinosaurs to life – the dystopic fantasy of the Crichton novel is to an extent made manifest in the Spielberg movie. Both have as their primary aim synthetic animation techniques of the highest verisimilitude. They are both concerned with producing virtual life. Like both the novel and the Park that is its subject, the film *Jurassic Park* is a form of entertainment. Film director Spielberg is consequently *doppelgänger* to the film character John Hammond, and their two respective *Jurassic Parks*, while simultaneously coincident, have opposite outcomes. Hammond's Jurassic Park goes down in ruins, his reputation is similarly demolished, and he is impoverished – both financially and morally. Spielberg's *Jurassic Park*, on the other hand, was both a technical and a commercial success, greatly enhancing the reputation and fortunes of its creator. This paradox is one of many contradictions the film presents to its viewers.

What is notable about the enormous efforts expended during the film's production to make the dinosaurs as life-like as possible, including taking the production crew to the zoo to watch giraffes, hiring animal behaviour specialists as consultants, and so forth, is that *this process itself is also made very visible and explicit*. On the one hand, the images of dinosaurs must obscure the means of their own fabrication to appear life-like, which puts the invisibility of cinematic production at a premium: it is imperative to remove all the traces of human fabrication from the on-screen spectacle. On the other hand, within the film narrative itself, the means of re-animating the once extinct dinosauria are themselves part of the show at Jurassic Park, which proudly incorporates the laboratory into its display of itself. Here again the efforts of Spielberg and his fictional counterpart Hammond are the opposite of one another. There is also thus a dual spectator thrill on offer for viewers of *Jurassic Park*: you get to see the spectacle and then you get to see how it was done.[12] Both the duplicity (in the sense of duplication) of the film's promise to offer a spectacle of the fantastic, and then to offer a realistic portrait of its creation, and the slippage between various levels of animation in the film establish a potential for a seemingly endless zig-zag, or relay, between surface and depth, or figure and ground, which underscore the cyclical repeat of life, death and re-animation.[13]

The theme of the fabricated spectacle structures the narrative of the film itself. The first sighting of the dinosaurs in the Park exemplifies this process. Weakened in the knees by the sight of a living dinosaur, Grant, one of the palaeontologists (played by Sam Neill), says to Hammond: 'You've created a miracle.' Eager to demonstrate his prowess by showing how this miracle was born and made, Hammond shepherds his guests back to the park headquarters for a brief screening of a film within the film, entitled *Mr DNA*,[14] featuring a cartoon account of how the dinosaurs were brought to life, using palaeo-DNA extracted from insects trapped in fossilised amber who fed on the blood of dinosaurs. A short explanation of genetic engineering is followed by a visit to the 'hatchery', where the guests watch a baby dinosaur being born. It is, again, a dual and somewhat contradictory promise which is part of the signature appeal of *Jurassic Park*, as though one were first shown the magician's display of conjuring, and then immediately thereafter educated in the mechanisms of its illusions.

This 'magical' dimension of the *Jurassic Park* spectacle is partly achieved through a layeredness of animation techniques, as mentioned above. Filmed with a combination of animatronics, morphing, texture mapping, and robotics using technology such as the Alias PowerAnimator™, Pixar's RenderMan™ and Reality Engine™, *Jurassic Park* literally involved a complex sequence of 'layering in' several dimensions of animated material in order to enable the dinosuars to 'come to life'. As stated above, what is notable about this process is that the necessity that it be *invisible* (that is, *not* appear to be a set of 'special effects') is juxtaposed against the constant return to the primal scene of (re)production in the film itself, where we are enabled to 'see how it was done'.

Jurassic Park: The Theme Park, the Ride and the Toy

The means by which the animation of the film 'brings to life' the promise of the narrative in the form of re-animating extinct dinosaurs allows *Jurassic Park* to offer a complex set of juxtapositions between fantasy and reality which, like many of Spielberg's films, play well to both very innocent and very knowing audiences. While delivering a set of reflexive, and at times moralistic, references to Hollywood cinema and the entertainment industry, Spielberg also provides a traditional context for the celebration of technoscience as both man-made and miraculous.

Recalling his original conception of *Jurassic Park*, author Michael Crichton notes:

> Whenever I come up with an idea like extracting dinosaur DNA and then growing a new animal from it, what naturally occurs to me is, 'Well, okay, who's going to pay for it?' The cost would most certainly be phenomenal – and what is it really worth to Stanford University to have a dinosaur? So part of the theme park idea had to do with how to pay for such a project. . . . I couldn't think of any other way to pay for it. I still can't. I think if dinosaurs ever *are* cloned, it will be done for entertainment.
>
> (quoted in Shay and Duncan, 1993: 4)

In notable contrast to Crichton's scepticism about the power of academic research scientists to mobilise sufficient funds to re-create an extinct dinosaur, he is confident the entertainment industry could do so, as, in a sense, they confirmed by investing huge sums in what many considered the improbable prospect of creating *Jurassic Park*. The self-ironical celebration in Crichton's acclaim for the movie industry is in contrast to his stated (if disingenuous) concern about the biotechnology industry: that 'the commercialization of genetic engineering [comprises] a very serious problem and one that we are still not facing' (quoted in Shay and Duncan, 1993: 4). One reading of these juxtaposed claims is that the film demonstrates the conscientiousness, and moral purpose, of the entertainment industry by offering a chilling denouncement of the biotechnology industries, and the scientific temptation to 'tinker' with the germplasm. A more cynical reading is that such claims are contradicted by the film's celebratory, 'gee whiz', depiction of biotechnology and genetic science, to which the moral reproach is mere narrative closure. Crichton has certainly benefited commercially from the hype surrounding biotechnologically assisted futures, at least through sales of his novel and the film.[15] Like *Schindler's List*, with which it overlapped in post-production, *Jurassic Park* offers moral denunciation – an attractive certainty in an age in which solid truths are hard to come by – and, even more importantly, good box office. Arguably it is precisely the excessive layering of this film, in both moral and entertainment terms, which renders both its reception and its 'message' so appropriately flexible.

In addition to the 'theme park' setting of *Jurassic Park*, with its ludic, self-referential relation to Hollywood, the cinema and the entertainment industry, it is significant that much of *Jurassic Park* is structured as a ride. Early in the film, the visiting party is swept across the ocean and plunged into a gut-wrenching drop by helicopter on to the landing pad at the base of a waterfall. Filmed on the island of Kauai at the western edge of the Hawaiian islands,[16] where tourists are invited to enjoy 'the most beautiful helicopter rides on earth' by at least a dozen flight-tour operators, the first 'ride' in *Jurassic Park* faithfully replicates an on-site tourist attraction. Subsequently, the visitors are transported by special 'tour cars' to the main headquarters. At headquarters, they take another 'ride' through the production of the dinosaurs in a series of 'behind-the-scenes' introductions to *Jurassic Park*, for which they are, as in the helicopter, literally strapped into their seats.[17] And, of course, the entire rest of the film from that point onwards is about a 'ride' that goes very wrong, as the tour cars stall and the visitors' escape from the theme park begins.

Remarking on the 'theme park model of consumption' exploited by Walt Disney in his creation of Disneyland, popular culture historian Mark Langer describes an 'integrated structure, which reached an international audience, [and] formed a transnational space for selling both goods and cultural images' (1995: 75). By dovetailing the opening of the Disneyland theme park with live television broadcasting, Disney was able to invite viewers in 1955 to:

> Dial 7 at 7:30 tonight for the biggest 'live' telecast in history, as Walt Disney himself guides you through the 160-acre wonderland he has created in Anaheim, California. You will steam down the rivers of America in a real old-fashioned stern-wheeler, *The Mark Twain*; trek to darkest Africa for a look at wild animals; ride a rocket to the moon – all in the comfort of your own living room.
>
> (Disney advertisement, quoted in Langer, 1995: 75)

Figure 6.2

The large 'toys' in the theme park are, of course, the dinosaurs themselves, which are in turn animated on film by both small and large puppets, such as the ill Triceratops shown in this scene.

Extending the Disneyland analogy of 'a movie that could be walked into' (Hine, 1986: 151), *Jurassic Park* offers a movie of a theme park which in turn becomes the main attraction of theme parks, set up by Universal Studios in 1994 in Florida and California – thus redeploying a similar series of dovetailings of rides-within-rides, theme parks-within-theme parks and movies-within-movies.[18]

The most important element of the theme park is, of course, its attractions: the 'living' dinosaurs of Jurassic Park, which are, like large puppets, its toys (Figure 6.2). As the hype factor within the film concerns the creation of animate dinosaurs, so did much of the media attention to *Jurassic Park* concern the state-of-the-art animation techniques necessary for its successful creation – the credibility of which was largely seen to determine the film's success or failure. 'Before too many months had elapsed, it became evident that *Jurassic Park* would need much more than the usual production in terms of preparation,' note Don Shay and Jody Duncan, authors of *The Making of Jurassic Park* (1993: 22). Denis Muren, of the special effects outfit Industrial Light and Magic founded by George Lucas to create *Star Wars*, recalls:

> At the time, Steven [Spielberg] was pretty much insistent on doing it all with full-size robotic dinosaurs that he was going to have made. He had seen the 'King Kong' ride at the Universal Studios tour in Florida and thought it was fabulous. He felt that if somebody could do that, then with some more direction they could make dinosaurs that would be able to do most of what he needed for this film.
>
> (quoted in Shay and Duncan, 1993: 18)

Production of the dinosaurs for *Jurassic Park* was eventually based on a combination of full-scale robotic devices and smaller puppet models, combined with computer-generated imagery.[19] The most daunting construction was the T-rex, which was ultimately built on a flight-simulator platform, adapted to conform in its movements to the manipulation of a fifth-scale T-rex replica. Designer Stan Winston explains:

> The mechanism was based on a flight simulator, but it's not a flight simulator – it's a 'dino-simulator'. It was built specifically for us, to our dimensions for this T-rex. But the concept is the same. We took all this hydraulic technology and spread it up through the simulator, into the body, out to the tip of the tail and the tip of the head.
>
> (quoted in Shay and Duncan, 1993: 29)

The aim was to achieve for the T-rex 'complete motion', adequate to convey the fluidity of organic musculature and bird-like rapidity. 'It was almost like sculpting motion rather than sculpting clay' noted one of the T-rex model-builders (Richard Landon, quoted in Shay and Duncan, 1993: 31). Dubbed 'go-motion animation', the techniques for animating the dinosaurs of *Jurassic Park* were successfully developed to maximise fluidity of movement and invisibility of technique. Animator Randy Dutra compiled a 'Dinosaur Bible' of movements, capable of being stored on computer and blurred into a cinema-finish through a use of motion control that eliminated the occasional 'strobing' effects of stop-motion techniques. Throughout, the primary aim in animating the dinosaurs for *Jurassic Park* was to convey a sense of warm-blooded, lithe, intelligent life forms in contrast to their lumbering, dim-witted and understandably extinct image. In addition, an emphasis on the behaviour of dinosaurs characterises both the narrative of the film and the depiction of the dinosaurs. 'What we tried to do', dinosaur creator Rick Carter claimed, 'was find the animal in the dinosaur as opposed to the monster in the dinosaur' (quoted in Shay and Duncan, 1993: 14).

Writing of the place of the toy between the animate and the inanimate, Susan Stewart describes it as 'the physical embodiment of fiction'.

> The toy . . . is a device for fiction: it is a device for fantasy, a point beginning for narrative. The toy opens an interior world. . . . The inanimate toy repeats the still life's theme of arrested life, the life of the tableau. But once the toy becomes animated, it initiates another world, the world of the daydream. The beginning of narrative time here is not an extension of the time of everyday life; it is the beginning of an entirely new temporal world.
>
> (1993: 57)

As a material-semiotic actor, the toy instantiates a fantasy temporality: that of the daydream. Its animation offers 'a point beginning for narrative' inviting 'an infinite pleasure', and it is thus directly keyed to the powers of imagination. Through the animation of the toy, an object 'comes to life': '[J]ust as the world of objects is always a kind of "dead among us", the toy ensures . . . the world of life "on the other side".' Stewart adds:

> It must be remembered that the toy moved late to the nursery, that from the beginning it was adults who made toys, and not only with regard to their other invention, the child.
>
> (1993: 57)

The spectre of the toy is inextricable from that of the machine, and in this sense, the toy is the ghost of industrialisation, 'the dream of the impeccable robot which has haunted the West' (Stewart, 1993: 57) as a kind of subtext to mechanisation, automation and the liveliness of machinery. How fitting Darwin should have proposed his redefinition of 'life itself' in the mid-nineteenth century, in an England seething with industrialisation, amidst the blur and hum of a mechanical liveliness all around him that was unprecedented until his era. Describing a Victorian table-top railway, Stewart suggests its amusement derives from the 'double stamp of culture brought about by introducing the mechanical to the natural and by traversing the natural with the mechanical at the same time that a reduction of scale is effected' (1993: 58). Nature is doubly transmogrified by such a display: '[T]he natural has moved from the forest to the individual trees of the park to the synthetic trees, barns, cows and farmers of the train set's landscape' (1993: 59). Toys could be said in this sense to represent an entire genre not only of second nature, but of seconded industrial culture.

This seconded, or 'toy-', nature inhabits an array of landscapes in *Jurassic Park*, in which both miniaturisation and the use of the gigantic were concealed mechanisms for the production of 'naturalistic' verisimilitude. From the mechanical hydraulics of the flight-simulator T-rex, to the delicate hand-held puppetry of the hatching Velociraptor, to the computer-generated animation of the Gallimimus herd, nature is seconded by a range of devices in pursuit not only of the amusements of a table-top reduction of scale, but of the view from the train-window which sweeps to the horizon point of landscape. The temporalities of live-action, mechanical simulation, virtual animation and their recombination post-production can be offered as a fluid cinematic spectacle, through which reorderings of scale, time and dimension are seamlessly re-unified.

Writing of the film's fluidity and movement, film theorist Peter Wollen suggests:

> It's all as if *Jurassic Park*, the film, was really designed to end up as *Jurassic Park* the ride. The strip of film unspooling through the projector is like the single-rail automated people-mover designed to shuttle tourists around the park.
>
> (1993: 8)

It is perhaps only fitting that visitors to Jurassic Park (in the film) should be transported by rail, as they are thus 'moved' by the 'mechanical dinosaurs' of the industrial age in their consumption of the great achievements of the age of genomics. Through consuming 'wildlife', as bio-tourists, such visitors witness the towering achievements of technoscience, indistinguishable from the 'real thing' save for the fact of their 65 million year disappearance.

As Stewart notes, the invention of the toy is proximate to that 'other invention': the child, and, consequently, the childlike. A complex positioning of the child operates within *Jurassic Park*, as in all Spielberg films, to which children are inevitably central. Superficially, children are important to *Jurassic Park* in the development of plotlines around the palaeontologist Grant, the palaeobotanist Ellie, and the Park owner, Hammond. More importantly, they are key to the establishment of point of view within the film, as well as the novel, which are notably childlike, although neither is particularly suitable for children. For both the author Crichton, and the director Spielberg, this centrality of the child and the childlike becomes closely associated with paternity, echoing the centrality of father–child bonds within the film. Michael Crichton recalls the turning point which led him to write *Jurassic Park*:

> My wife was pregnant with my first child, and I found I couldn't walk past a toy store without buying a stuffed toy. And what I was buying, more often than not, were stuffed dinosaurs. My wife couldn't understand it. We knew we were having a girl. Why was I buying all these dinosaurs? And I would say, 'Well girls like dinosaurs too.' But it was clear I was sort of obsessed with dinosaurs; and the whole idea of children and dinosaurs, and the meaning of what that was, was just on my mind a lot during that period.
>
> (quoted in Shay and Duncan, 1993: 3)

This extract is notable for several reasons, not least of which being the relationship between authorship and paternity signalled by the gifts purchased for his unborn daughter.[20] In a sense, the conception of *Jurassic Park*, its genesis or animation, has as its starting point a toy bought for a child – but perhaps not for the child. Upon reflection, the gift reveals an 'obsession' not only with dinosaurs, but with *children and dinosaurs*,[21] and indeed fathers giving dinosaurs as gifts to children. This fascination recapitulates the relation of author to text, long modelled on the idiom of paternity (Rose, 1993), in several senses. Certainly the character of Hammond, the entrepreneurial 'author' of Jurassic Park, demonstrates a pronounced paternal relation to the dinosaurs 'born' into his custody. 'I always try to be present at the birth,' he explains to his visitors in the hatchery. In a sense too, the Park is conceived by Hammond as a 'gift' to children and it is his own grandchildren he invites to visit the Park as a treat. Similarly, Spielberg's films centrally concern the relation of children to the miraculous, the monstrous and the father – who is often culpable, or flawed. As a celebrated cinematic *auteur*, Spielberg is particularly known for both appealing to children and terrifying them, much as Walt Disney did with films such as *Bambi*. As film critic Henry Sheehan points out, '[T]he two most terrifying scenes in the film revolve specifically around the children's near death at the hands first of the tyranno- saurus rex and then of the velociraptors', consistent with the signature Spielberg theme, present in both *Jaws* and *Schindler's List*, of 'the father or father figure trying to rescue a child just before it undergoes the death the father has unwittingly devised for it' (Sheehan, 1993: 10).

Whether or not, then, *Jurassic Park*, or other Spielberg films such as *Jaws*, are 'for' children, children are central to both his plotlines and his characterisations. Moreover, it is often noted that many of the pleasures associated with the work of Spielberg are distinctively childlike, and this is a defining feature of of *Jurassic Park*. As a fascination with dinosaurs may be described as childlike, so too is animation often described as a medium inextricable from the pleasures of childhood. Interviewed in *Art History Journal* for a special issue on 'Cartoon: Caricature: Animation', animator Irene Kotlarz describes the medium of animation as inevitably childlike because

> so many of the concerns of animation have been with the unfilmable, *or with aspects of the imagination* which are hard to represent in other media. Movement itself can be rendered in evocative ways, objects and people can be deformed, metamorphosed and dismembered. So many of its themes have come from fables or folklore or magic. Maybe there is something too about close attention to detail – an aspect of the process of production which promotes a kind of 'innocent' encounter with the world. . . . There is an obsessive and almost childlike interest in making things move – which often starts in early childhood.
>
> (quoted in Curtis, 1995: 25, emphasis added)

The uses of childhood, children and the childlike within *Jurassic Park* complement and enhance its invocation of the 'toy', the 'theme park' and the 'ride'. The essentially ludic space created through these devices is an important means through which the many juxtapositions offered by the film are explored. Closely linked to the imagina- tion, and to the 'unfilmable', an excess of animation offers a broad scope of possibility for re-imagining life, life's creation, and the re-creation of extinct life forms through the very medium itself.

● ● ● **The Making of *Jura$$ic Park***

The excesses of *Jurassic Park* at the level of the pre-production, production and post- production of the film were accompanied by an equally staggering market-making epic. 'If it's not *Jurassic Park*, it's extinct,' proclaimed the slogan for a host of tie-ins for the blockbuster dino-pic. More than 500 companies were licensed to sell more than 5000 products connected to *Jurassic Park* worldwide. In Britain alone, sales of the *Jurassic Park* dinosaur toy range exceeded £10 million by the end of 1993 – just over six months from the date of the film's US release. Many of these products were

Figure 6.3

The book about the making of the film featured in the Park's ill-fated gift shop is but one of many layering-in devices used in this very 'knowing' and highly reflexive film. The book cover features the Jurassic Park *brand – a no-show dino logo which withholds the vital ingredient it is marketing.*

featured in the film, which includes a slow pan of the Park's ill-fated gift shop, stacked with products emblazoned with the *Jurassic Park* logo (Figure 6.3).

Several aspects of the market-making efforts by Spielberg and MCA were as notable as the techniques used in production of the film itself. Just as *Jurassic Park*, the film, 'stretched the envelope' of animatronics and special effects, so too did the market saturation achieved for *Jurassic Park*, the global brand, overturn previous industry standards. By March 1994, less than a year after its release on 11 June 1993, the film had grossed over a billion dollars in merchandise alone. For a film that had cost $15 to $20 million to advertise, such returns could be seen only as overwhelmingly profitable. Moreover, in March 1994 *Jurassic Park* was still playing in over 900 movie theatres in the US alone, with the video yet to be released in the autumn of 1994.[22]

The aptly named marketing executive Brad Globe of Amblin Entertainment and Elizabeth Gelfand of MCA/Universal Studios led the marketing drive for what they described as 'the highest grossing movie of all time'.[23] Two departures from traditional market and release protocol were claimed to have been instrumental to the emergence of *Jurassic Park* as a 'global brand'. First, the usual timing between US and foreign release was significantly shortened, to within less than a month. This required that many of the merchandising companies were already signed on well in advance, which in turn generated approximately $60 million worth of domestic and international promotion exposure. Kenner, McDonald's, Sega and Nintendo were all early signers to the *Jurassic Park* 'Dinosaur Dream Team', as it was dubbed. Kmart, Weetabix, Kellogg's, PepsiCo and Coca-Cola joined later to represent different world markets. In turn, licensees of promotional products and tie-ins were invited to Amblin's Jurassic Park-style headquarters on the Universal Pictures lot in Studio City, California, to meet Spielberg, the producer Kathleen Kennedy, and other entertainment industry executives, and to view 'a rare screening of behind-the-scenes footage from *Jurassic Park*' (Magiera, 1994: S1–2). Once assembled, representatives from the various licensing firms were invited to contribute their own ideas to the Amblin/MCA 'Dream Team', enabling them to contribute directly to the promotion and marketing strategy.[24]

Key to the unification of 500 licensed products and more than eighty different marketing and promotional efforts was the *Jurassic Park* logo, the yellow, red and black shadow-profile of the upper part of a T-rex skeleton, standing with its jaws agape and claws raised. The logo, according to Brad Globe of Amblin, 'identified *Jurassic Park* as very special and very unique without actually showing the dinosaurs' (quoted in Magiera, 1994: S2). The no-show dino logo served two purposes, according to the marketing directors: it preserved the secrecy surrounding the appearence of the dinosaurs in the film, thus contributing to the suspense surrounding its release, and it clearly distinguished official *Jurassic Park* dinosaur products from their myriad saurian competitors. From early on, market managers were impressed by the worldwide appeal of the logo. According to MCA/Universal's Elizabeth Gelfand, 'I think that's the phenomenon of *Jurassic Park* – that around the world there is such a strong identity for this movie and its logo' (quoted in Magiera, 1994: S2). Market industry leaders were also impressed by the success of the *Jurassic Park* promotion, and the Amblin–MCA/Universal team was voted 'Promotional Marketer of the Year' by the influential trade journal *Advertising Age*.

As it not only met, but surpassed and transformed industry standards at the level of production, so too did the marketing and promotion of *Jurassic Park* exceed expectations and transform business-as-usual. It is difficult to account for the film's enormous worldwide popularity, and the effectiveness of the *Jurassic Park* 'global brand', which succeeded in creating an almost instantaneous global market. Clearly many films have vast promotion engines positioning them to become summer block-busters, and many are disastrous failures all the same. Other films, such as *Jurassic Park*, seem to attract not only the interest, attention and curiosity of the 'general public' but to generate momentum within the professional circles out of which they emerge – as this film seemed to do among advertisers and marketing executives, much as it had done among the cast and crew involved in its production. In more than one respect, and as a brand as much as a film, *Jurassic Park* somehow acquired a life of its own.

One way to begin to examine the bases of such fascination, curiosity and promise – the 'hook' of this film – is to shift attention away from its production and marketing to consider briefly at least one context of its consumption. In the following section, then, I examine the 'consumption' of *Jurassic Park* by the American Museum of Natural History in New York City. An unusual place for a tie-in to a major Hollywood motion picture, the American Natural History Museum was one of several prominent public institutions to 'jump on the *Jurassic Park* bandwagon'. In an ironic sense, the film put 'life itself' back into natural history through its occupation of an entire wing of one of America's most eminent scientific institutions, which is also home to one of the world's most celebrated departments of palaeontology.

• • • 'Press Screen to Start': Interacting with *Jurassic Park* in the Museum

> Michael Crichton's particular brand of science fiction is said to be distinguished by the very close proximity of his storylines to actual scientific plausibility, and this is a key component in the ability of [*Jurassic Park*] to promise artificial life. The storyline is so close to ongoing scientific research that actual scientific discoveries over the course of the film's production seemed as if deliberately planned to enhance its appeal.
>
> (text from a display at the American Natural History Museum's
> *Jurassic Park* exhibit)

As prominent science journals adapted their coverage of palaeontology to take advantage of the hype surrounding the production of *Jurassic Park*, so too did science museums create new displays timed to coincide with the film's release. Seamlessly recruited to do service for the pedagogically inclined institution of the science museum, model dinosaurs have long been a popular display item offered to consumers of official natural history. Towering like imperial giants over the vast scope of life's ancient majesty, model dinosaurs have a special place in the representation of ancient life forms.[25]

The successful extraction of palaeo-DNA from insects trapped in amber by scientists at the American Museum of Natural History in New York was one of several factors leading to the museum's adoption of the film as a basis for the exhibit 'The Dinosaurs of *Jurassic Park*' housed in their main building beside Central Park (Figure 6.4).[26] Outside the exhibit, a clip of the first-sighting scene in *Jurassic Park* repeated itself on a video monitor above the ticket office. In the first room, more clips from the film replayed themselves on a dozen monitors beside props from the film related to dinosaur re-creation and birth, including the embryo storage chamber and the hatchery. A display of storyboards from the film's production led on to a second room, dark with jungle foliage and containing replicas of the dinosaurs featured in the film, again with video monitors beside them playing relevant scenes from the movie. As a self-congratulatory denouement, the last room contained 'the evidence' provided by the museum's own collections. Insects trapped in amber, fossilised dinosaur eggs and skeletal remains were flanked by interactive computer terminals featuring the latest scientific findings about the dinosaurs: Were they related to birds? What did they eat? Did some of them have fur? How fast were they?

As a spectacle, the exhibit offered a 'behind-the-scenes' tour featuring a collection of authentic props (or artefacts) involved in the film's production, and illustrating these with relevant footage from the film itself. By employing the film as a 'lead-in' to the final exhibit displaying the museum's own collections, palaeontology was positioned as the ultimate 'behind-the-scenes' event.

The display of the museum's own 'contributions' to the film thus collapsed an origin story of a particular technique (the extraction of DNA from insects fossilised

Figure 6.4

In issuing an 'official guide' to the dinosaurs of Jurassic Park *the American Museum of Natural History sought both to attract customers by tail-backing on the film's appeal, and to reassert its authority as the 'true' source of the speculation necessary for dinosaurs to be discovered.*

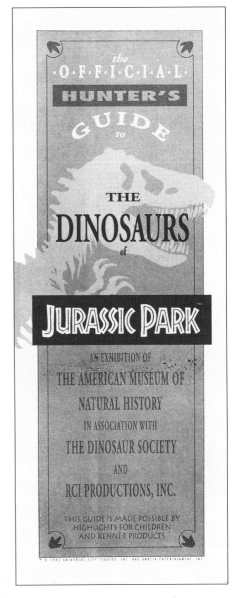

in amber) into an account of the origins for the film itself, positioning palaeontologists as the discoverers who inspired authors such as Crichton, and directors such as Spielberg, in the first place. In a sense, the display extended the film's credits by positioning palaeontology, rather than Michael Crichton (himself trained in anthropology), as its original inspiration. The display thus repositions the creativity behind *Jurassic Park* as derivative. The real author was natural history: the *raison d'être* for the museum itself. But the role of discoverer, of scientist, of 'modest witness' to the truth of nature's intimate genealogy, belongs to the palaeontologists, the high priests of fossilised life. For example, it was Henry Fairfield Osborn, then president of the museum, who named 'velociraptor', or 'quick seizer', in the scientific literature in 1924. The message is clear: without professional scientists, *Jurassic Park* would not exist. Or, as the museum itself chose to emphasise at the conclusion of its exhibit, in unintentionally ironic commercial language:

> Speculation as much as special effects was needed to bring dinosaurs to life in *Jurassic Park*. The most accurate speculations about dinosaurs and their worlds are based on fossil evidence gathered by scientists. There would be no *Jurassic Park*, no recreated dinosaurs for our entertainment without science.

Displayed under the headline: 'Dinosaurs – Dead or Alive?', this text asserts the primacy of scientific research in the power to create, the capacity to transcend extinction, and to re-create the living from the dead. In strikingly similar terms to authorship, the museum too stakes a claim in the resurrection of the extinct life forms celebrated in *Jurassic Park*. Instead of special effects, however, it is scientific knowledge, based on direct observation and disciplined research, which provides the animating spark or origin of life's re-creation.

Not surprisingly, given its immodesty, this claim proved controversial among members of the scientific community, such as Stephen Jay Gould, himself a palae-ontologist, who was stridently critical of the exhibit. In his review of 'Dinomania' in the *New York Review of Books* shortly after the exhibit opened, Gould protested that 'The Dinosaurs of *Jurassic Park*'

> dramatizes a conflict between institutions with disparate purposes – museums and theme parks. Museums exist to display authentic objects of nature and culture – yes, they must teach; and yes, they may certainly include all manner of computer graphics and other virtual displays and devices from the increasingly sophisticated arsenals of virtual reality to titillate, to scare, to thrill, even to teach. . . . But theme parks are in many ways the antithesis of museums. . . . [T]heme parks belong to the world of commerce, museums to the world of education. . . . For paleontologists, *Jurassic Park* is both our greatest opportunity and our most oppressive incubus – a spur for unparalleled general interest in our subject, and the source of a commercial flood that may truly extinguish dinosaurs by turning them from sources of awe into clichés and commodities.
>
> (1993: 56)

In contrast to Gould's 'two-cultures' view of science and its publics, British film critic Peter Wollen questions this very divide in a review of *Jurassic Park* that invokes quite a different scientific tradition. Writing about the Victorian fascination with dinosaurs in England in the mid-nineteenth century, he points out that the museum and the theme park have a closely intertwined history. Here he cites the celebrated 'dino-dinner' at the Great Exhibition of 1851, hosted by Richard Owen, who had coined the word 'dinosaur' (from the Greek meaning 'terrible lizard') at the annual meeting of the British Association for the Advancement of Science ten years earlier. Owen had life-sized dinosaur models built for the Exhibition site of the Crystal Palace in Hyde Park, London. As Wollen notes:

> To publicise the new attraction, a dinner was held on a platform inside the iguanodon, its back still open, with Owen seated at the head of the table in the dinosaur's head. The palaeontologists and geologists who gathered in the monster's 'socially loaded stomach', as the *Illustrated London News* reported, were there to form 'the best guarantee for the severe truthfulness' of [the replicas].
>
> (1993: 9)

Given Steven Spielberg's vigorous insistence upon the most 'severe truthfulness' of his dinosaurs, the discordance between the museum and the theme park cannot be said to lie in the traditions of natural history as a science. Neither was commerce absent from the earlier period of 'dinomania', as Wollen also points out:

> For the visitor to the dinosaur's island . . . there were tie-ins too: wall charts and small-scale models. Plainly the newly-minted dinosaur was in at the very birth of the theme park, mixing science with spectacle.
>
> (1993: 9)

At the American Museum of Natural History, there was as much to see in the gift shop as in the exhibition, to be sure. Beside *Jurassic Park* lunch-boxes (the lower end of the 'educational' spectrum) were several shelves stacked with literary dinosauria: *My Visit to the Dinosaurs*; *Dinosaurs of Long Ago*; *Dinosaur Babies*; *How Big is a Brachiosaurus?*; *The Day of the Dinosaur*; *Dinosaur Dreams*; *Fossils Tell of Long Ago*, and other titles were displayed before crowds of eager consumers.

Such tie-ins were undoubtedly an important source of revenue for museums struggling to become more entrepreneurial in an era of shrinking public funds. Like the American Museum of Natural History, the Carnegie Museum of Natural History in Pittsburgh, Pennsylvania, also took advantage of 'dinomania' by launching its own collection of 'museum quality' authentic replica dinosaurs (Figure 6.5). These colourful plastic commodisauria came with official pedigrees of their sober lineage:

> The original models were sculpted under the guidance of the paleontologists of the Carnegie Museum of Natural History, Pittsburgh, Pennsylvania. Each of these replicas is exactly to scale. Every detail is scientifically accurate. These replicas are a window onto a world that was. Not merely toys . . . but an unusual selection of collectible replicas. They are so authentic that each one has a diploma . . . a parchment tag suspended by a gold cord bearing a complete description.
>
> The Carnegie Collection – Collect them all before they become Extinct!
> (Manufactured by Safari Limited, Miami,
> Florida – made with 70% recycled materials.)

As the awkward disclaimer 'not merely toys' makes clear, this description once again attempts to combine the sobriety of learned scientific authority ('every detail is scientifically accurate') with both the trappings of commercialism ('a parchment tag suspended by a gold cord') and an appeal to the imagination ('a window onto a world that was'). Thus hybridising commerce, scientific authority and playfulness ('Collect them all before they become Extinct!), these scale models perform the dense artefactualism of global nature as forms of both commodity culture and scientific realism.

Like 'dinomania' more widely, the commercialisation of dinosaurs, both by the producers of *Jurassic Park*, and by the directors of prominent scientific institutions, would seem to have a 'life of its own'. The consumer appeal of dinosaurs, however, cannot itself explain why commerce, like so many other media, has become so vigorous a conduit for the expression of interest and fascination with the once extinct. Long before they were the subject of a major Hollywood motion picture, dinosaurs had become something of a 'trend'. This fascination has since been tapped by a range of enterprises, from the entertainment industry to the scientific establishment.[27]

Collect them all before they become Extinct!

The Carnegie Collection

Museum Quality Authentic Prehistoric Replicas
Made with 70% recycled materials.
Manufactured by:
Safari Limited • Box 630685 • Miami, Florida 33163 USA

DB 101

Figure 6.5

Like the American Museum of Natural History, the Carnegie Museum emphasised 'scientifically accurate' dinosaurs in its marketing of scale replicas 'sculpted under the guidance of paleontologists', as were the dinosaurs in the film Jurassic Park.

No. 423
Name: Corythosaurus
When: Late Cretaceous
Length: 33 feet (10 meters)
Weight: 2 tons

New for 1993

No. 420
Name: Mosasaurus
When: Late Cretaceous
Length: Up to 40 feet long (12 meters)
Weight: 4,000 lbs.

Scale: 1:40
Model: 10.5" (26.5 cm) long

No. 422
Name: Spinosaurus
When: Late Cretaceous
Length: 39 feet (12 meters)
Weight: 2-3 tons

No. 419
Name: Elasmosaurus
When: Late Cretaceous
Length: 48 feet (14 meters)
Weight: 5,100 lbs.

Scale: 1:40
Model: 6" (15 cm) long

No. 421
Name: Iguanodon
When: Jurassic/Cretaceous
Length: 30 feet (9 meters)
Weight: 5 tons

The Carnegie Collection

Maiasaura

They are so authentic that each one has a diploma...a parchment tag suspended by a gold cord bearing a complete description.

The original models were sculpted under the guidance of the paleontologists of the Carnegie Museum of Natural History, Pittsburgh, Pennsylvania. Each of these replicas is exactly to scale. Every detail is scientifically accurate. These replicas are a window into a world that was. Not merely toys...but an unusual selection of collectible replicas.

The Marketing of Life Itself

> Life itself is a capital accumulation strategy in the simultaneously marvelous and ordinary domains of New World Order, Inc.
>
> (Haraway 1997: 143)

In its blend of sober scientific prediction, speculative commercial ventures, virtual cinematic effects and popular narrative forms, *Jurassic Park* is a film which collapses distinctions between fact and fiction, life and art, science and entertainment. It thus performs a neat summary of the increasing ambiguity surrounding the concept of life itself in contemporary culture, where its increasingly explicit removal from its traditionally antithetical relation to the inanimate, or to death, is the occasion of both fascination and horror. *Jurassic Park* is a parable announcing the wrongs of disturbing the realms of the undead, the once extinct. Yet it is also a celebration of precisely this newfound technological capacity. It is not properly a secular film, but an almost biblical allegory. It collapses the trajectory of evolutionary time in a fantasy of re-creation, in which we stand beside our extinct genealogical brethren in awe at the miracle of (re-)creation, only to be reminded there was only one true Genesis which we mimic at our peril. But what it does best is to hold these two things together: the hubris of 'playing God' alongside its equally profound appeal.

This axis has many vectors of alignment with contemporary cultural practice, and the commercial success of *Jurassic Park* brings yet another set of meanings to the Foucauldian tradition of investigating 'life itself' as a singular indexical sign, and its conjugation as a distinctive turn-of-the-millennium grammar. In large part the production of *Jurassic Park* was commercially driven, yet its success cannot be explained by economic factors alone. It is the literally spectacular conjuncture between powerful economic forces, such as the entertainment industry, and conservative cultural institutions, such as science museums, which again demonstrates the excessiveness of the film's appeal. This excessiveness, I argue, must be understood to work imaginatively, much as it does commercially or pedagogically. Becoming literate in *Jurassic Park*'s many idioms turns out to be another way to read across the many-layered palimpsest that is global nature. Interpreting the success of this film requires a hermeneutics keyed to the wider cultural renegotiation of life itself, to the altered artefacts of its productive and reproductive strategies, and the non-linear routes of its distribution and consumption. Viable offspring of the antiquated authority of 'nature' it both displaces and revivifies, life itself emerges as a contested template of cultural values and social practice. Technology figures centrally in this process of denaturalisation, as do commercial forces – both of which are, in a sense, animating entities in their own right. In addition to the expanding stakes in global contests over ownership of life forms are the intimate and subjective dimensions of such contests, throwing into question fundamental social ties based on identity categories deeply rooted in the biological. In an era in which it has become a cliché to refer to these elementary units of sociality as being 'in crisis', I suggest instead that what is more useful is to become more literate in the syntax that now connects them. Whatever one thinks of *Jurassic Park* as a text, a parable, a product or a spectacle, one thing its excessiveness invites is a very broad array of reading strategies.

Jurassic Park is a film in which the central conceit involves not just exclusion, but exclusion of a very visible kind. The film relies fundamentally upon an axis of the visual in which everything depends on how much you don't see behind the scenes, and everything you do see as a result of this exclusion. What is of interest is the extent to which this axis does not hold steady, but becomes the central invitation of the film: both as a cinematic or museum spectacle, and as a commercial enterprise, the invitation to go 'behind the scenes' is the provocatively repeated refrain. From the constitution of its half-hidden brand image, to the lure offered to commercial investors of seeing 'behind the scenes' clips of the makings of the film, to the museum's reconstruction of its own 'behind the scenes' display, to the workings of the film itself, the invitation *to share in the secrets of its own making* is *Jurassic Park*'s predominant form of address. The film thus performs a very contemporary knowingness, speaking precisely to the knowledge of its audiences that there is more going on than meets the eye, and indeed that the invitation to call any bluff can be just another ruse. If such a form of cultural literacy is based on a certain scepticism, it is an overwhelmingly familiar one.

This repeated invitation to witness the making of *Jurassic Park* provides a powerful analogy for the forms of public witnessing which surround the remaking of life itself. Now that biology has become increasingly technologised, geneticised and informatic, its literal reconstruction in the lab has become increasingly public and visible, through episodes such as the worldwide publicity surrounding the creation of Dolly the cloned sheep. In newspaper diagrams and TV news show résumés of Dolly's creation, her made-in-the-lab origins were repeatedly made explicit through images of denucleated eggs, micro pipettes and petri dishes – an iconic biotechnological vocabulary with which the public has become increasingly familiar in the age of genomics. It is a measure of the extent to which life is no longer so much born and bred as manufactured and marketed that there is such popular interest in behind-the-scenes revelations of life's re-engineering – a feature of life in the age of genomics which is both attractive and disturbing.[28]

In this concluding section I turn to a set of general theoretical questions and proposals about what the genetic imaginary means for categories such as gender, sex and species which have in the past been grounded in a naturalised discourse of kinship and genealogy and remain so, while at the same time they also occupy a context of denaturalisation. More precisely, I want to ask what a refigured landscape of the genealogical augers in the way of cultural processes of signification – and, to be exact, of classification. What are the syntactics of difference through which reproductive and genetic ties are being re-circuited, re-calibrated and re-aligned as part of global nature, global culture?

Considering these questions, I also seek to return to the processes described at the outset of this volume – of naturalisation, denaturalisation and renaturalisation, building on Haraway's claim, in exploring the promises of monsters, that:

Nature for us is *made*, as both fiction and fact. If organisms are natural objects, it is crucial to remember that organisms are not born; they are made in world-changing technoscientific practices by particular collective actors in particular times and places. In the belly of the local/global monster in which I am gestating, often called the postmodern world, global technology appears to *denature* everything, to make everything a malleable matter of strategic decisions and mobile production and reproduction processes. Technological decontextualization is ordinary experience for hundreds of millions if not billions of human beings, as well as other organisms. I suggest that this is not *denaturing* so much as a *particular production* of nature. The preoccupation with productionism that has characterized so much parochial Western discourse and practice seems to have hypertrophied into something quite marvelous: the whole world is remade in the image of commodity production.

(1992a: 297, original emphasis, citations removed)

The question I am asking here imagines a parallel process for life itself, whereby it can be investigated as a set of emergent essentialising discourses interpellating subjects into new formations – including forms of identity, embodiment, connection and disconnection. These are resonant with, but also displacing of, certain more traditional formations associated with the natural and the biological. Undeniably, new forms of knowledge, power and practice associated with contemporary technologies to 'assist' reproduction, heredity and genealogy both draw upon and displace pre-existing beliefs associated with nature and the natural (Strathern, 1992a and b). Writing of the new genetic cartography, visual historian Barbara Stafford comments:

The genome project is routinely and metaphorically described as a lexicological enterprise. The task is systematically to collect the protein and chemical bits and pieces constituting a human being and making up the 'book of life'. The alphabet of DNA subunits will result, it is hoped, in the ultimate genetic compendium. Paradoxically, the trope of an inanimate catalogue or dead 'library' is used to talk about the original cells of existence. One of the purposes of this *ars combinatoria* would be to accelerate the identification of congenital defects. If the sequence of letters is out of order, the words are deranged. Consequently, reproduction has become part of the textualized and symbolized world of duplicable or disposable goods. Wanted ciphers can be kept, just as the diseased or unwanted ones can be discarded. Transposing living physiology into abstract language makes it easier, and less problematic, to justify manipulation. Like any dictionary, or digest, the consumer may refer, alter or combine decontextualized tiny elements at will.

(1991: 212)

The transposition of 'living physiology' into lexis, or text, comprises a shift of a particular kind: an axial transposition in the temporal and spatial orientation of life itself. If the modern definition of life itself derives, as Foucault suggests, from the

Darwinian model of life as a unified, consanguineous, interconnected *system*, then that system depended upon descent as its orientating axis, or even as its *telos*. In sum, genealogical descent is the vertical spine of the Darwinian model of life itself. When Darwin, for example, argues in *The Origin of Species* that life is indeed like a tree, the implication is that it is shared descent from a common, apical, ancestor which unifies life as a system that is not only consanguineous, but unified *as a genealogy*. Marilyn Strathern (1992b) amplifies this point by noting that it was the analogy of kinship which Darwin 'borrowed' to describe the significance of evolution. In this view, descent is the motor of selection – not just its axial orientation diagrammatically. Life itself derives its shape across the vertical passage of generations: it is distinctively, and necessarily, lineal. This lineal, vertical passage – seen to be unified, continuous and ubiquitous – is the source of the variation necessary for the invisible hand of evolutionary selection to operate (see note 9). Hence, variation provides the lateral axis of genealogy – the spread of the branches of the tree which denote the range of differences distinguishing distinct life forms. Importantly, for Darwin, life itself is vertically propriocentric: its progressive orientation is always in forward gear, and its ontological constitution as a force or principle of animate vitality is always composed through descent lines criss-crossed at the point of reproduction, but pointing downwards. Like the early Ford motor car, Darwin's genealogy didn't go into reverse.

Once life's variation is refigured as a sequence of letters, a catalogue of words, or a lexicon, the axis of transformation shifts from vertical to horizontal, as in the alphabets of magnetic letters so familiar from refrigerator doors. Recombination need no longer operate intergenerationally, through the downward (as if gravitational) lineal flow of descent. Selection need no longer operate like a weir across the river of life. Indeed the river need no longer 'flow' at all, since its mere width becomes at any given moment a source of greater horizontal variation than it ever was constrained within narrow, lineal, canal-like passages of gene transfer, tapering to their narrowest width at the point of recombination. As sexual reproduction is above all else the mechanism for genetic recombination under Darwin's scheme, so it is as definitively rendered insignificant by the advent of assisted heredity, cloned transgenics and the entire millennial menagerie of unfamiliar kinds.

This process can be described as the respatialisation of genealogy. Whereas, in the Darwinian model, genealogical order is the very order of life itself, in the post-Darwinian *ars recombinatoria* of the human genome project, genealogy is densely artefactual. Genealogical inevitability, once the master trope of sexual selection, becomes a thing of the past: it is a relic of an outdated recombinatory mechanism. Once upon a time, the breed was the outcome of generations of carefully selected lines, paired into haphazardly auspicious and unpredictably rewarding unions, and subsequently paired for the best of stock: the genetic capital, if there was any. OncoMouse™, the inaugural patented transgenic animal-apparatus for testing new cancer drugs, has no such pedigree. She and her sistren are a horizontal assemblage.

As it is, in a sense, flattened by the power of recombinant genetic technology to mix and match across species with the entire living lexical encyclopedia of proteins, enzymes and plasmid vectors to choose from, so genealogy is also re-temporalised after the fact of transgenic organisms such as OncoMouse^{TM}. Once upon a time, when the pure-bred and the hybrid were the breeder's only options, genealogy stood for lineage, and lineage stood for quality of livestock. Genealogy stood for the passage, or flow, of life across generations; good genealogy meant careful pedigrees ensuring profitable breedwealth. It referred to descent, and instrumentalised its graphology: the family tree, the lineage, the ancestral chart, the pedigree, the stud book. It was in the eighteenth century that a prized individual animal became fungible as breedwealth for its ancestry, and breeding could be said to have become modern, industrialised and organised in relation to individual genetic capital (Ritvo, 1995). All of that became old-fashioned when genealogy was replaced by the gene pool.

Genealogical time is also refigured by the newly exploitable *ars recombinatoria* made available through molecular biological techniques such as polymerase chain reaction (PCR). And time is passing quickly. A century ago, when biology was in its youthful period of confident expansion, genealogical time gave biology its authority in the form of its meta-trope: the mechanism of natural selection. At last freed from the trammels of merely categorical amusements, biology could offer *natural laws*. No longer constrained merely to describe the order of things (meticulously arrayed in their chaste museum boxes, each with a classificatory totem – like so many children's marble collections), biology could explain *origins*. Now, with hybrid vigour, biology has increasingly become biogenetics crossed with biotechnology to produce a biopower unparalleled in history. And in the age of PCR, immortal cell lines, DNA libraries, and Darwin Genetics, Inc., genealogical time is as irrelevant as species borders, reproductive strategies, sexual selection or shared descent in the manufacture of life's variation. Biodiversity has a new motor; it can be more diverse than ever before.

If sexual selection is no longer the name of the biological game, and life itself is no longer governed by sexual congress, does that mean it has been de-sexualised? Now that the organic is de-coupled from its *doppelgänger* – the reproductive *telos* of (hetero)sex – does that mean we are newly polymorphous? No longer perverse if we depart from the dutiful-but-rarely-beautiful sacred grove of nuclear familialism? What are the sexual politics proper to informational life, the virtual organic, transgenic desire, or Life Itself? If gender and kinship, like race, species, nation, ethnicity and sex, have traditionally been rooted in the given orders of the natural, the biological and the organic, then what is their function in the de-traditionalised loci of the Sequence Laboratory? Or, if class was never very far from pedigree in the Anglo-European traditions from which Darwin derived his original 'loan', what difference does it make that a high-class Ivy League Oncomouse has a trademark instead?

If the biological has been geneticised, and if that means that many of its former foundational fictions are now in the reliquary beside Lamarckism, then neither life nor sex is a branch on the same family tree that Darwin borrowed from the Bible to begin with. However, and as Steven Spielberg's ever-recombinant family fictions tempt us to imagine (only to punish the thought), the transition is more one of moving to a different register than of transposing the scale altogether.

● ● ●   The Re-sexualisation of Life Itself

The flip side of the behind-the-scenes invitations so important to the success of *Jurassic Park*, in all its varied manifestations, is the horror the film unleashes upon its audiences. As a monster movie, the film is designed to terrify its consumers. Within the consumption of this terror-as-entertainment lie many unexplored dimensions of dis-ease and anxiety. The narrative contains this threat through the storyline architecture of successful escape from the island, effecting a closure only reopened as a prelude to the film's sequel, *The Lost World*.

The sexual politics proper to *Jurassic Park* provide a figurative standpoint from which to consider the forms of traditional narrative closure which work to contain the disturbing imagery and derangements it releases. To begin with, sex is lexical for the dinosaurs of *Jurassic Park*, who have been genetically restricted to the female genre by means of prophylactic molecular programming. As feminised monstrous animatons, they play 'Mother Nature' in its many familiar guises from the bovine vegetarian brachiosaurs to the predatory and destructive T-rex.[29] Genealogically and reproductively they are deranged, and this includes their nascent hemaphroditic tendencies, *grâce à la grenouille*. The frog DNA spliced into their genome where insect hypodermic failure left crucial gaps at the protein level yields to that familiar Darwinian life force – the imperative for reproduction where Dr Wu's chastity helix would have there be none. The broken eggshells and little tiny baby dino footprints discovered by Grant, Alexis and Tim amidst their wanderings confirm what chaotician Ian Malcolm predicted was the only predictable thing: that 'life will find a way'. Life, then, emerges as reproductive and familial after all in *Jurassic Park*, just as Grant is forced to rediscover the deep paternal instincts he has supressed in his ordeal with the two children he must rescue.

As noted above, the sexual politics proper to genomic kin relations are centrally founded on paternity. As Stafford describes a textualisation of life itself, so is the life scientist positioned as author. As the 'romance' of the inquiring scientific voyeur is metaphorically structured by the Baconian *ur*-text of 'the masculine philosophy', so too does a sexualised discourse of discovery infuse prototypic modern biological narratives such as *The Double Helix*. In genomics, the masculine associations of 'original genius' proper to both authorship and invention may be literalised as progeny (Franklin, 1995).

As it is always debatable how successfully forms of narrative closure restore order in the wake of their transgression, so the horror created by *Jurassic Park* may be read as exceeding its own storyline. What is notable nonetheless is the restoration of family and paternity, of a deeply traditional sexual politics, in the space of its own displacement. Like the disruption of genealogy and its restorations, which we have argued is a defining charactistic of the workings of global nature, global culture, this film delivers both promising monsters and an escape route.

Critical to the establishment of the familiar identity categories based on race, gender, sex, nationality, species and family are distinctions of kind and type which make reference, if not to nature, then to biology and 'the facts of life'. These, in turn, comprise a reproductive model, as Marilyn Strathern notes: 'Kinship systems and family structures are imagined as social arrangements not just imitating, but based on and literally deploying processes of biological reproduction' (1992b: 3). She continues:

> It is no accident that thinking about intervention in this area should bring futuristic fantasies and (in some cases) doom-laden scenarios to people's minds. For the intervention is also into ideas, including ideas about the future itself – what it is we are laying or seeding for generations to come.
>
> (1992b: 5)

It is thus no accident that *Jurassic Park* attracted such enormous fascination coincident with the dramatic rise of biotechnology and genetic engineering as global economic industries. In thinking about the cultural dimensions of such developments, it is all but self-evident that a high level of social anxiety attends the renegotiation of 'life itself'. Another way to approach this question is to ask what kinship means in the context of instrumentalised genealogies, medicalised consanguinities and reconstituted biologies (which are, of course, the themes of *Jurassic Park*). Traditionally, anthropologically and conventionally, kinship is held to be based on ties established through reproduction, marriage or other legal means such as adoption. For Strathern, kinship is 'not just the ways in which relatives interact with one another, but how relationships as such are held to be constituted' (1992a: 5). As we described in Part One, Haraway offers yet another view: '[k]inship is a technology for producing the material and semiotic effect of natural relationship, of shared kind. . . . [It is] the question of taxonomy, category, and the natural status of artifactual entities. . . . Establishing identities is kinship work in action' (1997: 53, 67). This leads her to ask: 'How are natural kinds identified in the realms of late twentieth-century technoscience? What kinds of crosses and offspring count as legitimate and illegitimate? Who are my familiars?' (1997: 120). For Haraway, kinship is a taxonomic, classificatory device for the production of kind and type. She proposes that the denaturalisation of kinds brought about through the mix 'n match trans-genetics responsible for entities such as OncoMouse™ has made more evident how such beings are 'naturalised' as brands. The brand, or trademark, which connects OncoMouse™ to its parent company becomes the mark not only of its proper descent ('brought to you by Dupont, where better things for better living come to life'), but of its gender, kind. As Haraway first claimed in 1992, the cyborg animal or corporate bioscience are 'literate in quite a different grammar of gender' (1992b: 42).

Haraway thus claims that the gender of OncoMouse, and her transgenic kin, is in essence constituted by relations of propriety and paternity, rather than Mother Nature. Darwin's 'small, warm pond' matrix of life's creation is displaced in this view by the pure culture of the petri dish where embryos are re-fertilised with foreign DNA in order to carry other species' genetic signatures in the nuclear genome of every cell.

This corporately owned and produced corporeality is literally marked from within, and it is this altered flesh that the brand or trademark 'protects' as an ontological kind. Protected too by the paternal and authorial conventions of intellectual property, most notably patent, the transgenic mouse, like Dolly the cloned sheep, and like the dinosaurs in *Jurassic Park*, indeed inhabits a different grammar of genealogy, and its driving *telos* is unmistakably commercial.

It is in depicting precisely this sequence of events, of the creation of animals not only for profit, but to create entire new worlds of commodification of life itself, that *Jurassic Park* is, to put it literally, right on the money. Like Dolly, or OncoMouse^{TM}, or Jefferson the calf (or any other of the founder animals of new cloned transgenic lineages), the dinosaurs are not so much born as made. In a sense too, they are not so much beings as done-tos. The restrictions of a former genealogical ordering, whereby, for example, a mouse could not exchange genes with a human, have been removed, and in their place has emerged a cut-and-splice genealogy enabling almost any combination of genetic traits. The 'viable offspring' derived from the merger of corporate wealth generation and molecular biological techniques is driven not only by the viability of an animal in terms of being capable of life outside the womb, but by the viability of such animals as live-stock in a market organised around, as Haraway puts it, life as an accumulation strategy.

What is perhaps most notable about the genetic imaginary at work in *Jurassic Park* is the simultaneity of so many divergent and contradictory pathways offered up within its visual and narrative devices – and indeed the celebration of this excess. While it performs a denunciation of the potential abuses of new genetic technologies, it paradoxically mimics this same potency in its own visual technologies of animation. More pointedly, it is a film which punishes the *fictional* male, scientific inventor of these unfamiliar kinds (John Hammond), while celebrating the actual male *auteur* director's ability to deliver an animated allegory of the highest verisimilitude to 'real life'. While it is a film which achieves harmonious narrative closure through the production of a nuclear family, this itself is achieved in an oddly recombinant fashion. These contradictions are also evident in its circulation as a text endorsed by staid scientific establishments such as the American Museum of Natural History, for which actual props from the film itself are used to bolster a narrative about the power of scientific imagination and research. I have argued that the levels of creation being intertextually and artefactually annealed in this hybrid entertainment business help us to chart a distinctive genetic imaginary, made up of a multiplicity of options, much like the new genetic constructions that are its object.

It is in the archaeological layering of the genetic imaginary that global nature, global culture can be explored as a recombinant context, in which both being and doing are refigured. In sum, this context is as discursively recombinant as the dinosaurs themselves, brought into being by a range of devices that are both familiar and strange, transparent and opaque, animate, non-living and undead. It turns out that life itself is not only a wealth accumulation strategy, but a cultural technology as well.

Conclusion

Writing of the imagination, Arjun Appadurai claims that

> the image, the imagined, the imaginary – these are all terms that direct us to something critical and new in global cultural processes: *the imagination as social practice*. . . . The imagination is now central to all forms of agency, is itself a social fact, and is the key component of the new global order.
>
> (1996: 31, original emphasis)

In sum, he writes that 'the world we live in today is characterised by a new role for the imagination in social life' (1996: 31). In arguing that the imagery, narrative and consumption of *Jurassic Park* can alert us to new registers of social practice, such as the role of the genetic imaginary, I want not only to emphasise its importance to charting new calibrations of foundational, naturalised categories, such as gender, kinship or species. I am arguing not only that it demonstrates the means by which nature is remade as technique, but that it also offers a means of understanding how global nature and global culture emerge through specific processes of re-alignment. The argument in this sense is concerned not only with how we imagine genes, genetics or genealogy, but with a much wider set of orienting devices through which the world is both imagined and reproduced.

In arguing that *Jurassic Park* is a sign of the times, I am reaching well beyond the film itself to the many intertextualities which imbricate it within a wider social process of redefining the natural, the global, and the future. In its introduction of virtual natural history, its re-animation of extinct life forms, and its emphasis on blending state-of-the-art palaeontology with successful popular entertainment, *Jurassic Park* anticipated significant shifts not only in the perception of nature, but also in the production of knowledge. The appeal of the film's imaginative leap back into time was, as we have seen, celebrated within the scientific establishment in confirmation of its own speculative re-creations of lost worlds. Television series such as the BBC's *Walking with Dinosaurs*, screened to great fanfare in the autumn of 1999, push the envelope of this interchange more explicitly to create a new form of virtual palae-ontology. Self-consciously building on the success of animatronics in *Jurassic Park*, dinosaur models were 'taught' to walk, eat, mate, run, swim and fight for the highly successful series. Here, the imagination served not only the purposes of enter-tainment, but also the production of fact, engendering criticism by those who feared an abdication of scientific responsibility from one of the world leaders in nature documentaries. Was the BBC's *Walking with Dinosaurs* a 'natural history', as its publicity claimed and its realist narration implied? Was it a documentary at all? Palaeontologists who worked closely with the series' producer, Tim Haines, attested to having solved certain mysteries through the experimentation required to animate the dinosaurs convincingly based on scant fossil evidence. The Diplodicus featured in *Jurassic Park* eating from treetops was corrected in the BBC series, based on careful analysis of cervical vertebrae indicating that the animal could not raise its head above its body, and thus must have been a browser among low-lying shrubs and plants. In the virtual laboratory of computer-based animation, palaeontology-as-spectacle became 'the portrait of a lost world as it really was', revealing 'the behaviour behind the bones' and 'the living animal' itself (Haines, 1999).[30]

In this series, as in *Jurassic Park*, the imagination emerges as a 'key component' in the remaking of nature, and, as Appadurai claims, 'an organised field of social practices, a form of work . . . and a form of negotiation between sites of agency' (1996: 31). In such examples, and the many others we have explored throughout this book, the remaking of nature becomes apparent as cultural process in a manner which defies separation into 'real' versus 'imagined' life. That life itself has become the matrix for such a collapse between the spectacle and the actual, or the material and the virtual, only underscores its dense overdetermination as a domain of social practice, much like the domain of the natural in an earlier historical frame. Moreover, it is in tracing the work of the genetic imaginary that an essential critical dimension can be added to the analysis of global culture, global nature. Both what the imagination links together, through speculation (in both its senses), and what it keeps apart (for example, through the distancing effects of horror), are important reckoning devices for tracing the lives, worlds and selves that can be made and undone at the turn of the millennium.

● ● ●   **Notes**

1   Protesters in London in the spring of 1999 signalled their awareness of both the transnational and gender politics informing the worldwide competion to capitalise on new forms of bioengineering in their challenge to the British Prime Minister Tony Blair: 'Tony Don't Eat Bill's Seed.'
2   See also the work of Lily Kay (1993) on the rise of the 'new biology' and Evelyn Fox Keller (1995, 1996). See also further below.
3   The cultural dimensions of the introduction of transgenic animals is discussed at length by Haraway (1997). My argument here, and in this chapter generally, is that such animals represent a departure from familiar models of kinship and descent, by demonstrating that patterns of filiation and succession once considered irrevocable because they are fixed by nature can be transcended by technology (see further in Franklin 2001a and b).
4   Genealogical time in the sense of *intergenerational passage* can now be slowed down by cryopreservation or speeded up through mass cloning in a manner that demonstrates the increasing power of technology to transcend formerly 'natural' limits to reproduction. Similarly, the removal of the 'bar' once provided 'by nature' against not only inter-species, but also inter-kingdom, crossings, such as the splicing together of an eel and a strawberry, refigures genealogical space as more broadly recombinant, removing the limit point or horizon of former reproductive impossibility through the informationalisation and instrumentalisation of genetic codes as programmable procreative substance.
5   It is not only in the movies that extinction has become a thing of the past: much of our current zoological and botanical diversity is already preserved as genetic information, in banks, so that when populations of plants and animals become extinct, after the last living individual has expired, the genome of the species will continue to exist, or at least to be stored.
6   Collections of frozen tissue samples give new meaning to the concept of a population, and to the Foucauldian question of how sovereignty over populations is exercised, as has become evident in

debates both about the repatriation of human body parts (Bowyer, 1999), and about the controversial 'culling' of human embryos in storage (Franklin, 1999).

7   Van Dijck's *Imagenations: popular images of genetics* (1998) offers an insightful analysis of genetics as a space of theatre or performance. Although her book does not deal with animals or plants, and thus explictly not with *Jurassic Park* (see Van Dijck, 1998: 2–3), her analysis is highly relevant in its emphasis on narrative conventions and visual spectacle. As she notes: 'The theatre of genetics is defined by its story-tellers' (1998: 29).

8   As described in Chapter 2, Foucault's concept of the 'non-temporal rectangle' refers to the classificatory devices of the eighteenth century, whereby things were sorted by resemblances of form, and situated not within the chronotope of natural history, but in relation to the time of God's Creation (1970: 131).

9   The historical shift to a Darwinian paradigm of life as a unified, consanguineous system in a state of constant flux (evolution) is also noted by the authors of the US Government *Report* 'Patenting Life' in the context of debates about the ethics of commercialising life. Whereas Platonic thought pictured each species as a static, unitary and primordial unit defined by essential characteristics of form, they note, Darwin introduced a model of the species as a dynamic, polymorphous and temporal grouping (Office of Technology Assessment, 1987: 98–100). It is, thus, the Darwinian model of life which first prioritises the value of genetic diversity – as a necessary source of the advantageous mutations necessary for evolutionary survival. In turn, a concern with the value of genetic diversity for the survival of ecosystems and species both merges and is in tension with the increasing (commercial) value accorded to genetic or bio-'wealth'. Here, life as a 'productive' force interpolates with its (evolutionary) significance as a *re*-productive *telos*: an overdetermined junction in the context of contemporary struggles over biology-as-property.

10 Throughout this chapter I use italics to denote the film *Jurassic Park*, and roman type to denote the place Jurassic Park in the film and in the novel.

11 Domestic box-office sales in the US and Canada stood at $344.6 million, with international box-office sales at $537.5 million, creating a total worldwide box-office sales figure of $882.1 million.

12 As I discuss below, a hint of visibility of the making of *Jurassic Park*, the film, is present in one of the scenes where a shelf full of *Jurassic Park* products is (ironically) shown, including the book *The Making of Jurassic Park*, which was one of many texts produced and sold on the promise of being able to look 'behind the scenes' at the making of the film.

13 In turn, these features of the film are incorporated into its sequel, *The Lost World: Jurassic Park*, which went into film production in 1996 and was released the following year.

14 In the same way that Hammond is both *doppelgänger*, but also inferior, to Spielberg, so too is *Mr DNA* a kind of amateurish cartoon film, much the counterpoint of Spielberg's supreme cinematic *magnum opus*.

15 Scriptwriter David Koepp comments:

> Here I was writing about these greedy people who are creating a fabulous theme park just so they can exploit all these dinosaurs and make silly little films and sell stupid plastic plates and things. And I'm writing for a company that's eventually going to put this in their theme parks and make these silly little films and sell stupid plastic plates. I was really chasing my tail there for a while trying to figure out who was virtuous in this whole scenario – and eventually gave up. (quoted in Shay and Duncan, 1993: 56)

16 Spielberg is quoted as describing the decision to film on Kauai over Costa Rica, Puerto Rico, Mexico or the Philippines: 'I think it was my age. Had I been twenty-six instead of forty-five I might have gone to someplace really rugged. But the idea of staying in a Hawaiian hotel room with room service and a pool for the weekend was very appealing' (quoted in Shay and Duncan, 1993: 46).

17 The use of a 'ride' approach to the explanation of the scientific premise of *Jurassic Park* was also seen to be useful because of its expediency for exposition. Scriptwriter David Koepp explains:

> The most difficult part of the adaptation was determining how to deal with the exposition needed to explain the extraction of dinosaur DNA and the cloning of creatures that had not

walked the earth for millions of years. [The theme park-style ride] was brilliant. We could pop in for a few seconds here and there, put in some bits of information, and then get out. There was no need to have beginnings and middles and ends. We could do a lot of stuff that was fun to watch – *and* it would all make sense because it is part of the amusement park environment. (quoted in Shay and Duncan, 1993: 56)

18 Significantly, the makers of *Jurassic Park* explicitly sought to distinguish their theme park from theme parks such as Disneyland. As Rick Carter, dinosaur creator, comments: 'This is, after all, not Disneyland. What people want to go see in Jurassic Park would be the dinosaurs in their natural habitat, not a lot of man-made stuff' (Carter in Shay and Duncan, 1993: 45).

19 'Advanced morphing techniques' developed in the wake of the Oscar-winning special effects in *Terminator 2* aided in dispersing the 'lack of faith' in computer-generated animals pre-*Jurassic Park* (Shay and Duncan, 1993: 49). For the Gallimimus herding scenes, the creation of three-dimensional models in digital space was refined and developed to 'make the next quantum leap in computer graphics' (Shay and Duncan, 1993: 51). So successful were the computer graphics for *Jurassic Park*, that little of the 'go-motion' technique was used in the film – and indeed was considered all but 'extinct' due to the excitement generated by its animatronic successors.

20 In his classic account of the establishment of paternity, *Totemism and Exogamy* (1910), Frazer famously argued that it was the bringing of gifts to 'his' children which first alerts early man to the proprietary consequences of his physical paternity – until then unbeknownst to him, and afterwards the basis for exogamy. As Lévi-Strauss writes: 'It was thus not by chance that Frazer amalgamated totemism and physiological paternity: totemism assimilates men to animals, and the alleged ignorance of the role of the father in conception results in the replacement of the human genitor by spirits still closer to natural forces' (1962: 2).

21 Commenting on the film of *Jurassic Park*, palaeontologist and science writer Stephen Jay Gould complains that: 'This dinosaurian flooding of popular consciousness guarantees that no paleontologist can ever face a journalist and avoid what seems to be the most pressing question of the Nineties: Why are children so fascinated by dinosaurs?' (1993: 51). Yet, as Crichton's quandary suggests, it may not be *children*'s fascination with dinosaurs, but adults' fascination with this relation that is in part responsible for the flood of dinosaur replicas repopulating the domestic space of the western world.

22 After just one day on retailers' shelves, the home video of *Jurassic Park* set a new sales record for its parent company, surpassing MCA/Universal's previous record of 14 million units sold, held by Spielberg's *ET*.

23 *Jurassic Park* is not the highest grossing film of all time in terms of sales of film and video rights, which distinction belongs to *Gone with the Wind*, according to 1996 figures. However, *Jurassic Park* may well be the largest grossing film of all time if total merchandising sales per annum are used to measure its success.

24 In addition to tie-ins, 'merchandising' of *Jurassic Park* also extended into its packaging for retail cinema houses through discounts on Digital Theater Systems (DTS) enhanced audio facilities. Owned by MCA/Universal's parent company, Matsushita Electrical Industry Co., DTS utilised CD-ROM technology to produce a 'faithful reproduction' of the original soundtrack as it was mixed and recorded in the studio. Timed to be released to coincide with the distribution of *Jurassic Park*, Universal's promotional discount to cinema houses was accompanied by a letter from Steven Spielberg stating that *Jurassic Park* would be an 'experience you will never forget . . . thanks to DTS' (undated Universal Studios promotional packet).

25 A fascinating account of the importance of dinosaurs to the American Museum of Natural History (AMNH) is provided in the book-length account of the museum's extensive reorganisation of their dinosaur wing published in 1996. *Next of Kin*, by AMNH palaeontologist Lowell Dingus, is deserving of more commentary than I have provided in this chapter, in particular because of its account of the way cladistic genealogy structures the 'pathways' visitors follow through the exhibit, and because of the way in which its title denotes our 'relatedness' to dinosaurs.

26 One of several books authored by American Museum of Natural History palaeontologists in the wake of the success of the film *Jurassic Park* is entitled *The Science of* Jurassic Park *and* The Lost World: *or, how to build a dinosaur* (1997), by Rob DeSalle and David Lindley. Featuring on its cover

an insect trapped in amber set against a skeleton of a dinosaur, the book narrates the extraction of dinosaur DNA from amber in close proximity to an account of the film's production, foregrounding their inseparabiltiy. Though less prominently, AMNH palaeontologist Michael Novacek also makes references to the dinosaurs of *Jurassic Park* in his *Dinosaurs of the Flaming Cliffs* (1996).

27 Educationalists have not missed the unprecedented opportunity provided by the release of *Jurassic Park* to devise new means to 'kindle children's interest in science exploration with the interdisciplinary study of dinosaurs'. As Charlene M. Czerniak writes in *Science and Children*: 'Now that your students are abuzz with dinosaur fever, why not incorporate a few of the following interdisciplinary activities into your science lesson?' She suggests: 'Give each student a piece of beef jerky or a well-cooked 2.5-cm cube of beef and a piece of lettuce. Have the class try to eat each type of food using only their front teeth (incisors)', cautioning that, 'of course, the dinosaurs did not eat cooked meat, but we would not want students to eat raw meat'. Alternatively:

> Have children make 'insects in amber' by mixing two large boxes of orange or lemon gelatin dessert and 600 ml of hot water. Dissolve the gelatin completely and then pour it over a few raisins (representing insects) in small cups. When cool, remove it by running hot water over the outside of the cup. Students can see the 'insects embedded in *amber*' and have fun eating the finished product! (1993: 19–20, original emphasis)

28 Research conducted by the Wellcome Trust in London into public perceptions of cloning revealed high levels of scientific literacy concerning biotechnology, and that the more the public knew about the science of cloning the more sceptical they became, expressing grave scepticism towards the trustworthiness of either the scientific community or its regulatory mechanisms (Wellcome Trust, 1998).

29 Asking whether *Jurassic Park* is 'a work of covert misogynistic propaganda', author and art critic Marina Warner notes that 'female organisms, in the film, prove uncontrollably fertile, resistant to all the constraints of men of power. The story can be reduced to a naked confrontation between nature-coded female and culture-coded male' (1994: 5, and see also Creed, 1993).

30 The effort to re-create extinct life forms is made even more vivid in the project funded by the Discovery Channel to remove a frozen mammoth from permafrost in Siberia and extract its cells for use in an attempt either to clone a mammoth by nuclear transfer, or to fertilise an elephant's egg to produce a hybrid pachyderm.

Bibliography

Abu Lughod, Janet (1991) 'Going Beyond Global Babble', in Anthony D. King (ed.), *Culture, Globalization and the World-System*, London: Macmillan, pp. 131–8.

Adorno, Theodor and Horkheimer, Max (1979) *Dialectic of Enlightenment* (trans. John Cumming), London: Verso.

Ahmed, Sara (2000) *Strange Encounters: embodied others in post-coloniality*, London: Routledge.

American Heritage Dictionary (1992) 2nd edition, New York: Houghton Mifflin.

Anderson, Benedict (1983) *Imagined Communities: reflections on the origin and spread of nationalism*, London: Verso.

Appadurai, Arjun (1990) 'Disjuncture and Difference in the Global Cultural Economy', in Mike Featherstone (ed.), *Global Culture: nationalism, globalization and modernity*, London: Sage, pp. 295–310.

Appadurai, Arjun (1996) *Modernity at Large: cultural dimensions of globalization*, Minneapolis: University of Minnesota Press.

Ardener, Edwin (1972) 'Belief and the Problem of Women', in Jean S. LaFontaine (ed.), *The Interpretation of Ritual*, London: Tavistock.

Armstrong, Stephen (1996) 'Yobs for the Boys', *The Guardian*, 26 February, pp. 24–5.

Ausubel, Kenneth (1994) *Seeds of Change: the living treasure*, San Francisco: HarperCollins.

Back, Les and Quaade, Vibeke (1993) 'Dream Utopias, Nightmare Realities: imaging race and culture within the world of Benetton advertising', *Third Text* 22: 65–80.

Balibar, Etienne (1991) 'Is There a "Neo-Racism"?', in Etienne Balibar and Immanuel Wallerstein (eds), *Race, Nation and Class: ambiguous identities*, London: Verso, pp. 17–28.

Barker, Martin (1984) *The New Racism*, London: Junction Books.

Barnes, Max (1993) 'Serious Message in Benetton Ads', letter, *The Independent*, 14 January.

Barthes, Roland (1977) *Image/Music/Text* (trans. Stephen Heath), New York: The Noonday Press.

Barthes, Roland (1981) *Camera Lucida: reflections on photography* (trans. R. Howard), New York: Hill and Wang.

Barthes, Roland (1985) *The Fashion System* (trans. Matthew Ward and Richard Howard), London: Cape.

Battersby, Christine (1989) *Gender and Genius: towards a feminist aesthetics*, Bloomington: Indiana University Press.

Baudrillard, Jean (1993) *Symbolic Exchange and Death* (trans. Ian Hamilton Grant), London: Sage.

Baudrillard, Jean (1994a) *Simulacra and Simulation* (trans. Sheila Fari Glaser), Ann Arbor: University of Michigan Press.

Baudrillard, Jean (1994b) *The Illusion of the End* (trans. Chris Turner), Cambridge: Polity.

Baudrillard, Jean (1998) *The Consumer Society: myths and structures* (trans. Chris Turner), London: Sage.

Bauman, Zygmunt (1992) 'Survival as a Social Construct', *Theory, Culture and Society* 9 (1): 1–36.

Bauman, Zygmunt (1999) *Globalization: the human consequences*, Cambridge: Polity.

Beck, Ulrich (1992) *Risk Society: towards a new modernity* (trans. Mark Ritter), London: Sage.

Beck, Ulrich (2000) *What Is Globalization?* (trans. Patrick Camiller), Cambridge: Polity.

Bell, Emily (1995) 'The Big Hard Sell', *Media Guardian*, 13 February, p. 13.

Benjamin, Walter (1970) *Illuminations* (trans. Harry Zotin), London: Fontana.

Benjamin, Walter (1983) *Das Passagen-Werk* (edited by Rolf Tiedemann), Frankfurt am Main: Suhrkamp.

Berlant, Lauren (1993) 'National Brands/National Body: *Imitation of Life*', in Bruce Robbins (ed.), *The Phantom Public Sphere*, Minneapolis: University of Minnesota Press, pp. 173–208.

Bhabha, Homi (1988) 'The Commitment to Theory', *New Formations* 5: 5–24.

Bhabha, Homi (1990) 'The Third Space', in Jonathan Rutherford (ed.), *Identity*, London: Lawrence and Wishart, pp. 207–21.

Bhabha, Homi (ed.) (1993) *Nation and Narration*, London: Routledge.

Bhabha, Homi (1994) *The Location of Culture*, London: Routledge.

Birke, Lynda (1986) *Women, Feminism, and Biology: the feminist challenge*, Brighton: Wheatsheaf.

Birke, Lynda and Hubbard, Ruth (eds) (1995) *Reinventing Biology: respect for life and the creation of knowledge*, Bloomington: Indiana University Press.

Body Shop Team (1994) *The Body Shop Book: skin, hair and body care*, London: Little, Brown.

Borges, Jorge (1964) 'On Rigor in Science', in *Dreamtigers*, Austin, TX: University of Texas Press.

Bowyer, Susannah (1999) 'Talking to the Dead: what bodies in museums tell us', M.Phil. dissertation submitted to the Department of Social Anthropology, Cambridge University.

Braidotti, Rosi (1994) *Nomadic Subjects: embodiment and sexual difference in contemporary feminist theory*, New York: Columbia University Press.

Brown, Wendy (1995) *States of Injury: power and freedom in late modernity*, Princeton: Princeton University Press.

Buck-Morss, Susan (1989) *The Dialectics of Seeing: Walter Benjamin and the arcades project*, Cambridge, MA: MIT Press.

Budd, Susan and Sharma, Ursula (1994) *The Healing Bond: the patient-practitioner and therapeutic responsibility*, London: Routledge.

Busch, A. (1997) 'Globalisation: some evidence on approaches and data', Globalization Workshop, Department of Politics, University of Birmingham, March.

Butler, Judith (1990) *Gender Trouble: feminism and the subversion of identity*, New York: Routledge.

Butler, Judith (1993) *Bodies That Matter: on the discursive limits of 'sex'*, New York: Routledge.

Campbell, Colin (1999) 'The Easternisation of the West', in Bryan Wilson and Jamie Cresswell (eds), *New Religious Movements: challenge and response*, London: Routledge, pp. 35–48.

Canguilhem, Georges (1994) 'The Concept of Life', in François Delaporte (ed.), *A Vital Rationalist: selected writings from Georges Canguilhem* (trans. Arthur Goldhammer), New York: Zone, pp. 303–20.

Carr-Gomm, Philip (1998) *The Druid Renaissance*, London: Thorsons.

Carter, Erica and Watney, Simon (eds) (1989) *Taking Liberties: AIDS and cultural politics*, London: Serpent's Tail.

Cartwright, Lisa (1995) *Screening the Body: tracing medicine's visual culture*, Minneapolis: University of Minnesota Press.

Castañeda, Claudia (1996) 'Worlds in the Making: the child body in the production of difference', PhD dissertation submitted to the History of Consciousness Program, University of California at Santa Cruz.

Castañeda, Claudia (2001) *Worlds in the Making: child, body, globe*, Durham, NC: Duke University Press.

Castells, Manuel (1996) *The Rise of the Network Society*, Oxford: Blackwell.

Chaitow, Leon (1983) *An End to Cancer: the nutritional approach to its prevention and control*, 2nd edn, Wellingborough, Northants: Thorsons.

Charles, Rachel (1990) *Mind, Body and Immunity*, London: Methuen.

Chopra, Deepak (1989) *Quantum Healing: exploring the frontiers of mind-body medicine*, London: Bantam.

Chopra, Deepak (1993) *Ageless Body, Timeless Mind: a practical alternative to growing old*, London: Rider.

Collier, Jane and Yanagisako, Sylvia (eds) (1987) *Gender and Kinship: essays toward a unified analysis*, Stanford, CA: Stanford University Press.

Coombe, Rosemary (1998) *The Cultural Life of Intellectual Properties: authorship, appropriation and the law*, Durham, NC: Duke University Press.

Cope, Julian (1998) *The Modern Antiquarian: a field guide to over 300 prehistoric sites around Britain*, London: Thorsons.

Corrias, Piño (1993) 'Beneath Jumpers', *The Guardian*, 8 June, p. 16.

Cosgrove, Denis (1994) 'Contested Global Visions: *One-World, Whole Earth* and the Apollo space photographs', *Annals of the Association of American Geographers* 84 (2): 270–94.

Bibliography

Cousteau, Jacques-Yves (1988) 'Foreword', in Kevin W. Kelley (ed.), *The Home Planet*, Reading, MA: Addison-Wesley.

Coward, Rosalind (1989) *The Whole Truth: the myth of alternative health*, London: Faber and Faber.

Crary, Jonathan and Kwinter, Sanford (eds) (1992) *Incorporations*, New York: Zone.

Crawford, Robert (1985) 'A Cultural Account of "Health": control, release and the social body', in John B. McKinlay (ed.), *Issues in the Political Economy of Health Care*, London: Tavistock, pp. 60–103.

Creed, Barbara (1993) *The Monstrous Feminine: film, feminism and psychoanalysis*, London: Routledge.

Cronin, Anne (1999) 'Seeing Through Transparency: performativity, vision and intent', *Cultural Values* 3 (1): 54–72.

Cronon, William (ed.) (1995) *Uncommon Ground: toward reinventing nature*, New York: W.W. Norton.

Crouch, Martha L. (1998) 'How the Terminator Terminates: an explanation for the non-scientist of a remarkable patent for killing second-generation seeds of crop plants', an occasional paper of the Edmonds Institute, Washington: Edmonds Institute.

Curtis, Barry (1995) '"In Betweening": an interview with Irene Kotlarz', *Art History* 18 (1): 24–36.

Czerniak, Charlene (1993) 'The Jurassic Spark', *Science and Children*, October, pp. 19–22.

DeLanda, Manuel (1992) 'Nonorganic Life', in Jonathan Crary and Sanford Kwinter (eds), *Incorporations*, New York: Zone, pp. 128–67.

Delaney, Carol (1986) 'The Meaning of Paternity and the Virgin Birth Debate', *Man* 21: 494–593.

Delaporte, François (ed.) (1994) *A Vital Rationalist: selected writings from Georges Canguilhem* (trans. Arthur Goldhammer), New York: Zone.

de Lauretis, Teresa (1987) *Technologies of Gender: essays on theory, film and fiction*, Bloomington: Indiana University Press.

Deleuze, Gilles (1992) 'Mediators', in Jonathan Crary and Sanford Kwinter (eds), *Incorporations*, New York: Zone, pp. 280–95.

DeSalle, Rob and Lindley, David (1997) *The Science of Jurassic Park: or, how to build a dinosaur*, New York: Basic Books.

Descola, Philippe and Palsson, Gisli (eds) (1996) *Nature and Society: anthropological perspectives*, London: Routledge.

Dickens, Peter (1996) *Reconstructing Nature: alienation, emancipation and the division of labour*, London: Routledge.

Dingus, Lowell (1996) *Next of Kin: great fossils at the American Museum of Natural History*, New York: Rizzoli.

Doane, Mary Ann (1990) 'Information, Crisis and Catastrophe', in Patricia Mellencamp (ed.), *Logics of Television: essays in cultural criticism*, Bloomington: Indiana University Press and London: British Film Institute, pp. 222–40.

Doward, Jamie (1999) 'A Splash of Colour in Cyberspace', *The Observer*, 11 April, p. 7.

Dreyfuss, Rochelle (1990) 'Expressive Genericity: trademarks as language in the Pepsi generation', *Notre Dame Law Review* 65: 397–424.

Duden, Barbara (1993) *Disembodying Women: perspectives on pregnancy and the unborn* (trans. Lee Hoinacki), Cambridge, MA: Harvard University Press.

Dyer, Wayne W. (1998) *Manifest Your Destiny: the 9 spiritual principles for getting everything you want*, London: Thorsons.

Easlea, Brian (1980) *Witch Hunting, Magic and the New Philosophy*, Brighton: Harvester.

Easlea, Brian (1981) *Science and Sexual Oppression: patriarchy's confrontation with women and nature*, London: Weidenfeld and Nicolson.

Edwards, Jeanette, Franklin, Sarah, Hirsch, Eric, Price, Frances and Strathern, Marilyn (1993) *Technologies of Procreation: kinship in the age of assisted conception*, Manchester: Manchester University Press.

Edwards, Jeanette, Franklin, Sarah, Hirsch, Eric, Price, Frances and Strathern, Marilyn (1999) *Technologies of Procreation: kinship in the age of assisted conception*, 2nd edition, London: Routledge.

Evans, Caroline and Thornton, Minna (1989) *Women and Fashion: a new look*, London: Quartet.

Falk, Pasi (1996) 'The Benetton-Toscani Effect', in Mica Nava, Andrew Blake, Iain MacRury and Barry Richards (eds), *Buy This Book: studies in advertising and consumption*, London: Routledge, pp. 64–86.

Fausto-Sterling, Anne (1985) *Myths of Gender: biological theories about women and men*, New York: Basic Books.

Featherstone, Mike (ed.) (1990a) *Global Culture: nationalism, globalization and modernity*, London: Sage.

Featherstone, Mike (1990b) 'Global Culture: an introduction', in Mike Featherstone (ed.), *Global Culture: nationalism, globalization and modernity*, London: Sage, pp. 1–14.

Featherstone, Mike and Lash, Scott (1995) 'Globalization, Modernity and the Spatialization of Social Theory: an introduction', in Mike Featherstone, Scott Lash and Roland Robertson (eds), *Global Modernities*, London: Sage, pp. 1–24.

Featherstone, Mike, Lash, Scott and Robertson, Roland (eds) (1995) *Global Modernities*, London: Sage.

Fee, Elizabeth and Fox, Daniel (eds) (1988) *AIDS: the burdens of history*, Berkeley: University of California Press.

Fenton, Sasha (1998) *How to Read Your Star Signs*, London: Thorsons.

Flatley, Jonathan (1996) 'Warhol Gives Good Face: publicity and the politics of prosopopoeia', in Jennifer Doyle, Jonathan Flatley and José Esteban Muñoz (eds), *Pop Out: queer Warhol*, Durham, NC: Duke University Press, pp. 101–33.

Foucault, Michel (1970) *The Order of Things: an archaeology of the human sciences*, New York: Vintage.

Foucault, Michel (1973) *The Birth of the Clinic: an archaeology of medical perception* (trans. Alan M. Sheridan), London: Tavistock.

Foucault, Michel (1980) *History of Sexuality: Volume 1: an introduction* (trans. Robert Hurley), New York: Vintage.

Foucault, Michel (1988a) *History of Sexuality: Volume 3: the care of the self* (trans. Robert Hurley), New York: Vintage.

Foucault, Michel (1988b) 'Technologies of the Self', in Luther H. Martin, Huck Gutman and Patrick H. Hutton (eds), *Technologies of the Self: a seminar with Michel Foucault*, London: Tavistock, pp. 16–49.

Franklin, Sarah (1995) 'Romancing the Helix: nature and scientific discovery', in Lynne Pearce and Jackie Stacey (eds), *Romance Revisited*, London: Lawrence and Wishart, pp. 63–77.

Franklin, Sarah (1996) 'Introduction', in Sarah Franklin (ed.), *The Sociology of Gender*, Cheltenham: Edward Elgar, pp. ix–xlvii.

Franklin, Sarah (1997a) *Embodied Progress: a cultural account of assisted conception*, London: Routledge.

Franklin, Sarah (1997b) 'Dolly: a new form of transgenic breedwealth', *Environmental Values* 6 (4): 427–37.

Franklin, Sarah (1999) 'Dead Embryos: feminism in suspension', in Lynn Morgan and Meredith Michaels (eds), *Fetal Subjects, Feminist Positions*, Philadelphia: University of Pennsylvania Press, pp. 61–83.

Franklin, Sarah (2001a) 'Biologization Revisited: kinship in the context of the new biologies', in Sarah Franklin and Susan McKinnon (eds), *Relative Values: new directions in kinship study*, Durham, NC: Duke University Press.

Franklin, Sarah (2001b) 'Kinship, Genes, and Cloning: life after Dolly', in Alan Goodman and Deborah Heath (eds), *Anthropology in the Age of Genetics*, Berkeley: University of California Press.

Franklin, Sarah, Lury, Celia and Stacey, Jackie (eds) (1991a) *Off-Centre: feminism and cultural studies*, London: HarperCollins.

Franklin, Sarah, Lury, Celia and Stacey, Jackie (1991b) 'Feminism and Cultural Studies: pasts, presents, futures', in Sarah Franklin, Celia Lury and Jackie Stacey (eds), *Off-Centre: feminism and cultural studies*, London: HarperCollins, pp. 1–20.

Franklin, Sarah, Lury, Celia and Stacey, Jackie (eds) (1991c) 'Feminism, Marxism and Thatcherism', in Sarah Franklin, Celia Lury and Jackie Stacey (eds), *Off-Centre: feminism and cultural studies*, London: HarperCollins, pp. 21–48.

Frazer, J.G. (1910) *Totemism and Exogamy*, 4 volumes, London.

Friedland, Roger and Boden, Deirdre (eds) (1994) *NowHere: space, time and modernity*, Berkeley: University of California Press.

Friedman, Jonathan (1994) *Cultural Identity and Global Process*, London: Sage.

Frow, John (1996) 'Information as Gift and Commodity', *New Left Review*, September/October, no 219: 89–108.

Gaines, Jane (1990) 'Superman and the Protective Strength of the Trademark', in Patricia Mellencamp (ed.), *Logics of Television: essays in cultural criticism*, Bloomington: Indiana University Press and London: British Film Institute, pp. 173–93.

Gaines, Jane (1991) *Contested Culture: the image, the voice and the law*, Chapel Hill: University of North Carolina Press.

Bibliography

Galanti, Marina (1993) 'Serious Messages in Benetton Ads', letter, *The Independent*, 14 January.

Giddens, Anthony (1990) *The Consequences of Modernity*, Cambridge: Polity.

Giddens, Anthony (1991) *Modernity and Self Identity: self and society in the late modern age*, Cambridge: Polity.

Giddens, Anthony (1999) *Reith Lectures*, www.bbc.co.uk.

Gillick, Muriel, R. (1984) 'Health Promotion, Jogging and the Pursuit of the Moral Life', *Journal of Health Politics, Policy and the Law* 9: 369–87.

Ginsburg, Faye (1989) *Contested Lives: the abortion debate in an American community*, Berkeley: University of California Press.

Giroux, Henry (1994) *Disturbing Pleasures*, New York: Routledge.

Goodman, Martin (1998) *In Search of the Divine Mother*, London: Thorsons.

Gould, Stephen Jay (1993) 'Dinomania', *The New York Review of Books*, 12 August, pp. 51–6.

Grewal, Inderpal and Kaplan, Caren (eds) (1994a) *Scattered Hegemonies: postmodernity and transnational feminist practices*, Minneapolis: University of Minnesota Press.

Grewal, Inderpal and Kaplan, Caren (1994b) 'Introduction: transnational feminist practices and questions of postmodernity', in Inderpal Grewal and Caren Kaplan (eds), *Scattered Hegemonies: postmodernity and transnational feminist practices*, Minneapolis: University of Minnesota Press, pp. 1–33.

Grossberg, Lawrence, Nelson, Cary and Treichler, Paula (eds) (1992) *Cultural Studies*, London: Routledge.

Grove, Richard H. (1995) *Green Imperialism: colonial expansion, tropical islands, Edens and the origins of environmentalism, 1600–1860*, Cambridge: Cambridge University Press.

Guattari, Félix (1992) 'Regimes, Pathways, Subjects', in Jonathan Crary and Sanford Kwinter (eds), *Incorporations*, Cambridge, MA: Zone, pp. 16–35.

Guillaumin, Collette (1995) *Racism, Sexism, Power and Ideology*, London: Routledge.

Haines, Tim (1999) *Walking with Dinosaurs: a natural history*, London: BBC.

Hall, Stuart (1990) 'Cultural Identity and Diaspora', in Jonathan Rutherford (ed.), *Identity*, London: Lawrence and Wishart, pp. 222–37.

Hall, Stuart (1991a) 'The Local and the Global: globalization and ethnicity', in Anthony D. King (ed.), *Culture, Globalization and the World-System*, London: Macmillan, pp. 19–40.

Hall, Stuart (1991b) 'Old and New Identities, Old and New Ethnicities', in Anthony D. King (ed.), *Culture, Globalization and the World-System*, London: Macmillan, pp. 41–68.

Hannerz, Ulf (1987) 'The World in Creolization', *Africa* 57 (4): 546–59.

Hannerz, Ulf (1990) 'Cosmopolitans and Locals in World Culture', in Mike Featherstone (ed.), *Global Culture: nationalism, globalization and modernity*, London: Sage, pp. 237–52.

Hannerz, Ulf (1991) 'Scenarios for Peripheral Cultures', in Anthony D. King (ed.), *Culture, Globalization and the World-System*, London: Macmillan, pp. 107–28.

Haraway, Donna (1989a) 'The Biopolitics of Postmodern Bodies: determinations of self in immune system discourse', *differences: a journal of feminist cultural studies* 1 (1): 3–45.

Haraway, Donna (1989b) *Primate Visions: gender, race and nature in the world of modern science*, New York: Routledge.

Haraway, Donna (1989c) 'A Manifesto for Cyborgs: science, technology and socialist feminism in the 1980s', in Elizabeth Weed (ed.), *Coming to Terms: feminism, theory, politics*, London: Routledge, pp. 173–204.

Haraway, Donna (1991) *Simians Cyborgs and Women: the reinvention of nature*, New York: Routledge.

Haraway, Donna (1992a) 'The Promises of Monsters: a regenerative politics for inappropriate/d others', in Lawrence Grossberg, Cary Nelson and Paula Treichler (eds), *Cultural Studies*, New York: Routledge, pp. 292–337.

Haraway, Donna (1992b) 'When Man^{TM} is on the Menu', in Jonathan Crary and Sanford Kwinter (eds), *Incorporations*, New York: Zone, pp. 38–43.

Haraway, Donna (1997) *Modest_Witness@Second_Millennium: FemaleMan©_Meets_OncoMouse^{TM}*, New York: Routledge.

Hartouni, Valerie (1992) 'Fetal Exposures: abortion politics and the optics of illusion', *camera obscura* 29: 131–50.

Hartouni, Valerie (1997) *Cultural Conceptions: on reproductive technologies and the remaking of life*, Minneapolis: University of Minnesota Press.

Harvey, David (1989) *The Condition of Postmodernity*, Oxford: Blackwell.

Haug, W.F. (1986) *Critique of Commodity Aesthetics*, Cambridge: Polity.

Hay, Louise (1988) *You Can Heal Your Life*, London: Eden Grove.

Hay, Louise (1989) *Heal Your Body: the mental causes of physical illness and the metaphysical way to overcome them*, London: Eden Grove.

Hayles, N. Katherine (1999) *How We Became Posthuman: virtual bodies in cybernetics, literature, and informatics*, Chicago: University of Chicago Press.

Heelas, Paul (1996) *The New Age Movement: the celebration of the self and the sacralisation of modernity*, Oxford: Blackwell.

Heelas Paul, Lash, Scott and Morris, Paul (eds) (1996) *Detraditionalization: critical reflections on authority and identity at a time of uncertainty*, Oxford: Blackwell.

Herbert, Marie (1996) *Healing Quest: journey of transformation*, London: Random House.

Hine, Thomas (1986) *Populuxe*, New York: Alfred A. Knopf.

Holbeche, Soozi (1997) *Changes: a guide to personal transformation and new ways of living in the next millennium*, London: Piatkus.

Holquist, Michael (1989) 'From Body Talk to Biography: the chronobiological bases of narrative', *The Yale Journal of Criticism* 3 (1): 1–36.

hooks, bell (1992) *Black Looks: race and representation*, London: Turnaround.

Hope, Murray (1998) *The Ancient Wisdom of Egypt*, London: Thorsons.

Hubbard, Ruth (1990) *The Politics of Women's Biology*, New Brunswick, NJ: Rutgers University Press.

Hubbard, Ruth (1995) *Profitable Promises: essays on women, science and health*, Monroe, ME: Common Courage Press.

Hubbard, Ruth, Henifen, Mary Sue and Fried, Barbara (eds) (1982) *Biological Women – the Convenient Myth*, Cambridge, MA: Schenckman.

Hubbard, Ruth and Wald, Elijah (1993) *Exploding the Gene Myth*, Boston: Beacon.

Ingold, Tim (1993) 'Globes and Spheres: the topology of environmentalism', in Kay Milton (ed.), *Environmentalism: the view from anthropology*, London: Routledge, pp. 31–42.

Jalan, Rajika (1997) 'An Asian Orientalism? *Libas* and the textures of postcolonialism', in Alan Scott (ed.), *The Limits of Globalization: cases and arguments*, London: Routledge, pp. 90–115.

Jameson, Fredric (1991) *Postmodernism, or the Cultural Logic of Late Capitalism*, London: Verso.

Jameson, Fredric (1999) 'Notes on Globalization as a Philosophical Issue', in Fredric Jameson and Masao Miyoshi (eds), *The Cultures of Globalization*, Durham, NC: Duke University Press, pp. 54–80.

Jameson, Fredric and Miyoshi, Masao (eds) (1999) *Cultures of Globalization*, Durham, NC: Duke University Press.

Jordanova, Ludmilla (1980) 'Natural Facts: a historical perspective on science and sexuality', in Carol MacCormack and Marilyn Strathern (eds), *Nature, Culture and Gender*, Cambridge: Cambridge University Press, pp 42–69.

Jordanova, Ludmilla (ed.) (1986) *Languages of Nature: critical essays on science and literature*, London: Free Association Books.

Jordanova, Ludmilla (1989) *Sexual Visions: images of gender in science and medicine between the eighteenth and nineteenth centuries*, Hemel Hempstead: Harvester Wheatsheaf.

Kalman, Timor (1996) 'Timor Kalman. Interview with Moira Cullen', in *Eye* 20: 10–16.

Kaplan, Caren (1995) '"A World Without Boundaries": the Body Shop's trans/national geographies', *Social Text* 13 (2): 45–66.

Kaplan, Caren (1996) *Questions of Travel: postmodern discourses of displacement*, Durham, NC: Duke University Press.

Kaplan, Caren and Grewal, Inderpal (1994) 'Transnational Feminist Cultural Studies: beyond the marxism/poststructuralist/feminism divides', *Positions: East Asia cultures critique* 2 (2): 430–45.

Kay, Lily (1993) *The Molecular Vision of Life: Caltech, the Rockefeller Foundation, and the rise of the new biology*, New York: Oxford University Press.

Keller, Evelyn Fox (1990) 'From Secrets of Life to Secrets of Death', in Mary Jacobus, Evelyn Fox Keller and Sally Shuttleworth (eds), *Body/Politics: women and the discourses of science*, London: Routledge, pp. 177–91.

Keller, Evelyn Fox (1992) *Secrets of Life, Secrets of Death: essays on language, gender and science*, New York: Routledge.

Bibliography

Keller, Evelyn Fox (1995) *Refiguring Life: metaphors of twentieth-century biology*, New York: Columbia University Press.

Keller, Evelyn Fox (1996) 'The Biological Gaze', in George Robertson, Melinda Mash, Lisa Tickner, Jon Bird, Barry Curtis and Tim Putnam (eds), *Future Natural: nature, science, culture*, London: Routledge, pp. 107–21.

Kelley, Kevin W. (ed.) (1988) *The Home Planet*, Reading, MA: Addison-Wesley.

Kelly, Kevin (1998) 'I do have a brain', interview with Martha Stewart, *Wired*, August, pp. 114–15.

Kenton, Leslie (1998) *Journey into Freedom*, London: Thorsons.

King, Anthony (ed.) (1991) *Culture, Globalization and the World-System*, London: Macmillan.

Kitzinger, Sheila (1986) *Being Born*, London: Dorling Kindersley.

Kleinman, Arthur and Kleinman, Jane (1996) 'The Appeal of Experience, the Dismay of Images: cultural appropriations of suffering in our times', *Daedalus* 125 (1): 1–23.

Koch, Gertrud (1993) 'Mimesis and Bilderverbot', *Screen* 34 (3): 211–22.

Kracauer, Siegfried (1995) *The Mass Ornament: Weimar essays* (trans. Thomas Y. Levin), Cambridge, MA: Harvard University Press.

Landis, Robyn with Khalsa, Karta Purkh Singh (1998) *Herbal Defence to Illness*, London: Thorsons.

Langer, Mark (1995) 'Why the Atom is Our Friend: Disney, General Dynamics and the USS *Nautilus*', *Art History* 18 (1): 63–96.

Lash, Scott and Urry, John (1987) *The End of Organized Capitalism*, Cambridge: Polity.

Lash, Scott and Urry, John (1994) *Economies of Signs and Space*, London: Sage.

Latour, Bruno (1987) *Science in Action: how to follow scientists and engineers through society*, Cambridge, MA: Harvard University Press.

Law, John (1994) *Organizing Modernity*, Oxford: Blackwell.

Lévi-Strauss, Claude (1962) *The Savage Mind*, London: Weidenfeld.

Levin, Roger (1987) 'Cancer and the Self: how illness constellates meaning', in David M Levin (ed.), *Pathologies of the Modern Self: postmodern studies on narcissism, schizophrenia and depression*, New York: New York University Press, pp. 163–97.

Lewis, Reina (1996) *Gendering Orientalism: race, femininity and representation*, London: Routledge.

Longman's English Dictionary (1984) London: Longman.

Lowenthal, David (1995) 'The Forfeit of the Future', *Futures* 27 (4): 385–95.

Luhmann, Niklas (1989) *Ecological Communication*, Cambridge: Polity.

Lukács, Georg (1968) *History and Class Consciousness: studies in Marxist dialectics* (trans. Rodney Livingstone), London: Merlin.

Lury, Adam (1993) 'Advertising: moving beyond the stereotypes', in Nicholas Abercrombie, Russell Keat and Nigel Whiteley (eds), *The Authority of the Consumer*, London: Routledge, pp. 91–102.

Lury, Celia (1993) *Cultural Rights: technology, legality and personality*, London: Routledge.

Lury, Celia (1996) *Consumer Culture*, Cambridge: Polity.

Lury, Celia (1998) *Prosthetic Culture: photography, memory and identity*, London: Routledge.

Lury, Celia (1999) 'Marking Time with Nike: the illusion of the durable', *Public Culture* 11 (3): 499–526.

Lury, Giles (1998) *Brandwatching: lifting the lid on the phenomenon of branding*, Dublin: Blackhall.

Lutz, Catherine A. and Collins, Jane L. (1993) *Reading National Geographic*, Chicago: University of Chicago Press.

Lyotard, Jean-François (1984) *The Postmodern Condition: a report on knowledge* (trans. Geoff Bennington and Brian Massumi), Manchester: Manchester University Press.

McClintock, Anne (1995) *Imperial Leather: race, gender and sexuality in the colonial contest*, London: Routledge.

MacCormack, Carol and Strathern, Marilyn (eds) (1980) *Nature, Culture and Gender*, Cambridge: Cambridge University Press.

McKibben, Bill (1989) *The End of Nature*, New York: Viking.

Macnaghten, Phil and Urry, John (1995) 'Towards a Sociology of Nature', *Sociology* 29: 203–20.

Macnaghten, Phil and Urry, John (1998) *Contested Natures*, London: Sage.

McNeil, Maureen and Litt, Jacqueline (1992) 'More Medicalizing of Mothers: fetal alcohol syndrome in the U.S.A. and related developments', in Steve Platt, Sue Scott, Hilary Thomas and Gareth Williams (eds), *Private Risks and Public Dangers*, Aldershot: Avebury, pp. 112–32.

Magiera, Mark (1994) 'Promotional Marketer of the Year', *Advertising Age*, 21 March, pp. S-1, S-2, S-8.

Mantle, Jonathan (1999) *Benetton: the family, the business and the brand*, London: Little, Brown.

Martin, Emily (1991) 'The Egg and the Sperm: how science has constructed a romance based on stereotypical male/female roles', *Signs* 16 (3): 485–501.

Martin, Emily (1992) 'Body Narratives: Body Boundaries', in Lawrence Grossberg, Cary Nelson and Paula Treichler (eds), *Cultural Studies*, London: Routledge, pp. 409–19.

Martin, Emily (1994) *Flexible Bodies: tracking immunity in American culture from the days of polio to the days of AIDS*, Boston: Beacon.

Massey, Doreen (1999) 'Imagining Globalization: power-geometrics of time-space', in Avtar Brah, Mary J. Hickman and Mairtin Mac an Ghaill (eds), *Global Futures: migration, environment and globalization*, London: Macmillan, pp. 27–44.

Mattei, Francesca (n.d.) 'A Matter of Style', *News: United Colors of Benetton*, pp. 4–5.

Mattelart, Armand (1979) *Multinational Corporations and the Control of Culture: the ideological apparatuses of imperialism* (trans. Michael Chanan), Brighton: Harvester.

Mauss, Marcel (1992) 'Techniques of the Body', in Jonathan Crary and Sanford Kwinter (eds), *Incorporations*, New York: Zone, pp. 454–77.

Mellencamp, Patricia (ed.) (1990a) *Logics of Television: essays in cultural criticism*, Bloomington: Indiana University Press and London: British Film Institute.

Mellencamp, Patricia (1990b) 'TV Time and Catastrophe, or *Beyond the Pleasure Principle* of Television', in Patricia Mellencamp (ed.), *Logics of Television: essays in cultural criticism*, Bloomington: Indiana University Press and London: British Film Institute, pp. 240–67.

Merchant, Carolyn (1980) *The Death of Nature: women, ecology and the scientific revolution*, San Francisco: Harper and Row.

Metchnikoff, Elie (1905) *Immunity in Infective Diseases* (trans. F.G. Binney), Cambridge: Cambridge University Press.

Mitchell, William J. (1992) *The Reconfigured Eye: visual truth in the postmodern era*, Cambridge, MA: MIT Press.

Moir, Jan (1995) 'Ad Nauseum', *The Guardian Weekend*, 11 February, pp. 38–9.

Morgan, Lynn M. and Michaels, Meredith (eds) (1999) *Fetal Subjects, Feminist Positions*, Philadelphia: University of Pennsylvania Press.

Morris, Betsy (1996) 'The Brand's the Thing', *Fortune*, 4 March, pp. 28–38.

Morse, Margaret (1990) 'An Ontology of Everyday Distraction', in Patricia Mellencamp (ed.), *Logics of Television: essays in cultural criticism*, Bloomington: Indiana University Press, pp. 193–222.

Morton, Chris and Thomas, Ceri Louise (1998) *The Mystery of the Crystal Skulls*, London: Thorsons.

Myers, Greg (1999a) *Ad Worlds: brands, media, audiences*, London: Arnold.

Myers, Greg (1999b) 'Cosmopolitanism in Everyday Lives' (mimeo, unpublished: Centre for the Study of Environmental Change, Lancaster University).

Myerson, Jeremy (1998) 'Designs on Britain's Future', *Independent on Sunday*, 29 March, pp. 58–60.

Myss, Caroline (1997) *Anatomy of the Spirit: the seven stages of power and healing*, London: Bantam.

Nelkin, Dorothy and Lindee, M. Susan (1995) *The DNA Mystique: the gene as a cultural icon*, New York: W.H. Freeman.

New Formations (special issue on hybridity) (1992), no. 18, Winter.

Novacek, Michael (1996) *Dinosaurs of the Flaming Cliffs*, New York: Doubleday.

O'Barr, William M. (1994) *Culture and the Ad: exploring otherness in the world of advertising*, Boulder, CO: Westview.

Office of Technology Assessment (1987) *Patenting Life*.

Ohmae, Kenichi (1987) *Beyond National Borders: reflections on Japan and the world*, Tokyo: Kodansha.

O'Neill, John (1990) 'AIDS as a Globalizing Panic', in Mike Featherstone (ed.), *Global Culture: nationalism, globalization and modernity*, London: Sage, pp. 329–42.

O'Reilly, John (1998) 'Advertising or exploitation?', *The Guardian*, 21 September, pp. 4–5.

Ortner, Sherry (1974) 'Is Female to Nature as Male is to Culture?', in Louise Lamphere and Michelle Rosaldo (eds), *Women, Culture and Society*, Stanford: Stanford University Press, pp. 67–96.

Ortner, Sherry and Whitehead, Harriet (eds) (1981) *Sexual Meanings: the cultural construction of gender and sexuality*, Cambridge: Cambridge University Press.

Oudshoorn, Nelly (1994) *Beyond the Natural Body: the archaeology of sex hormones*, London: Routledge.

Oyama, Susan (1985) *The Ontogeny of Information: developmental systems and evolution*, Cambridge: Cambridge University Press.

Parsons, Talcott, Fox, Renée C. and Lidz, Victor M. (1972) 'The "Gift of Life" and Its Reciprocation', *Social Research* 39: 367–415.

Patton, Cindy (1990) *Inventing AIDS*, London: Routledge.

Perry, Nick (1998) *Hyperreality and Global Culture*, London: Routledge.

Petchesky, Rosalind Pollack (1987) 'Foetal Images: the power of visual culture in the politics of reproduction', in Michelle Stanworth (ed.), *Reproductive Technologies: gender, motherhood and medicine*, Cambridge: Polity, pp. 57–80.

Phelan, Peggy (1993) *Unmarked: the politics of performance*, New York: Routledge.

Phizacklea, Anne (1990) *Unpacking the Fashion Industry: gender, racism, and class in production*, London: Routledge.

Pieterse, Jan Nederveen (1995) 'Globalization as Hybridization', in Mike Featherstone, Scott Lash and Roland Robertson (eds), *Global Modernities*, London: Sage, pp. 45–68.

Pietroni, Patrick (1990) *The Greening of Medicine*, London: Victor Gollancz.

Plumwood, Val (1993) *Feminism and the Mastery of Nature*, London: Routledge.

Pollan, Michael (1999) 'In My Own Backyard', *The Sunday Review, The Independent on Sunday*, 4 April, pp. 8–12.

Popham, Peter (1993) 'Cunning Stunts', *The Independent Magazine*, 31 July, pp. 24–7.

Popham, Peter (1996) 'A World That Still Washes Whiter', *The Independent*, 27 February, pp. 14–15.

Poppi, Cesare (1997) 'Wider Horizons With Larger Details: subjectivity, ethnography and globalisation', in Alan Scott (ed.), *The Limits of Globalisation*, London: Routledge, pp. 284–305.

Quinn, Malcolm (1994) *The Swastika: constructing the symbol*, London: Routledge.

Rabinow, Paul (1992) 'Artificiality and Enlightenment: from sociobiology to biosociality', in Jonathan Crary and Sanford Kwinter (eds), *Incorporations*, New York: Zone, pp. 234–52.

Rabinow, Paul (1994) 'Introduction: a vital rationalist', in François Delaporte (ed.), *A Vital Rationalist: selected writings from Georges Canguilhem*, New York: Zone, pp. 11–24.

Rabinow, Paul (1996a) *Essays on the Anthropology of Reason*, Berkeley: University of California Press.

Rabinow, Paul (1996b) *Making PCR: a story of biotechnology*, Chicago: University of Chicago Press.

Rawson, Gloria and Callinan, David (1998) *The 10 Minute Miracle: the quick fix survival guide for mind and body*, London: Thorsons.

Renaud, Alain (1995) 'From Photography to Photology: concerning certain philosophical implications of digital transformation of the photographic image', in Cypres (ed.), *Art/Digital Photography*, Aix-en-Provence: École d'Art d'Aix-en-Provence, pp. 178–220.

Renouf, Jane (1993) *Jimmy: no time to die*, London: Fontana/HarperCollins.

Revel, Jean-François and Richard, Matthieu (1998) *The Monk and the Philosopher: East meets West in a father–son dialogue*, London: Thorsons.

Ritchin, Fred (1990) 'Photojournalism in the Age of Computers', in Carole Squiers (ed.), *The Critical Image*, Seattle: Bay Press, pp. 28–37.

Ritvo, Harriet (1995) 'Possessing Mother Nature: genetic capital in eighteenth-century Britain', in John Brewer and Susan Staves (eds), *Early Modern Conceptions of Property*, New York: Routledge, pp. 413–26.

Ritzer, George (1995) *The McDonaldization of Society: an investigation into the changing character of contemporary social life*, London: Pine Forge.

Ritzer, George and Liska, Allan (1997) '"McDisneyization" and "Post-Tourism": complementary perspectives on contemporary tourism', in Chris Rojek and John Urry (eds), *Touring Cultures*, London: Routledge, pp. 96–109.

Robertson, George, Mash, Melinda, Tickner, Lisa, Bird, Jon, Curtis, Barry and Putnam, Tim (eds) (1996) *Future Natural: nature, science, culture*, London: Routledge.

Robertson, Roland (1990) 'Mapping the Global Condition: globalization as the central concept', in Mike Featherstone (ed.), *Global Culture: nationalism, globalization and modernity*, London: Sage, pp. 15–30.

Robertson, Roland (1992) *Globalization: social theory and global culture*, London: Sage.

Robertson, Roland (1995) 'Glocalization: time-space and homogeneity-heterogeneity', in Mike Featherstone, Scott Lash and Roland Robertson (eds), *Global Modernities*, London: Sage, pp. 25–44.

Roddick, Anita (1991) *Body and Soul*, London: Ebury Press.

Roddick, Anita (1994) 'Introduction', in The Body Shop Team, *The Body Shop Book: skin, hair and body care*, London: Little, Brown, pp. 9–15.

Roger, John and McWilliams, Peter (1996) *You Can't Afford the Luxury of a Negative Thought*, London: Thorsons.

Rose, Mark (1993) *Authors and Owners: the invention of copyright*, Cambridge, MA: Harvard University Press.

Rosenblum, Barbara (1991) '"I have begun the process of dying"', in Jo Spence and Patricia Holland (eds), *Family Snaps: the meanings of domestic photography*, London: Virago, pp. 239–44.

Roseneil, Sasha (1997) 'The Global Common: the global, local and personal dynamics of the women's peace movement in the 1980s', in Alan Scott (ed.), *The Limits of Globalization: cases and arguments*, London: Routledge, pp. 55–74.

Rothman, Barbara Katz (1986) *The Tentative Pregnancy: pre-natal diagnosis and the future of motherhood*, New York: Viking.

Rubin, Gayle (1975) 'The Traffic in Women: notes on the "political economy" of sex', in Rayna Reiter (ed.), *Toward an Anthropology of Women*, New York: Monthly Review Press, pp. 157–210.

Rudwick, Martin J.S. (1976) *The Meaning of Fossils: episodes in the history of paleontology*, 2nd edition, Chicago: University of Chicago Press.

Rusk, Tom and Rusk, Natalie (1998) *Coach Yourself to Success: how to overcome hurdles and free yourself from mindtraps*, London: Thorsons.

Russell, Nicholas (1986) *Like Engendering Like: heredity and animal breeding in early modern England*, Cambridge: Cambridge University Press.

Sachs, Wolfgang (1994) 'The Blue Planet: an ambiguous modern icon', *The Ecologist* 25: 170–5.

Said, Edward (1978) *Orientalism: western concepts of the orient*, London: Routledge and Kegan Paul.

Sassen, Saskia (1991) *The Global City: New York, London, Tokyo*, Princeton: Princeton University Press.

Sassen, Saskia (1998) *Globalization and Its Discontents: essays on the new mobility of people and money*, New York: The New Press.

Scheper-Hughes, Nancy and Lock, Margaret (1987) 'The Mindful Body: a prolegomenon to future work in medical anthropology', *Medical Anthropology Quarterly* 1 (1): 6–41.

Schulman, Sarah (1994) 'And Now for a Word from Our Sponsor: the emergence of a gay management class and its impact on the print media', paper presented at the University of California, San Diego, 17 January.

Scott, Alan (ed.) (1997) *The Limits of Globalization: cases and arguments*, London: Routledge.

Shapiro, Michael (1994) 'Images of Planetary Danger: Luciano Benetton's ecumenical fantasy', *Alternatives* 19 (4): 433–54.

Sharma, Ursula (1992) *Complementary Medicine Today: practitioners and patients*, London: Tavistock/Routledge.

Shay, Don and Duncan, Jody (1993) *The Making of Jurassic Park: an adventure 65 million years in the making*, New York: Ballantine.

Sheehan, Henry (1993) 'The Fears of Children', *Sight and Sound*, July, p. 10.

Shiva, Vandana (1989) *Staying Alive: women, ecology and development*, London: Zed.

Shiva, Vandana (1991) *The Violence of the Green Revolution: third world agriculture, ecology and politics*, London: Zed.

Shohat, Ella (1992) '"Laser for Ladies": endodiscourse and the inscription of science', *camera obscura* 29: 57–90.

Sholl, Simon (1996) 'Basic Instinct', *Design Week*, 5 July, pp. 14–15.

Siegel, Bernie (1993) *Living, Loving and Healing: a guide to a fuller life, more love and greater health*, London: Aquarian Press/HarperCollins.

Simonton, Carl O., Matthews-Simonton, Stephanie and Creighton, James, L. (1978) *Getting Well Again*, London: Bantam Books.

Sklair, Leslie (1991) *Sociology of the Global System*, Baltimore: Johns Hopkins University Press.

Sklair, Leslie (1993) '"Going Global": competing models of globalisation', *Sociological Review* 3 (2): 7–10.

Slingsby, Helen (1994) 'Distinguishing Marks', *Marketing Week*, 11 November, pp. 40–1.

Smith, Neil (1996) 'The Production of Nature', in George Roberston, Melinda Mash, Lisa Tickner, Jon

Bibliography

Bird, Barry Curtis and Tom Putnam (eds), *Future Natural: nature, science, culture*, London: Routledge, pp. 35–54.

Sofia, Zoe (1984) 'Exterminating Fetuses: abortion, disarmament, and the sexo-semiotics of extraterrestrialism', *Diacritics* 4 (2): 331–41.

Solomon-Godeau, Abigail (1991) *Photography at the Deck: essays on photographic history, institutions and practices*, Minneapolis: University of Minnesota Press.

Sontag, Susan (1977) *On Photography*, New York: Farrar, Straus and Giroux.

Spanier, Bonnie (1991) '"Lessons" from "Nature": gender ideology and sexual ambiguity in biology', in Julia Epstein and Kristina Straub (eds), *Body Guards: the cultural politics of gender ambiguity*, New York: Routledge, pp. 329–50.

Spanier, Bonnie (1995) *Im/partial Science: gender and the politics of molecular biology*, Bloomington: Indiana University Press.

Spillers, Hortense (1987) 'Mama's Baby, Papa's Maybe: an American grammar book', *Diacritics* 17 (2): 65–81.

Spivak, Gayatri (1999) *A Critique of Postcolonial Reason: toward a history of the vanishing present*, Cambridge, MA: Harvard University Press.

Stabile, Carole (1992) 'Shooting the Mother: fetal photography and the politics of disappearance', *camera obscura* 28: 179–206.

Stacey, Jackie (1997) *Teratologies: a cultural study of cancer*, London: Routledge.

Stafford, Barbara (1991) *Body Criticism: imaging the unseen in enlightenment art and medicine*, Cambridge, MA: MIT Press.

Stewart, Susan (1993) *On Longing*, Durham, NC: Duke University Press.

Stolcke, Verena (1993) 'Is Sex to Gender as Race is to Ethnicity?', in Teresa de Valle (ed.), *Gendered Anthropology*, London: Routledge, pp. 17–38.

Stolcke, Verena (1995) 'Talking Culture: new boundaries, new rhetorics of exclusion in Europe', *Current Anthropology* 36 (1): 1–24.

Strathern, Marilyn (1980) 'No Nature, No Culture: the Hagen case', in Carol MacCormack and Marilyn Strathern (eds), *Nature, Culture and Gender*, Cambridge: Cambridge University Press, pp. 174–222.

Strathern, Marilyn (1988) *The Gender of the Gift: problems with women and problems with society in Melanesia*, Berkeley: University of California Press.

Strathern, Marilyn (1991) *Partial Connections*, Savage, MD: Rowan and Littlefield.

Strathern, Marilyn (1992a) *After Nature: English kinship in the late twentieth century*, Cambridge: Cambridge University Press.

Strathern, Marilyn (1992b) *Reproducing the Future: anthropology, kinship and the new reproductive technologies*, Manchester: Manchester University Press.

Strathern, Marilyn (ed.) (1995a) *Shifting Contexts: transformations in anthropological knowledge*, London: Routledge.

Strathern, Marilyn (1995b) 'The Nice Thing about Culture is that Everyone has It', in Marilyn Strathern (ed.), *Shifting Contexts: transformations in anthropological knowledge*, London: Routledge, pp. 153–76.

Strathern, Marilyn (1998) 'What Is Intellectual Property After?', in John Law and John Hassard (eds), *Actor Network Theory and After*, Oxford: Blackwell, pp. 156–80.

Strathern, Marilyn (1999) *Property, Substance and Effect: anthropological essays on persons and things*, London: Athlone.

Sum, Ngai-Ling (1999) 'New Orientalisms, Global Capitalism, and the Politics of Synergetic Differences: discursive construction of trade relations between the USA, Japan and East Asian NICs', in Avtar Brah, Mary J. Hickman and Mairtin Mac an Ghaill (eds), *Global Futures: migration, environment and globalization*, London: Macmillan, pp. 99–121.

Szerszynski, Bronislaw (1996) 'The Varieties of Ecological Piety', paper delivered at '*Nature Religion Today*' conference at Lancaster University, 9–12 April.

Szerszynski, Bronislaw and Toogood, Mark (2000) 'Global Citizenship, the Environment and the Mass Media', in Stuart Allan, Barbara Adam and Cynthia Carter (eds), *The Media Politics of Environmental Risk*, London: University College London Press, pp. 218–28.

Szerszynsksi, Bronislaw, Lash, Scott and Wynne, Brian (1996) 'Introduction: ecology, realism and the social sciences', in Scott Lash, Bronislaw Szerszynski and Brian Wynne (eds), *Risk, Environment and Modernity: towards a new ecology*, London: Sage.

Tagg, John (1991) 'Globalization, Totalization and the Discursive Field', in Anthony D. King (ed.), *Culture, Globalization and the World-System*, London: Macmillan, pp. 155–60.

Tauber, Alfred I. (1994) *The Immune Self: theory or metaphor?*, Cambridge: Cambridge University Press.

Taubes, Gary (1996) 'Conversations in a Cell', *Discover*, February, pp. 49–54.

Taussig, Michael (1993) *Mimesis and Alterity: a particular history of the senses*, London: Routledge.

Thompson, John (1995) *The Media and Modernity: a social theory of the media*, Cambridge: Polity.

Thurman, Robert (1998) *The Tibetan Book of the Dead*, London: Thorsons.

Tomlinson, John (1999) *Globalisation and Culture*, Cambridge: Polity.

Toogood, Mark and Myers, Greg (1999) 'Banal Globalism and the Media: images of belonging, responsibility and citizenship', (mimeo, unpublished).

Toscani, Oliviero (1995) 'Taboos for Sale', interview with Michel Guerrin, *Guardian Weekly*, 26 March, p. 20.

Treichler, Paula (1988) 'AIDS, Gender and Biomedical Discourse: current contests for meaning', in Elizabeth Fee and Daniel Fox (eds), *AIDS: the burdens of history*, Berkeley: University of California Press, pp. 190–266.

Tsing, Anna (1995) 'Empowering Nature, or: some gleanings in bee culture', in Sylvia Yanagisako and Carol Delaney (eds), *Naturalizing Power: essays in feminist cultural analysis*, New York: Routledge, pp. 113–43.

Tutsell, Glen (eds) (1995) 'Shade Trade', *Marketing*, 9 November, pp. 27–9.

UNESCO (1993) *The Multi-Cultural Planet: the report of a UNESCO International Expert Group* (ed. Ervin Laszlo), Oxford: Oneworld.

Urry, John (2000) *Sociology Beyond Societies: mobilities for the twenty-first century*, London: Routledge.

Van Dijck, José (1998) *Imagenation: popular images of genetics*, New York: New York University Press.

Virilio, Paul (1991) *The Lost Dimension* (trans. Julie Rose), New York: Semiotext(e).

Virilio, Paul (1994) *The Vision Machine* (trans. Julie Rose), London: British Film Insititute.

Wallerstein, Immanuel (1991) 'The National and the Universal: can there be such a thing as world culture?', in Anthony King (ed.), *Culture, Globalization and the World-System*, London: Macmillan, pp. 91–106.

Ware, Vron (1992) *Beyond the Pale: white women, racism and history*, London: Verso.

Warner, Marina (1994) *Six Myths of Our Time: little angels, little monsters, beautiful beasts, and more*, London: Vintage.

Weil, Andrew (1997) *Spontaneous Healing*, London: Warner Books.

Weindling, Paul (1981) 'Theories of the Cell State in Imperial Germany', in Charles Webster (ed.), *Biology, Medicine and Society 1840–1940*, Cambridge: Cambridge University Press, pp. 99–155.

Weiner, Annette (1995) 'Culture and Our Discontents', *American Anthropologist* 97 (1): 14–40.

Wellcome Trust, Medicine and Society Programme (1998) *Public Perceptions of Cloning*, London: Wellcome Trust.

Wernick, Andrew (1991) *Promotional Culture*, London: Sage.

White, Hayden (1987) *The Content of the Form: narrative, discourse and historical representation*, Baltimore: Johns Hopkins University Press.

Williams, Patricia (1993) *The Alchemy of Race and Rights*, London: Virago.

Williams, Raymond (1976) *Keywords: a vocabulary of culture and society*, Fontana: London.

Williams, Raymond (1980) 'Ideas of Nature', in *Problems in Materialism and Culture*, London: Verso, pp. 67–85.

Wilson, Alexander (1992) *The Culture of Nature: North American landscape from Disney to the Exxon Valdez*, Cambridge, MA: Blackwell.

Wittig, Monique (1992) *The Straight Mind and Other Essays*, Hemel Hempstead: Harvester Wheatsheaf.

Wolff, Janet (1991) 'The Global and the Specific: reconciling conflicting theories of culture', in Anthony D. King (ed.), *Culture, Globalization and the World-System*, London: Macmillan, pp. 161–74.

Wollen, Peter (1993) 'Theme Park and Variations', *Sight and Sound*, July, pp. 7–10.

Yanagisako, Sylvia (1985) 'The Elementary Structure of Reproduction in Gender and Kinship Studies', paper presented at the annual meeting of the American Anthropological Association, Washington, DC, 4–8 December.

Bibliography

Yanagisako, Sylvia and Delaney, Carol (eds) (1995a) *Naturalizing Power: essays in feminist cultural analysis*, New York: Routledge.

Yanagisako, Sylvia and Delaney, Carol (1995b) 'Naturalizing Power', in Sylvia Yanagisako and Carol Delaney (eds), *Naturalizing Power: essays in feminist cultural analysis*, New York: Routledge, pp. 1–24.

Young, Robert M. (1985) *Darwin's Metaphor: nature's place in Victorian culture*, Cambridge: Cambridge University Press.

Yoxen, Edward (1981) 'Life as a Productive Force: capitalising the science and technology of molecular biology', in Les Levidow and Robert Young (eds), *Science, Technology and the Labour Process*, London: Free Association Books, pp. 66–122.

Index

Page numbers in *italics* refer to figures and tables.

Index

Index

Index